THE ADDRESS BOOK

THE
ADDRESS
BOOK

How to Reach Anyone Who *Is* Anyone

MICHAEL LEVINE

A Perigee Book

Every effort has been made to provide the most current mailing addresses.
Addresses, however, do change, and neither publisher nor author is responsible for
misdirected or returned mail.

We regret that when this book went to press,
it was too late to include the names of the recently
elected United States public officials.

A Perigee Book
published by
The Berkley Publishing Group
200 Madison Avenue
New York, NY 10016

Library of Congress Cataloging-in-Publication Data

Levine, Michael
    The address book : how to reach anyone who is anyone / Michael Levine.
        p. cm.
    "A Perigee book."
    ISBN 0-399-52149-6
    1. United States—Directories.   2. Social registers—United
States.   3. Celebrities—United States—Directories.
4. Associations, institutions, etc.—United States—Directories.
5. Associations, institutions, etc.—Directories.   I. Title.
E154.5.L48   1995
917.3'0025—dc20   94-33188
                                                                 CIP

Cover design by Richard Rossiter

Printed in the United States of America

1   2   3   4   5   6   7   8   9   10

Acknowledgments

I'm lucky. I get to say publicly to the special people in my life how much they mean to me. To each of them, my appreciation for their help with this book and, most of all, their unwavering friendship and love.

My literary agent, Alice Martell, and her assistant, John Sanful.

My friends at Putnam (where I have been published since 1984): Julie Merberg, John Duff, and Rena Walner.

My father, Arthur O. Levine, stepmother, Marilyn, and sister, Patty.

My special friends Rana Bendixen and Sorrell, Toby Berlin, Ken Bostic, Bill Calkins, Richard Impressia, Bette Geller Jackson, Karen Kansion, Richard Lawson, Nancy Mager, John McKillop, Dennis Prager, and Erline White.

My business partners, Mitchell Schneider and Monique Moss.

My office family, Kristine Ashton, Chris Blake, Todd Brodginski, Amanda Cagan, Deb Coquillette, Naomi Goldman, Kamale Gray, Susan Jacobs, Kathy Koehler, Denise McIver, Julie Nathanson, Robert Pietranton, Tresa Redburn-Cody, Marcee Rondan, Susan Schoepe, Melissa Spraul, Dana Stibor, and Lesley Zimmerman.

To my business associates Alan Edwards, Laura Herlovich, Sal Manna, Chris Poole, Terrie Williams, Howard Wisnicki and Cheryl Hollimon.

Special thanks to Kathleen Conner for incredible commitment to excellence in the researching of this book.

The Guilt:
Garrison Keillor on Letter Writing

The first step in writing a letter is to get over the guilt of not writing. You don't "owe" anybody a letter. Letters are a gift. The burning shame you feel when you see unanswered mail makes it harder to pick up a pen and makes for a cheerless letter, too. I feel bad about not writing, but I've been so busy, etc. Skip this. Few letters are obligatory, and they are *Thanks for the wonderful gift* and *I am terribly sorry to hear about George's death* and *Yes, you're welcome to stay with us next month,* and not many more than that. Write those promptly if you want to keep your friends. Don't worry about others, except love letters, of course. When your true love writes, *Dear Light of My Life, Joy of My Heart, O Lovely Pulsating Core of My Sensate Life,* some response is called for.

From *We Are Still Married*
by Garrison Keillor
(Viking Press, 1989)

Letter-writer's Campaign Led to Increased Hiring of Black Scholars

A recently discovered cache of letters tells how one man—through an ambitious letter-writing campaign—helped integrate northern universities just after World War II.

The correspondence between Fred G. Wale and hundreds of college and university presidents brought at least 150 distinguished black scholars to the attention of the universities and led to jobs for 50 of them. Nevertheless, the letters, found in the Fisk University archives, also tell a story about the role of institutional racism in American academia during the post-war years and shed light on current hiring attitudes, says Michael Levine, author of the reference book for letter-writers, *The Address Book: How to Reach Anyone Who Is Anyone* (Putnam/Perigee).

The study of the Wale correspondence leads him to believe that the post-war rationales used to justify the exclusion of blacks from white academia placed on African-American scholars "a badge of inferiority that continues to some degree in our own present," stated Levine.

Wale, education director of the Julius Rosenwald Fund, contacted some 600 presidents in the summer of 1945, asking if they would hire qualified applicants who were black. In a follow-up letter, Wale included a list he compiled of some 150 African-American scholars who were qualified to hold faculty posts "in the most outstanding" American schools. Over the course of two years, Wale carried out an "extensive correspondence" with administrators from Maine to Oregon—even met with many of them.

By the mid-1940s, about 3,000 African-Americans had earned master's degrees and more than 550 had earned doctorates—nearly all of them at northern white or European universities. Still, only one black—Allison Davis—had a tenure-track position at a northern white university.

In response to his first letter, Wale received only 200 replies, most of them ardent defenses of racially neutral hiring practices. In response to his second, he again received 200 replies, many from presidents who affirmed their belief in meritocratic principles and hiring procedures, and then searched for reasons unrelated to race to account for the longstanding exclusion of such outstanding African-American scholars from their faculties. Many presidents attributed exclusion to geographical or demographic factors, institutional need or community attitudes.

As proof of the absence of group prejudice on his campus, one California president offered: "We have employed a Negro for a part-time coaching position with the football team for many years." An Ohio school president wrote that "The man who trains many of our students [in] the Dining Hall is a Negro."

As a result of Wale's campaign, 23 black scholars were given permanent faculty positions in northern white universities, and another 27 picked up temporary appointments.

"The research shows yet again the power of letter writing," said Levine.

Operation Address Book

There are several million names not appearing in this address book, but they may be among the most important people of all: the countless dedicated men and women serving in our armed forces around the world. There's nothing that means more to our troops than a letter from home, and though most of them certainly correspond with their families, they also enjoy hearing from other Americans as well.

The following are several addresses you can write to that guarantee your letter or package will reach our defenders of freedom at their lonely outposts. Please take the time to write them.

America Remembers the Army
c/o Commander
2nd ACR
ATTN: S-5/PAO
APO New York, NY 09093

America Remembers Enterprise (CVN-65)
c/o Commander Enterprise (CVN-65)
ATTN: PAO
FPO San Francisco, CA 96636-2610

America Remembers the Forrestal (CV-59)
c/o Commander, Forrestal (CV-59)
ATTN: PAO
FPO Miami, FL 34080-2730

America Remembers 435th Tactical Air Wing
c/o 435th TAW
Rhein-Main Air Base
APO New York, NY 09057

America Remembers the Marines
c/o Camp Foster USO
P.O. Box 743
FPO Seattle, WA 98774

America Remembers U.S. Forces in Korea
c/o Chaplain
APO San Francisco, CA 96202

Introduction

A couple of years ago, I proudly accepted an invitation to deliver a speech at the Harvard Business School. Never having visited an Ivy League school, I wasn't quite sure what to expect.

The audience of America's best and brightest took me completely by surprise—and damn near gave the faculty a collective heart attack—when they stood and cheered my concluding observation: "Some ideas are so stupid, only intellectuals can believe them."

I came to appreciate this truism about twelve years ago when I first approached New York's publishing elite with my admittedly simple idea to create a series of address books. One by one, they peered down from their thrones, rejecting the idea as "far too simple," and suggesting that in this hurry-up world, only fools would be naive enough to write to people they didn't know.

Finally, Putnam saw its worth, and today, it is estimated over 2,000,000 letters have been successfully delivered, thanks to this best-selling series of address books.

I've heard from desperate medical patients who have received help from blood donors thanks to the book, from lost lovers reunited, from consumers battling and beating corporate villains, and, of course, from fans hearing from their heroes.

By the way, a few years ago I visited the White House, and never in my life did I feel prouder than when I saw *The Address Book* on the desks in several executive offices.

Yes, the address book was a simple idea; an idea that works. But, how can you make it work for you?

*How can you make sure the notable receives your letter? The number-one reason mail to notables is left unanswered is that it is addressed improperly and never reaches its intended destination. A letter addressed simply to "Barbra Streisand, Hollywood, California" will find its way only to the dead-letter file of the post office. The complete, accurate addresses in this book will get your mail to the offices, agents, studios, managers, or even homes of the addressees, and I have been unable to find one notable, no matter how busy or important, who doesn't personally read some of his or her mail—

even the President of the United States. That doesn't mean notables read and answer every single piece, but it should offer encouragement to people who write to them.

*Politicians have a standard rule of thumb: for every letter they receive, they estimate that one hundred people who didn't take the time to write are thinking the same thought as the letter expresses. So you can calculate the effect of your single letter by multiplying it by one hundred! And all entertainment figures keep a close watch on their mail. It is a real indication of what people are thinking and feeling. Often, the notable is surrounded by a small group of associates who tend to isolate the star from the public. Your letter helps break down this barrier. Amazing things have been accomplished with letters as long as they have the proper mailing address.

*Here are several important things to remember in writing notables: Always include a self-addressed stamped envelope. This is the single most important factor in writing a letter if you want a response. Because of the unusually high volume of mail notable people receive, anything you can do to make it easier for them to respond is going to work in your favor. Keep your letters short and to the point. Notables are usually extremely busy people, and long letters tend to be set aside for "future" consideration. For instance, if you want an autographed picture of your favorite TV personality, don't write three pages of prose to explain your request.

*Make your letters as easy to read as possible. This means type it or, at the very least, handwrite it very neatly. Avoid crayons, markers, or even pencils. And don't forget to leave some margins on the paper.

*Be sure to include your name and address (even on all materials that you include with your letter) in the event the materials are separated from your letter. You would be amazed how many people write letters without return addresses and then wonder why they never hear from the person to whom they wrote.

*Never send food to notables. Due to spoilage and security matters, it cannot be eaten anyway. (Would you eat a box of homemade brownies given to you by a total stranger?) If you send gifts, don't wrap them in large boxes with yards of paper, string, and tape around them. (They may not have a crowbar on hand.) Again, don't forget to include your name and address on all material you send. Of course, don't send—or ask for—money.

*In writing to corporation heads, remember most of them rose to their lofty positions because they were better problem-solvers than their company peers. Good corporation heads are zealous about finding solutions to written complaints (especially if you have sent copies of your complaint letters to appropriate consumer organizations). A recent survey of corporation heads showed that 88 percent of all letters of complaint were resolved. Therefore, the old adage, "When you have a problem, go to the top," appears to be accurate. Likewise, corporation executives greatly appreciate hearing good news (satisfaction, extra service, helpful employees, and so forth).

But nowhere is it written that mail should only be filled with praise and congratulations. You may enjoy shaking a fist at your favorite villain, so I have included infamous people in my book.

Most people are usually very kind and sincere in their letters. They write what they would say or ask if they had the opportunity to do so in person. This is especially true of children, who are extremely honest. On the other hand, infamous people and others who are out of favor with the public predictably receive hostile and angry letters.

Most of the people, famous and infamous, listed in *The Address Book* are movers and shakers, and thus highly transient, changing their addresses far more often than the average person. Their mail is usually forwarded to them, but occasionally a letter may be returned to the sender. If this should happen to your letter, first check to make sure that you have copied the address correctly. If you wish to locate another address for the person to whom you are writing, begin your search by writing to him or her in care of the company or association with which they may have been most recently associated. For example, if a musician or singer has last recorded an album with a specific record company, write in care of that company; a sports figure might be contacted through the last team he or she was associated with; an author through his or her most recent publisher; and so forth.

According to 1987 statistics, about 90 million pieces of mail land in the dead-letter pile because the carrier couldn't make out the address, so write clearly.

Remember, *a person who writes to another makes more impact than ten thousand who are silent.*

—Michael Levine
Los Angeles, CA

And none will hear the postman's knock without a quickening of the heart. For who can bear to feel himself forgotten?

—W. H. AUDEN, from "Night Mail"

A & E
Arts and Entertainment
    Network
555 Fifth Ave.
New York, NY 10017

A & M Records, Inc.
1416 N. LaBrea Ave.
Hollywood, CA 90028
Record company

(New York Office)
595 Madison Ave.
New York, NY 10022

A & R Records
900 19th Ave. S., #207
Nashville, TN 37212
Ruthie Steele, Owner
Independent record label

A & W Restaurants
17197 N. Laurel Park Dr.,
    #500
Livonia, MI 48152
E. Dale Mulder, CEO
Fast-food chain

A. C. Nielsen Co.
Nielsen Plaza
Northbrook, IL 60062
N. Eugene Harden, President
TV ratings company

a-ha
c/o Warner Bros.
3300 Warner Blvd.
Burbank, CA 91510
Recording group

Aaron, Betsy
CBS News
524 W. 5th St.
New York, NY 10019-2902
Journalist

Aaron, Chester
P.O. Box 388
Occidental, CA 95465
Author of Gideon *and* Hello to
    Bodega

Aaron, Hank
P.O. Box 4064
Atlanta, GA 30302-4064
Baseball legend

AAU Youth Sports Program
3400 W. 86th St.
P.O. Box 68207
Indianapolis, IN 46268
Stan Hooley, Executive
    Director

ABA Center on Children and the Law
1800 M St., NW
Washington, DC 20036
Howard Davidson, Director
Lawyers for kids

Abba
Box 26072 S-100 41
Stockholm, Sweden
Recording group

Abbado, Claudio
c/o Columbia Artists Mgmt.
165 W. 57th St.
New York, NY 10019-2201
Conductor

Abbott, Bruce
c/o M. Rosenberg
8428 Melrose Place, #C
Los Angeles, CA 90069
Actor

Abbott, George
10 Rockefeller Plaza, #1009
New York, NY 10020
*One-hundred-ten-year-old
playwright, director, producer*

Abbott, Jim
Yankee Stadium
E. 161 St. & River Ave.
Bronx, NY 10451
Baseball player

Abbott, Wilton Robert
Bldg. 150, 70-01
P.O. Box 504
Sunnyvale, CA 94086-0001
Aerospace engineer

Abboud, Joseph M.
650 Fifth Ave., 32nd Fl.
New York, NY 10019
Fashion designer

ABC
Capital Cities/ABC Inc.
77 W. 66th St.
New York, NY 10023
TV network

**Capital Cities/ABC Inc.
(Hollywood)**
4151 Prospect Ave.
Los Angeles, CA 90027

Abdul, Paula
Third Rail Entertainment
Tri-Star Bldg.
10202 W. Washington Ave.,
#26
Culver City, CA 90232
Singer, dancer, choreographer
birthdate 6/19/62

**Abdul-Jabbar, Kareem
(Lewis Ferdinand Alcindor)**
P.O. Box 10
Inglewood, CA 90306-0010
Basketball player

Abelson, Alan
Barron's Magazine
200 Liberty St.
New York, NY 10281-1003
Columnist

Abercrombie, Neil
1440 Longworth House Office
Bldg.
Washington, DC 20515-1101
*Representative from Hawaii,
Democrat
First District*

Abrams, Elliot
Hudson Inst.
1015 18th St. NW, #200
Washington, DC 20036
Writer, foreign affairs analyst

Abramson, Leslie H.
4929 Wilshire Blvd., #940
Los Angeles, CA 90010
*Attorney (part of Menendez
defense team)*

Abshire, David Manker
Strategic and International
    Studies
1800 K St. NW, #1014
Washington, DC 20006-2202
Diplomat, research executive

AC/DC
11 Leonminster Road, Morden
Surrey SM4 England
Recording group

ACA Joe, Inc.
148 Townsend St.
San Francisco, CA 94107
Alice Wany Lam, CEO
Chain of clothing stores

Academy of American Poets
584 Broadway, #1208
New York, NY 10012
Beth McCabe, Program
    Director

Academy of Country Music
6255 Sunset Blvd., #923
Hollywood, CA 90028
Fran Boyd, Executive Secretary

Academy of Country Music
    Awards Programs
Entertainment Media Corp.
Box 2772
Palm Springs, CA 92263
Published lists

Academy of Family Films and
    Family Television
334 W. 54th St.
Los Angeles, CA 90037
Dr. Donald A. Reed, Director

Academy of Family Mediators
P.O. Box 10501
Eugene, OR 97440
James C. Melamed, Executive
    Director

Academy of Model
    Aeronautics
1810 Samuel Morse Dr.
Reston, VA 22090
Vince Mankowski, Executive
    Director

Academy of Motion Picture
    Arts and Sciences
8949 Wilshire Blvd.
Beverly Hills, CA 90211
Bruce Davis, Executive
    Director
Oscar's parents

Academy of Science Fiction,
    Fantasy and Horror Films
334 W. 54th St.
Los Angeles, CA 90037
Dr. Donald A. Reed, President

Academy of Television Arts
    and Sciences
5220 Lankershim Blvd.
N. Hollywood, CA 91601
James L. Loper, Executive
    Director
Emmy's parents

Accordion Federation of
    North America
11438 Elmcrest St.
El Monte, CA 91732
Peggy Milme, Executive
    Secretary

Accountant, The
Lafferty Publications
2970 Clairmont Rd. NE, #800
Atlanta, GA 30329-1634
Paul Byrne, Publisher
Magazine for accountants

Accountants Directory
American Business Directories,
    Inc.
5711 S. 86th Circle
Box 27347
Omaha, NE 68127-4146
Sharon Hallett, Publisher

Accuracy in Media
1275 K St. NW, #1150
Washington, DC 20005
Reed Irvine, Chairman
Watchdog group

Ace
Box 11201
Shawnee Mission, KS 66207
*Magazine for people interested in
underground and pirate radio
stations*

Acheson, James
Sandra Marsh Mgmt.
9150 Wilshire Blvd., #220
Beverly Hills, CA 90212-3414
Costume designer

Achilles Track Club
1 Times Sq., 10th Fl.
New York, NY 10036
R. Trum, President
Track for the physically challenged

Ackerley, Barry
800 Fifth Ave.
Seattle, WA 98104
*Professional basketball team
executive, communications
company executive*

Ackerman, Gary L.
2445 Rayburn House Office
Bldg.
Washington, DC 20515-3205
*Representative from New York,
Democrat
Fifth District*

Ackerman, Helen Page
405 Hilgard Ave.
Los Angeles, CA 90024-1301
Librarian, educator

Acoustic Alchemy
c/o GRP
555 W. 57th St.
New York, NY 10019
Recording group

Acoustic Guitar
The String Letter Corp.
412 Red Hill Ave., #15
San Anselmo, CA 94960
David A. Lusterman, Publisher
Magazine

Acousticats, The
c/o Carlin
411 Ferry St., #4
Martinez, CA 94533
Recording group

ACT UP
**AIDS Coalition to Unleash
  Power**
135 W. 29th St., 10th Fl.
New York, NY 10001
Robert Rygr, Contact
AIDS activists

Action for Child Protection
2724C Park Rd.
Charlotte, NC 28209
Wayne Holder, Executive
  Director
*Lobbies to strengthen and improve
  child protection efforts*

Activist
Democratic Socialists of
  America
15 Dutch St., #500
New York, NY 10038
Ginny Coughlin, Editor
Political magazine

Actor's Fund of America
1501 Broadway, #518
New York, NY 10036
Joseph P. Benincasa, General
  Manager
*Human service organization for
  the entertainment industry*

Actors and Others for Animals
5510 Cahuenga Blvd.
N. Hollywood, CA 91601
Cathy Singleton, Executive
  Officer
Animal rights group

Actors Studio
432 W. 44th St.
New York, NY 10036
Patty Ewald, Executive
  Director

Ada, Joseph Franklin
Office of the Governor
  Guam Territory
Agana, GU 96910
Territorial governor

Adair, Red
(Paul Neal)
Red Adair Oil Well Fires and
  Blowouts Control Co.
8101 Pinemont Dr.
Houston, TX 77040-6591
Oil-well problem-control specialist

Adam Walsh Child Resource
  Center
11911 U.S. Hwy. 1, #301
N. Palm Beach, FL 33408
Nancy A. McBride, Executive
  Director
*Helps coordinate efforts to find
  lost children*

Adam, Ken
10100 Santa Monica Blvd.,
  #700A
Los Angeles, CA 90067
Film production designer

Adam, Prince II
Schloss Vaduz
Principality of Liechtenstein
Ruler of Liechtenstein

Adams, Bryan
1416 N. LaBrea Ave.
Hollywood, CA 90028
Vocalist, composer

Adams, Michael
Washington Bullets
Capitol Center
Hyattsville, MD 20785
Basketball player

Adams, Richard George
26 Church St.
Whitechurch, Hampshire,
  England
Author of Watership Down

ADC Band
17397 Santa Barbara
Detroit, MI 48221
Recording group

Addams Family, The
Hanna-Barbera Cartoons, Inc.
3400 Cahuenga Blvd.
Hollywood, CA 90068
Animated series

Adelman, Rick
Portland Trail Blazers
700 NE Multnomah St.
Portland, OR 97232-2131
Basketball coach

Adidas USA, Inc.
15 Independence Blvd.
Warren, NJ 07060
Ann Occie, Director of Public
  Relations
Manufacturer of sportswear

Adirondack Council
Box D-2
Church St.
Elizabethtown, NY 12932
Timothy Burke, Executive
  Director
Environmental group

Adjodhia, Jules
Office of the President
Paramaribo, Suriname
President of Suriname

Adler, Freda Schaffer
Rutgers University School of
  Criminal Justice
15 Washington St.
New York, NY 10004-1018
Criminologist, educator

Adler, Richard
8 E. 83rd St.
New York, NY 10028
Composer, lyricist

Admiration Toy Co., Inc.
60 McLean Ave.
Yonkers, NY 10705
S. Newman, President
*Manufacturer of dolls and stuffed
toys*

Adolfo
(Adolfo F. Sardina)
36 E. 57th St.
New York, NY 10022-2500
Fashion designer

Adoptees in Search
P.O. Box 41016
Bethesda, MD 20824
Joanne W. Small, Director
*Adoptees in search of biological
parents*

Adoptive Families of America
3333 Hwy. 100 N.
Minneapolis, MN 55422
Susan Freivalds, Executive
Director

Adult Video Association
270 N. Canon Dr., #1370
Beverly Hills, CA 90210
David Kastens, President
Anti-censorship

Adulyadej, King Bhumibol
Chitralada Villa
Bangkok, Thailand
Ruler of Thailand

**Adventures of Brisco County
Jr., The**
Warner Bros. Television
4000 Warner Blvd.
Burbank, CA 91522
TV series

Advertising Council
261 Madison Ave.
New York, NY 10016-2303
Ruth A. Wooden, President
Public service ad campaigns

Aerosmith
c/o Fan Club
P.O. Box 4668
San Francisco, CA 94101
Recording group

Aesthetic Realism Foundation
141 Greene St.
New York, NY 10012
Ellen Reiss, Class Chairman
*"The art of liking the world and
oneself at the same time
by seeing the world and oneself
as aesthetic opposites"*

Affirmative Action
c/o Rainforest
225 N. New Hampshire Ave.
Los Angeles, CA 90004
Ed Davis
Rock group

African Skies
c/o Atlantic Films
227 Broadway, #300
Santa Monica, CA 90401
TV series

After the Stork, Inc.
1501 12th St., NW
Albuquerque, NM 87104
Alan Stopper, President
Children's clothing store chain

Aftershock
c/o Virgin
1790 Broadway, 20th Fl.
New York, NY 10019
Rock group

AFTRA
American Federation of TV and Radio Artists
260 Madison Ave.
New York, NY 10016
John C. Hall, Jr., Executive Secretary

Aga Khan IV, J.H. Prince Karim
Aiglemont
60270 Gouvieux, France
Spiritual leader and Iman of Ismailian Muslims

Agassi, Andre
ATP Tour North America
200 ATP Tour Blvd.
Ponte Vedra Beach, FL 32082
Tennis player

Agatha Christie Appreciation Society: Postern of Murder
61 E. Northhampton St., #206
Wilkes-Barre, PA 18701
Dorothy M. Carr, President

Agerwala, Tilak Krishna Mahesh
IBM Corp.
Neighborhood Rd.
Kingston, NY 12401
Computer company executive

Aging in America
1500 Pelham Pkwy. S.
Bronx, NY 10461
Ralph Hall, President
Gerontology researchers

Agitpop
c/o Twin/Tone
2541 Nicollet Ave.
Minneapolis, MN 55404
Recording artists

Agoraphobics Anonymous
P.O. Box 43082
Upper Montclair, NJ 07043
Patricia Steffens, Director

Aguilera, Richard Warren
Minnesota Twins
501 Chicago Ave. S.
Minneapolis, MN 55415
Baseball player

AGVA
American Guild of Variety Artists
184 5th Ave.
New York, NY 10010
Entertainment union

Ahmed, Kyle
Joffrey Ballet
130 W. 56th St.
New York, NY 10019-3818
Dancer

Aiello, Danny
10000 Santa Monica Blvd., #305
Los Angeles, CA 90067
Actor
birthdate 6/20/33

Aikman, Troy
Cowboys Ctr.
1 Cowboys Pkwy.
Irving, TX 75063-4727
Football player

Air Supply
1990 S. Bundy Dr., #590
Los Angeles, CA 90025
Rock group

Aircraft Owners and Pilots Association
421 Aviation Way
Frederick, MD 21701
Phil Boyer, President

Airwalk
Division of Items International
2042 Corte Del Nogal, Suite A
Carlsbad, CA 92009
William Mann, President
Importer of sports equipment, skateboarding shoes

Akaka, Daniel K.
720 Senate Hart Office Bldg.
Washington, DC 20510-1103
Senator from Hawaii, Democrat

Akayev, Askar
Office of the President
Bishkek, Kyrgyz Reespublikasy
President of Kyrgyzstan

Akiyoshi, Toshiko
Sony Music Entertainment
550 Madison Ave.
New York, NY 10022
Jazz composer, pianist

**Al-Anon Family Group
   Headquarters**
P.O. Box 862, Midtown Station
New York, NY 10018
Carle Kuney, Contact

Alabama
Box 529
Ft. Payne, AL 35967
Country music group

Aladdin
Walt Disney Television
   Animation
5200 Lankershim Blvd.
N. Hollywood, CA 91601
Animated series

Alaska Coalition
408 C St., NE
Washington, DC 20002
Mike Matz, Chairman

Albee, Edward Franklin
14 Harrison St.
New York, NY 10013
Author, playwright

Albert, Marv
NBC Sports
30 Rockefeller Plaza, #1411
New York, NY 10112
Sportscaster

Albrecht, Duane Taylor
Aspenwood Animal Hospital
1290 S. Colorado Blvd.
Denver, CO 80222-2904
Veterinarian

Albrecht, Kay Montgomery
Innovations in Early
   Childhood Education
P.O. Box 82087
Houston, TX 77282-0687
*Early childhood educator, child
   advocate*

**Alcoholics Anonymous World
   Services**
475 Riverside Dr.
New York, NY 10163

Alcott, Amy Strum
LPGA
2570 Volusia Ave., #B
Daytona Beach, FL 32114-1113
Golfer

Alderson, Richard Lynn
Oakland Athletics
Oakland Coliseum
Oakland, CA 94621
Baseball team executive

Aldredge, Theoni Vachliotis
350 W. 50th St.
New York, NY 10019
Costume designer

Alexander, Jason
151 El Camino
Beverly Hills, CA 90212
Actor
birthdate 9/23/59

Alexopoulos, Helene
New York City Ballet, Inc.
N.Y. State Theater
Lincoln Center Plaza
New York, NY 10023
Ballet dancer

Alfa Candy Corporation
P.O. Box 344
New York, NY 10034
George Atstaedter, President
Healthy candy company

Alfred Hitchcock's Mystery Magazine
Bantam Doubleday Dell
Publishing Group
666 5th Ave.
New York, NY 10103
Mystery magazine

Ali, General Zine al-Abidine Ben
Presidence de la Republique
Tunis, Tunisia
President of Tunisia

Ali, Muhammad
Ali Farm
Berrien Springs, MI 49103
Boxing legend

All-American Amateur Baseball Association
c/o Tom J. Checkush
340 Walker Dr.
Zanesville, OH 43701

All American Association of Contest Judges
1627 Lay Blvd.
Kalamazoo, MI 49001
Judges of high school music: bands, chorus, etc.

All Star Sporting Goods
Subsidiary of Ampac
Enterprises, Inc.
1 Main St.
P.O. Box 1356
Shirley, MA 01464
David J. Holden, President
Manufacturer of baseball equipment

Allard, Wayne
422 Cannon House Office
Bldg.
Washington, CA 20515-0604
Representative from Colorado, Republican
Fourth District

Allen, Chad
6212 Banner Ave.
Los Angeles, CA 90038
Actor

Allen, Debbie
Wolf Kasteler
1033 Gayley Ave., #208
Los Angeles, CA 90024
Actress, director, dancer, choreographer, producer
birthdate 1/16/51

Allen, Eric Andre
Philadelphia Eagles
3501 S. Broad St.
Philadelphia, PA 19148-5298
Football player

Allen, Frances Elizabeth
P.O. Box 704
Yorktown Heights, NY 10598-0704
Computer scientist

Allen, Jay Presson
1051 Broadway, #1614
New York, NY 10036-5503
Writer, producer

Allen, Karen
151 El Camino
Beverly Hills, CA 90212
Actress
birthdate 10/5/51

Allen, Marcus
Kansas City Chiefs
One Arrowhead Dr.
Kansas City, MO 64129
Football player

Allen, Nancy
15301 Ventura Blvd., #345
Sherman Oaks, CA 91403
Actress
birthdate 6/24/50

Allen, Steve
(Stephen Valentine Patrick
William Allen)
15201 Burbank Blvd.
Van Nuys, CA 91411
Humorist, author, songwriter
birthdate 12/26/21

Allen, Tim
ABC
77 W. 66th St.
New York, NY 10023
Actor, comedian

Allen, Woody
930 Fifth Ave.
New York, NY 10021
Director, writer, actor
birthdate 12/1/35

Alley, Kirstie
9320 Wilshire Blvd., 3rd Fl.
Beverly Hills, CA 90212
Actress
birthdate 1/12/55

Alliance Against Fraud in
Telemarketing
c/o National Consumers
League
815 15th St. NW, #928N
Washington, DC 20005
John Barker, Coordinator

Alliance of Motion Picture and
Television Producers
14144 Ventura Blvd., 3rd Fl.
Sherman Oaks, CA 91423
J. Nicholas Counter, III,
President

Alliance of Resident Theatres/
New York
131 Varick St., #904
New York, NY 10013
Howard J. Aibel, Board
Chairman

Allied Underwear Association
100 E. 42nd St.
New York, NY 10017
Sidney Orenstein, Executive
Director

Alligator Records
P.O. Box 60234
Chicago, IL 60660
Bruce Iglauer, President
Independent record label

Allison, Bobby
140 Church Ave.
Bessemer, AL 35023-2409
Retired stock-car driver

Allman Brothers Band, Inc.
18 Tamworth Rd.
Waban, MA 02168
Rock group

Allman, Gregg
1801 Century Park W.
Los Angeles, CA 90067
Musician
birthdate 12/7/47

Almighty, The
825 8th Ave.
New York, NY 10019
Recording artists

Alomar, Roberto Velazquez
Toronto Blue Jays
300 Brenner Blvd., Gate 9
Toronto, ON Canada
    M5V 3B3
Baseball player

Alomar, Sandy, Jr.
Cleveland Indians
Cleveland Stadium
Cleveland, OH 44114
Baseball player

Alonso, Maria Conchita
1999 Ave. of the Stars, #2850
Los Angeles, CA 90067
Actress
born 1957

Alou, Felipe Rojas
P.O. Box 500, Station M
Montreal, PQ Canada
H1V 3P2
Baseball manager

Alpert, Herb
Rondor Publications
360 N. La Cienega Blvd.
Los Angeles, CA 90048
*Music publishing company
executive, musician*
birthdate 3/31/35

Alpha Flight
Marvel Entertainment Group
387 Park Ave. S.
New York, NY 10016
Comic

Alpo Petfoods, Inc.
P.O. Box 2187
Lehigh Valley, PA 18001
Franklin Krum, CEO
Pet food manufacturer

Alt and the Lost Civilization
c/o Atlantic Records
75 Rockefeller Plaza
New York, NY 10019
Recording artists

Alt, Carol
9169 Sunset Blvd.
Los Angeles, CA 90069
Model, actress

Alt, John
1 Arrowhead Dr.
Kansas City, MO 64129-1651
Football player

Alter, Jonathan Hammerman
c/o Newsweek
444 Madison Ave.
New York, NY 10022-6903
Journalist

Altern 8
c/o Virgin
1790 Broadway, 20th Fl.
New York, NY 10019
Rock group

**Alternative Dispute Resolution
Committee**
c/o American Bar Association,
Family Law
750 N. Lake Shore Dr.
Chicago, IL 60611
Marshal J. Wolf, Chairman

Alternative Music Hotline
10 Center St.
Califon, NJ 78301
Newsletter

Altman, Robert
Sandcastle 5 Productions
502 Park Ave., #15G
New York, NY 10022-1108
Film director, writer, producer
birthdate 2/20/25

Altura, Burton Myron
450 Clarkson Ave.
Brooklyn, NY 11203-2098
Physiologist, educator

**Aluminum Recycling
Association**
1000 16th St. NW, #603
Washington, DC 20036
Richard M. Cooperman,
Executive Director

Alurista
(Alberto Baltazar Urista-
Heredia)
522 University Ave.
Santa Barbara, CA 93106-0001
Educator, poet, writer

Alvin and the Chipmunks
MWS
4222 W. Burbank Blvd.
Burbank, CA 91505
Comic singing group

Amateur Astronomers, Inc.
Union County College
William Sperry Observatory
1033 Springfield Ave.
Cranford, NJ 07016
Linda M. Horning, President

Amateur Organists and
Keyboard Association
International
6436 Penn Ave. S.
Richfield, MN 55423

Amateur Softball Association
of America
2801 NE 50th St.
Oklahoma City, OK 73111
Don E. Porter, Executive
Director

Amateur Speedskating Union
of the United States
1033 Shady Lane
Glen Ellyn, IL 60137
Shirley A. Yates, Executive
Secretary

Ambitious Lovers
c/o Elektra
345 Maple Dr., #123
Beverly Hills, CA 90210
Recording artists

Ambler, Eric
14 Bryanston Sq.
London W1H 7FF England
Writer

AMC Entertainment, Inc.
106 W. 14th St.
Kansas City, MO 64105
Stanley H. Durwood, CEO
Movie theater chain

AMEND
(Abusive Men Exploring New
Directions)
777 Grant St., #600
Denver, CO 80203
Robert C. Gallup, Executive
Director

Amergroid Society of America
P.O. Box 30149
Baltimore, MD 21270
R. Lewis, President
Society of people of two or more
races

America
8730 Sunset Blvd., Penthouse
Los Angeles, CA 90069
Rock group

America the Beautiful Fund
219 Shoreham Bldg., NW
Washington, DC 20005
Paul Bruce Dowling, Executive
Director

America's Funniest Home
Videos
Vin Di Bona Productions
12233 W. Olympic Blvd.
Los Angeles, CA 90064
TV series

America's Funniest People
Vin Di Bona Productions
12233 W. Olympic Blvd.
Los Angeles, CA 90064
TV series

**American Academy and
Institute of Arts and Letters**
633 W. 155th St.
New York, NY 10032
Virginia Dajani, Executive
Director

**American Academy of
Diplomacy**
1726 M St. NW, #800
Washington, DC 20036
David H. Popper, President

**American Academy of
Matrimonial Lawyers**
150 N. Michigan Ave., #2040
Chicago, IL 60601
Lorraine J. West, Executive
Director

**American Academy of Natural
Family Planning**
615 S. New Ballas Rd.
St. Louis, MO 63141
Charmain Champanine,
President

**American Accordion
Musicological Society**
334 S. Broadway
Pitman, NJ 08071
Stanley Darrow, Secretary

**American Accounting
Association**
5717 Bessie Dr.
Sarasota, FL 34233-2399
Paul L. Gerhardt, Executive
Director

**American Alliance for Theatre
and Education**
Arizona State University
Theatre Department
Tempe, AZ 85287-3411
Barbara Salisbury Wills,
Executive Director

**American Amateur Baseball
Congress**
118-19 Redfield Plaza
Marshall, MI 49068
Joseph R. Cooper, President

**American Amateur Karate
Federation**
1930 Wilshire Blvd., #1208
Los Angeles, CA 90057
Hidetaka Nishiyama, President

**American Amateur Racquetball
Association**
815 N. Weber, #101
Colorado Springs, CO 80903
Luke St. Onge, Executive
Director

**American Amusement Machine
Association**
12731 Directors Loop
Woodbridge, VA 22192
Robert C. Fay, Executive Vice-
President

**American Anti-Vivisection
Society**
Noble Plaza, #204
801 Old York Rd.
Jenkintown, PA 19046
Margaret B. Eldon, President

**American Arbitration
Association**
140 W. 51st St.
New York, NY 10020
Robert Coulson, President

American Armwrestling
Association
c/o Bob O'Leary
P.O. Box 132
Scranton, PA 18504

American Arts Alliance
1319 F St. NW, #500
Washington, DC 20004
Judith Golub, Executive
Director
*Dance, theater, opera, symphony,
etc. lobbyists*

American Association for the
Improvement of Boxing
86 Fletcher Ave.
Mt. Vernon, NY 10552
Stephen Acunto, Chairman

American Association for
Leisure and Recreation
1900 Association Dr.
Reston, VA 22091
Dr. Christen G. Smith,
Executive Director

American Association of
Backgammon Clubs
P.O. Box 12359
Las Vegas, NV 89121
Linda Kruegel, Executive
Officer

American Association of
Community Theatre
c/o Ross Rowland
8209 N. Costa Mesa Dr.
Muncie, IN 47303

American Association of
Museums
1225 Eye St. NW, #200
Washington, DC 20005
Edward H. Able, Executive
Director

American Association of
Police Polygraphists
c/o Henry L. Canty
1918 Sleepy Hollow
Pearland, TX 77581-5740
Henry L. Canty, Secretary-
Treasurer

American Association of
Retired Persons
601 E St. NW
Washington, DC 20049
Horace B. Deets, Executive
Director

American Association of
Suicidology
2459 S. Ash
Denver, CO 80222
Julie Perlman, Executive
Director

American Athletic Association
for the Deaf
3607 Washington Blvd., #4
Ogden, UT 84403
Shirley H. Platt, Secretary-
Treasurer

American Aviation Historical
Society
2333 Otis St.
Santa Ana, CA 92704
Harry Gann, President

American Ball Manufacturing
Corp.
1225 Tappan Circle
Carrollton, TX 75006
William V. Brown, President
*Sporting goods and athletic
equipment manufacturer*

American Ballet Competition
Box 328
Philadelphia, PA 19105
F. Randolph Swartz, Executive
  Director
*Committee established to select and
  prepare U.S. Team for Olympics
  of Dance*

American Ballet Theatre
890 Broadway
New York, NY 10003-1211

American Banjo Fraternity
271 McKinley St.
Pittsburgh, PA 15221
Norman W. Azinger, Executive
  Secretary

American Bankers Association
1120 Connecticut Ave. NW
Washington, DC 20036
Don Ogilvie, Executive Vice-
  President

American Bar Association
750 N. Lake Shore Dr.
Chicago, IL 60611
David J. A. Hayes, Jr.,
  Executive Director

**American Bar Association
Center for Professional
Responsibility**
541 N. Fairbanks Ct.
Chicago, IL 60611-3314
Jeanne P. Gray, Director
Lawyer watchdog organization

**American Bartender's
Association**
P.O. Box 15527
Sarasota, FL 34277
Douglas Ferguson, Director
  and President

**American Bed and Breakfast
Association**
10800 Midlothian Turnpike
Richmond, VA 23235-4700
Sara Sonke, Director

**American Beefalo World
Registry**
116 Executive Park
Louisville, KY 40207
*Registers the offspring of cattle
  and buffalo matings*

American Bicycle Association
P.O. Box 718
Chandler, AZ 85244
Clayton John, President

American Blimp Corporation
1900 N.E. 25th Ave., #5
Hillsboro, OR 97124
James R. Thiele, President
Blimp manufacturer

**American Blind Bowling
Association**
c/o Alice Hoover
411 Sheriff
Mercer, PA 16137

**American Blind Skiing
Foundation**
610 S. William St.
Mt. Prospect, IL 60056
Sam Skobel, Executive
  Director

**American Boat and Yacht
Council**
3069 Solomons Island Rd.
Edgewater, MD 21037-1416
Lysle B. Gray, Executive
  Director

**American Booksellers
Association**
560 White Plains Rd.
Tarrytown, NY 10591
Bernard E. Rath, Executive
  Director

American Bowling Congress
5301 S. 76th St.
Greendale, WI 53129
Darold Dobs, Executive
  Director

American Bread Company
P.O. Box 100390
Nashville, TN 37210
Charles K. Evers, CEO
*Cookies and crackers
manufacturer*

American Camping Association
5000 State Rd., 67N
Martinsville, IN 46151
Ruth List, Communications
Director

**American Cannabis Research
Experiment**
P.O. Box 3240
Charlottesville, VA 22903
Ellis Godard, Executive
Director
Strives to legalize marijuana

American Canoe Association
7432 Alban Station Rd., #B226
Springfield, VA 22150
Don Sorensen, Commodore

**American Cat Fanciers
Association**
P.O. Box 203
Point Lookout, MO 65726
Wini Keuler, Executive
Director

**American Cave Conservation
Association**
131 Main and Cave Sts.
P.O. Box 409
Horse Cave, KY 42749
David G. Foster, Executive
Director

**American CB Radio
Association**
3478 Main St.
Hartford, CT 06120
Mark E. Wertheim, President

American Checker Federation
P.O. Drawer 365
Petal, MS 39465
Charles Walker, Secretary

American Cheese Society
c/o Food Work
34 Downing St.
New York, NY 10014
Anna Herman, Executive
Director

American Chess Foundation
353 W. 46th St.
New York, NY 10036
Allen Kaufman, Executive
Director

American Chewing Gum, Inc.
Eagle and Lawrence Rds.
Havertown, PA 19083
Edward L. Fenimore,
President
Chewing gum manufacturer

American Chicle Group
810 Main St.
Cambridge, MA 02139
Donald R. Eberhart, Manager
Candy manufacturer

**American Civil Defense
Association, The**
118 S. Court St.
P.O. Box 1057
Starke, FL 32091
Max Klinghoffer, M.D.,
President

**American Civil Liberties
Union**
132 W. 43rd St.
New York, NY 10036
Ira Glasser, Executive Director

American Coaster Enthusiasts
P.O. Box 8226
Chicago, IL 60680
Ray J. Ueberroth, President
Roller coaster fans

American Conservation Association
30 Rockefeller Plaza, #5402
New York, NY 10112
George Lamb, Executive
Director

American Council of Spotted Asses
P.O. Box 121
New Melle, MD 63365
John Counter, President
Donkey breeders

American Counseling Association
5999 Stevenson Ave.
Alexandria, VA 22304-3300
Dr. Theodore P. Remley, Jr.,
Executive Director

American Countertrade Association
P.O. Box 31432
St. Louis, MO 63131
Dan West, Chairman
Assisting countries in the generation of hard currency to purchase U.S. products

American Crossbow Association
3245 W. Walnut St.
Springfield, MO 65802
Dick Marchand, President

American Crossword Federation
P.O. Box 69
Massapequa Park, NY 11762
Stanley Newman, President

American Cryptogram Association
18789 W. Hickory St.
Mundelein, IL 60060
Rebecca Kornbluh, Treasurer
Code breakers club

American Custom Gunmakers Guild
P.O. Box 812
Burlington, IA 52601-0812
Jan Billeb, Executive Director

American Dairy Association
O'Hare International Center
10255 W. Higgins Rd., #900
Rosemont, IL 60018-5616
Gordon McDonald, Senior
Vice-President

American Dance Guild
31 W. 21st St., 3rd Fl.
New York, NY 10010
Muriel Manings, President

American Darts Organization
7603 E. Firestone Blvd., #E-6
Downey, CA 90241
Tom Fleetwood, Executive
Director

American Deaf Volleyball Association
c/o Farely Warshaw
300 Roxborough St.
Rochester, NY 14619

American Dinner Theatre Institute
P.O. Box 7057
Akron, OH 44306
William Lynk, Executive
Director

American Double Dutch League
P.O. Box 776
Bronx, NY 10451
David A. Walker, President
Jump ropers

American Facsimile Association
1528 Walnut St.
Philadelphia, PA 19102
G. L. Brodsky, Executive
Director
FAX group

American Fancy Rat and Mouse Association
9230 64th St.
Riverside, CA 92509
Karen Hauser, Founder
Mouse and rat breeders

American Federation of Pueri Cantores
(Children in Roman Catholic Church Choirs)
5445 11th Ave., N.
St. Petersburg, FL 33710
William Tapp, Executive Officer

American Fighter Aces Museum Foundation
4636 Fighter Aces Dr.
Mesa, AZ 85205
James W. Boyce, Executive Director

American Film Institute
John F. Kennedy Center for the Performing Arts
Washington, DC 20566
Jean Firstenberg, Director

American Folk Music & Folklore Recordings
American Folklife Center
Library of Congress
Washington, DC 20540
Annual list

American Forestry Association
1516 P St. NW
Washington, DC 20005
R. Neil Sampson, Executive Vice-President

American Friends of Lafayette
c/o Daniel A. Evans
Skillman Library
Lafayette College
Easton, PA 18042

American Fur Industry
363 7th Ave., 4th Fl.
New York, NY 10001
Sandra Blye, Executive Vice-President

American Fur Merchant's Association
101 W. 30th St.
New York, NY 10001
Sandra Blye, Executive Director

American Gas Association
1515 Wilson Blvd.
Arlington, VA 22209
Michael Baly, III, President

American Gladiators
1041 N. Formosa Ave.
Los Angeles, CA 90046
TV show

American Gramaphone Records
9130 Mormon Bridge Rd.
Omaha, NE 68152
Michael Delich, National Sales Director
Independent record label

American Greetings Corporation
10500 American Rd.
Cleveland, OH 44144
Morry Weiss, CEO
Greeting card manufacturer

American Gun Trade Association
181 World Trade Center
P.O. Box 581043
Dallas, TX 75258
Peggy Willett, Executive Director

American Handwriting Analysis Foundation
c/o Dorothy W. Hodos
1211 El Solyo Ave.
Campbell, CA 95008

American Hardwood Export Council
1250 Connecticut Ave. NW, #200
Washington, DC 20036
Betsy Ward, Executive Director

American Harp Society
6331 Quebec Dr.
Hollywood, CA 90068
Dorothy Remsen, Executive Secretary

American Hearing Impaired Hockey Association
1143 W. Lake St.
Chicago, IL 60607
Stan Mikita, President

American Hockey League
425 Union St., #D-3
West Springfield, MA 01089
Jack A. Butterfield, President

American Horse Shows Association
220 E. 42nd St., #409
New York, NY 10017
Bonnie J. Blake, Executive Director

American Horticultural Society
7931 E. Boulevard Dr.
Alexandria, VA 22308
Helen L. Walutes, Executive Director
Plant group

American Hot Rod Association
111 N. Haford Rd.
Spokane, WA 99204
Orville Moe, Executive Vice-President

American Humane Association
Children's Division
63 Inverness Dr. E.
Englewood, CO 80112
Patricia Schene, Ph.D., Director
Protects children from neglect and abuse

American Institute of Graphic Arts
1059 3rd Ave.
New York, NY 10021
Caroline Hightower, Director

American Journal
King World Productions Inc.
1700 Broadway, 35th Fl.
New York, NY 10019
TV series

American Junior Gold Association
2415 Steeplechase Lane
Roswell, GA 30076
Stephen A. Hamblin, Executive Director

American Kennel Club
51 Madison Ave.
New York, NY 10010
Robert Maxwell, CEO
Dog breeders

American Kiddie Ride Association
3800 Nicollet Ave. S.
Minneapolis, MN 55409
Anita Bennett, Executive Director

American Kitefliers Association
1559 Rockville Pike
Rockville, MD 20852
David Gomberg, President

American Lawn Bowling Association
c/o Merton Isaacman
17 Buckthorn
Irvine, CA 92714

American League of
Professional Baseball Clubs
350 Park Ave.
New York, NY 10022
Robert W. Brown, M.D.,
President

American Legion Baseball
P.O. Box 1055
Indianapolis, IN 46206
James R. Quinlan,
Coordinator

American Library Association
50 E. Huron St.
Chicago, IL 60611
Peggy Sullivan, Executive
Director

American Life League
P.O. Box 1350
Stafford, VA 22554
Judie Brown, President
Pro-life

American Marketing
Association
250 S. Wacker Dr., #200
Chicago, IL 60606
Jeffrey Heilbrunn, President

American Meat Institute
P.O. Box 3556
Washington, DC 20007
J. Patrick Boyle, President

American Mensa
2626 E. 14th St.
Brooklyn, NY 11235
Sheila Skolnik, Executive
Director
*Social organization for brainy
people*

American Mime Theatre, The
61 4th Ave.
New York, NY 10003-5202
Paul J. Curtis, Founder and
Director

American Mining Congress
1920 N St. NW, #300
Washington, DC 20036
John A. Knebel, President

American Mobilehome
Association
12929 W. 26th Ave.
Golden, CO 80401
R. Eranest White, CAE,
President

American Model Soldiers
Society
1390 El Camino
San Carlos, CA 94070
Frank G. Frisella, Director

American Model Yachting
Association
c/o Harry Robertson
2793 Shellwick Ct.
Columbus, OH 43234

American Motorcyclist
Association
P.O. Box 6114
Westerville, OH 43081
Ed Youngblood, President

American Music Center
(U.S. Information Center for
American Music)
30 W. 26th St., #1001
New York, NY 10010
Nancy Clarke, Executive
Director

American Music Conference
303 E. Wacker Dr., #1214
Chicago, IL 60601
Paul Bjorneberg, Director
Sponsors school and church music

American Music Scholarship
Association
1826 Carew Tower
Cincinnati, OH 45202
Gloria Ackerman, Executive
Director

American Musical Instrument Society
c/o The Shrine to Music Museum
414 E. Clark St.
Vermillion, SD 57069
Margaret Downie Banks, Registrar

American Name Society
c/o Prof. Wayne H. Finke
Baruch College
Department of Modern Languages and Comparative Literature
Box 340
New York, NY 10010
Professional onomalologists

American Needlepoint Guild
P.O. Box 3525
Rock Hills, SC 29732
Nancy Bowers, President

American Nuclear Insurers
Town Center
29 S. Main St., #300-S
West Hartford, CT 06107-2445
Robert J. Clark, Executive Vice-President

American Numismatic Association
818 N. Cascade Ave.
Colorado Springs, CO 80903
Robert J. Leuver, Executive Director
Coin collectors

American Orff-Schulwerk Association
P.O. Box 391089
Cleveland, OH 44139
Cindi Wobig, Executive Secretary
Music for children

American Petroleum Institute
1220 L St. NW
Washington, DC 20005
Charles J. DiBona, President

American Philatelic Society
100 Oakwood Ave.
P.O. Box 8000
State College, PA 16803
Keith A. Wagner, Executive Director
Stamp collectors

American Planning Association
1776 Massachusetts Ave. NW, #400
Washington, DC 20036
Israel Stollman, Executive Director
Community development

American Poolplayers Association
1000 Lake St. Louis Blvd., #325
Lake St. Louis, MO 63367
Terry L. Bell, Executive Officer

American Power Boat Association
P.O. Box 377
17640 E. 9 Mile Rd.
Eastpointe, MI 48021
Gloria J. Urbin, Executive Administrator

American Puffer Alliance
c/o Foster Gunnison, Jr.
1 Gold St., #22-ABC
Hartford, CT 06103
Promotes smokers' rights

American Quilt Study Group
660 Mission St., #400
San Francisco, CA 94105-4007
Sarah K. Howard, Executive Director

American Quilter's Society
P.O. Box 3290
Paducah, KY 42001
Meredith Schroeder, Executive

American Record Guide
Salem Research
R.D. 1, Box 183
Stoddard Hollow Rd.
Delancey, NY 13752
Magazine

American Recorder Society
580 Broadway, #1107
New York, NY 10012
Alan G. Moore, Executive
Director

American Recreational Equipment Association
P.O. Box 395
Mason, OH 45040
R. C. Fussner, Sr., Executive
Director
Amusement-riding devices

American Red Cross National Headquarters
431 18th St. NW
Washington, DC 20006
Elizabeth Dole, President

American Restitution Association
232 Horton Hall
P.O. Box 70099
Shippenburg University
Charleston, SC 29415
Elizabeth Watson, President
Strives for accountability in the juvenile justice system

American Rivers
801 Pennsylvania Ave. SE, #400
Washington, DC 20003
Kevin J. Coyle, President

American Roque and Croquet Association
P.O. Box 2304
Richmond, IN 47375
Jack R. Roegner, President
(Roque is billiards combined with croquet)

American Sailing Association
13922 Marquesas Way
Marina del Rey, CA 90292
Leonard Shabes, Executive
Director

American Sammy Corporation
2421 205th St., Suite D-104
Torrance, CA 90501
Manufactures software for electronic games

American Seating Co.
901 Broadway
Grand Rapids, MI 49504
Albert H. Meyer, President
Manufactures stadium and arena seating

American Senior Citizens Association
P.O. Box 41
Fayetteville, NC 28302
Ben Sutton, Executive Vice-President

American Sewing Guild
P.O. Box 8476
Medford, OR 97504
Edie Von Kamecke, Director

American Shore and Beach Preservation Association
P.O. Box 279
Middletown, CA 95461
Orville T. Magoon, President

American Shortwave Listeners Club
16182 Ballad Lane
Huntington Beach, CA 92649
Stewart Mackenzie, General
Manager

American Ski Association
P.O. Box 480067
Denver, CO 80248
Michael Marston, President

American Society for Amusement Park Security and Safety
c/o Robert Brauner
Universal Studios Florida
1000 Universal Studios
Orlando, FL 32819-8330
Thomas Hugh Latimer,
Executive Vice-President

ASPCA
American Society for the Prevention of Cruelty to Animals
424 E. 92nd St.
New York, NY 10128
Dr. Stephen Zawistowski,
Executive Vice-President

American Society of Association Executives
1575 Eye St. NW
Washington, DC 20005-1168
R. William Taylor, CAE,
President

American Society of Cinematographers
1782 N. Orange Dr.
Hollywood, CA 90028
William A. Fraker, President

ASCAP
American Society of Composers, Authors and Publishers
1 Lincoln Plaza
New York, NY 10023
Morton Gould, President

American Society of Interior Designers
608 Massachusetts Ave. NE
Washington, DC 20002
Robert H. Angle, Executive
Director

American Society of Journalists and Authors
1501 Broadway, #302
New York, NY 10036
Alexandra S. E. Cantor,
Executive Director

American Society of Music Arrangers and Composers
P.O. Box 11
Hollywood, CA 90078
Bonnie Janofsky, Executive
Secretary

American Society of Photographers
P.O. Box 3191
Spartanburg, SC 29304
Randy Bradford, Executive
Director

American Society of Roommate Services
250 W. 57th St., #1629
New York, NY 10019
Michael Santomauro,
Executive Officer
Cheaper living through roommates

American Society of Theater Consultants
c/o Ned Lustig
12226 Mentz Hill Rd.
St. Louis, MO 63128

American Society of Travel Agents
1101 King St.
Alexandria, VA 22314
Phil Davidoff, President

American Songwriter Magazine
42 Music Square W.
Nashville, TN 37203
Jim Sharp, Publisher

American Sportscasters
Association
5 Beekman St., #814
New York, NY 10038
Louis O. Schwartz, Executive
Director and President

American Stamp Dealers
Association
3 School St., #205
Glen Cove, NY 11542
Joseph B. Savarse, Executive
Officer

American Stock Exchange
86 Trinity Place
New York, NY 10006
James R. Jones, Chairman

American Traffic Safety
Services Association
ATSSA Bldg.
5440 Jefferson Davis Hwy.
Fredericksburg, VA 22407
Robert M. Garrett, Executive
Director

American Truck Stop Owners
Association
P.O. Box 4949
Winston-Salem, NC 27115-
4949
Lloyd L. Golding, President

American Tunaboat
Association
1 Tuna Lane
San Diego, CA 92101
Richard C. Atchison, Contact

American Vaulting Association
P.O. Box 3663
Saratoga, CA 95070
Judith S. Bryer, Executive
Secretary

American Victims of Abortion
419 7th St. NW, #500
Washington, DC 20004
*People who regret having had
abortions*

American Watchmakers
Institute
3700 Harrison Ave.
Cincinnati, OH 45211
Milton C. Stevens, Executive
Secretary

American Water Ski
Association
799 Overlook Dr.
Winter Haven, FL 33884
Duke Cullimore, Executive
Director

American Wheelchair Bowling
Association
3620 Tamarack Dr.
Redding, CA 96003
Walt Roy, Executive Secretary-
Treasurer

American Whitewater
Affiliation
P.O. Box 85
Phoenicia, NY 12464
Phyllis Horwitz, Executive
Director
Whitewater rafters

American Wildlands
3609 S. Wadsworth Blvd., #123
Lakewood, CO 80235
Tracy Lehnan, Executive
Assistant

American Woman's Economic
Development Corporation
641 Lexington Ave.
New York, NY 10022
Rosalind Paaswell, CEO

American Yoga Association
3130 Mayfield Rd., #W-103
Cleveland Heights, OH 44118

American Youth Foundation
1315 Ann Ave.
St. Louis, MO 63104
Robert S. MacArthurs,
President
Strives to develop personal best

American Youth Soccer Organization
5403 W. 138th St.
Hawthorne, CA 90250
Burton K. Haimes, President

Americans for Decency
871 Post Ave.
Staten Island, NY 10310
Paul J. Gangemi, Founder
Conservative traditionalists

Americans for Effective Law Enforcement
5519 N. Cumberland Ave., #1008
Chicago, IL 60656-1498
Wayne W. Schmidt, Executive Director

Americans for International Aid
435 Wavetree
Roswell, GA 30075
Jodie R. Darragh, Director
Aids international adoptions

Americans for Religious Liberty
P.O. Box 6656
Silver Spring, MD 20916
Edd Doerr, Executive Director

Americans for Safe Food
1875 Connecticut Ave. NW, #300
Washington, DC 20009-5728
Roger Blobaum, Director
Advocates contaminant-free food

America's Boychoir Federation
120 S. 3rd St.
Connellsville, PA 15425
Rodolfo Torres, President

America's Most Wanted
151 El Camino
Beverly Hills, CA 90212
Rock group

Amerman, John W.
Mattel, Inc.
333 Continental Blvd.
El Segundo, CA 90245-5012
Toy company executive

Ames, Louise Bates
Gesell Institute of Child Development
310 Prospect St.
New Haven, CT 06511-2188
Child psychologist

Amis, Sir Kingsley
c/o Jonathan Clowes & Co. Ltd.
Iron Bridge House
Bridge Approach
London NW1 8BD England
Novelist

AMOA International Flipper Pinball Association
c/o Doug A. Young
141 W. Vine St.
Milwaukee, WI 53212

Amonte, Anthony Lewis
NY Rangers
MSG4, Pennsylvania Plaza
New York, NY 10001
Hockey player

Amory, Cleveland
200 W. 57th St.
New York, NY 10019-3211
Writer

Amos, James Lysle
P.O. Box 118
Centreville, MD 21617-0118
Photographer

Amos, Tori
c/o Atlantic Records
75 Rockefeller Plaza
New York, NY 10019
Singer

Amputee Shoe and Glove Exchange
P.O. Box 27067
Houston, TX 77227
Dr. Richard E. Wainerdi, Director

Amusement and Music Operators Association
401 N. Michigan Ave.
Chicago, IL 60611-4267
John M. Schumacker, Executive Vice-President

An Claidheamh Soluis—The Irish Arts Center
553 W. 51st St.
New York, NY 10019
Nye Heron, Executive Director

An Emotional Fish
c/o Atlantic Records
75 Rockefeller Plaza
New York, NY 10019
Musical group

And All That Jazz
New Orleans Jazz Club
Box 1225
Kerrville, TX 78029
Magazine

And Why Not?
c/o Island
8920 Sunset Blvd., 2nd Fl.
Los Angeles, CA 90069
Recording artists

Andersen, Morten
New Orleans Saints
6928 Saints Dr.
Metairie, LA 70003
Football player

Anderson, Bradley Jay
United Features Syndicate
200 Park Ave.
New York, NY 10166
Cartoonist

Anderson, Harry
9830 Wilshire Blvd.
Beverly Hills, CA 90212
Actor, magician
birthdate 10/14/49

Anderson, Jack
United Features Syndicate
200 Park Ave.
New York, NY 10166-0005
Newspaper columnist

Anderson, Kevin
9830 Wilshire Blvd.
Beverly Hills, CA 90212
Actor

Anderson, Loni
Capell Coyme & Co.
2121 Ave. of the Stars, #1240
Los Angeles, CA 90067-5009
Actress
birthdate 8/5/46

Anderson, Lynn (Rene)
c/o Buddy Lee Attractions
38 Music Sq. E.
Nashville, TN 37203-4304
Singer
birthdate 9/26/47

Anderson, Neal
Chicago Bears
55 E. Jackson Blvd., #1200
Chicago, IL 60604-4105
Football player

Anderson, Pamela Denise
8730 Sunset Blvd., #220
Los Angeles, CA 90069
Actress

Anderson, Poul William
c/o Scott Meredith
845 3rd Ave.
New York, NY 10022
Science fiction author

Anderson, Richard Dean
8942 Wilshire Blvd.
Beverly Hills, CA 90211
Actor
birthdate 1/23/53

Anderson, Robert
Roxbury, CT 06783
Playwright, novelist, screenwriter

Anderson, Sparky
Detroit Tigers
Tiger Stadium
Detroit, MI 48216
*First baseball manager to win 100
games in a season in both
leagues*

Andretti, John
P.O. Box 34156
Indianapolis, IN 46234
Race car driver

Andretti, Mario
53 Victory Lane
Nazareth, PA 18064
*Race car driver and racing
patriarch*

Andrews, Julie
P.O. Box 666
Beverly Hills, CA 90213
Singer
birthdate 10/1/35

Andrews, Michael A.
303 Cannon House Office
Bldg.
Washington, DC 20515-4325
*Representative from Texas,
Democrat
Twenty-fifth District*

Andrews, Robert E.
1005 Longworth House Office
Bldg.
Washington, DC 20515-3001
*Representative from New Jersey,
Democrat
First District*

Andrews, Thomas H.
1530 Longworth House Office
Bldg.
Washington, DC 20515-1901
*Representative from Maine,
Democrat
First District*

Andrews, V. C.
c/o Pocket Books
1230 Ave. of the Americas
New York, NY 10020
Author

Andrus, Cecil Dr.
State Capitol
Boise, ID 83720
Governor of Idaho

Angelou, Maya
Dave LaCamera Lordly and
Dame Inc.
51 Church St.
Boston, MA 02116
Author and poet

Animal Logic
c/o IRS
3939 Lankershim Blvd.
Studio City, CA 91604
Recording artists

Animal Man
DC Comics, Inc.
1325 Ave. of the Americas
New York, NY 10019
Comic

Animaniacs
Warner Bros. Animation
15303 Ventura Blvd., #1100
Sherman Oaks, CA 91403
Animated series

Anka, Paul
9000 Sunset Blvd., 12th Fl.
Los Angeles, CA 90069
Singer
birthdate 7/30/41

**Ann-Margret
(Olsson)**
3111 Bel Air Dr., #20H
Las Vegas, NV 89109
Singer, actress
birthdate 4/28/41

Annenberg, Walter
Box 98
Rancho Mirage, CA 92270
VIP

Annette Funicello Fan Club
Box 134
Nestleton, Ontario L0B 1LO
   Canada
Mary Lou Fitton, President

Annihilator
c/o Roadrunner
225 Lafayette, #709
New York, NY 10012
Recording artists

**Anonymous Arts Recovery
   Society**
380 W. Broadway
New York, NY 10012
Ivan C. Karp, President and
   Founder
*Preserves sculpture by unknown
   artists, usually architectural
   ornaments*

Ansen, David B.
Newsweek
11835 W. Olympic Blvd.
Los Angeles, CA 90064
Critic, writer

Ant, Adam
1801 Ave. of the Stars, #1250
Los Angeles, CA 90067
Performer
birthdate 11/3/54

Ant Banks
c/o Jive
6777 Hollywood Blvd., 6th Fl.
Hollywood, CA 90028
Recording artists

Antenna
c/o Mammoth
Carr Mill, 2nd Fl.
Carrboro, NC 27510
Rock group

Anthrax
c/o Island
8920 Sunset Blvd.
Los Angeles, CA 90069
Heavy metal group

Anti-Defamation League
823 United Nations Plaza
New York, NY 10017
Abraham H. Foxman, Director

**Antiquarian Booksellers
   Association of America**
50 Rockefeller Plaza
New York, NY 10020
Liane Wood-Thomas,
   Executive Director

Anton, Susan
9300 Wilshire Blvd., #410
Beverly Hills, CA 90212
Actress
birthdate 10/12/50

Antonucci, John
Colorado Rockies
1700 Lincoln St., #4100
Denver, CO 80203-4541
Professional sports team executive

Antupit, Samuel Nathaniel
100 5th Ave.
New York, NY 10011-6903
Art director

Apache
c/o Warner Bros.
3300 Warner Blvd.
Burbank, CA 91510
Recording artists

Apollo Comedy Hour
801 Second Ave.
New York, NY 10017
TV series

Apostles
151 El Camino
Beverly Hills, CA 90212
Recording artists

Appier, Kevin
P.O. Box 419969
Kansas City, MO 64141
Baseball player

Applause
132 Liverpool Rd.
London N1 1LA England
Music magazine

Apple Computer, Inc.
20525 Mariami Ave.
Cupertino, CA 95014
John Sculley, CEO
*Manufactures Apple and
Macintosh computer hardware
and software*

Applegate, Douglas
2183 Rayburn House Office
Bldg.
Washington, DC 20515-3518
*Representative from Ohio,
Democrat
Eighteenth District*

APSCO Enterprises
50th St. and First Ave.
Bldg. #57
Brooklyn, NY 11232
Rudy DiPietro, President
*Manufactures, distributes, and
imports official caps, pennants
and T-shirts for NBA, NCAA,
NHL, NFL and major
league baseball*

Aptidon, Hassan Gouled
Presidence de la Republique
Djibouti, Republic of Djibouti
President of Djibouti

Arbour, Alger
NY Islanders
Uniondale, NY 11553
Hockey coach

Arcaro, Eddie
ABC Sports
1330 Ave. of the Americas
New York, NY 10019
*Sports broadcasting journalist,
former jockey*

Archer, Anne
8942 Wilshire Blvd.
Beverly Hills, CA 90211
Actress
birthdate 8/25/50

Archer, Bill
1236 Longworth House Office
Bldg.
Washington, DC 20515-4307
*Representative from Texas,
Republican
Seventh District*

Archerd, Army
Daily Variety
5700 Wilshire Blvd., #120
Los Angeles, CA 90036
Columnist, TV commentator

**Archie Comics (Archie, Betty,
Veronica, and Jughead)**
Archie Comic Publications
325 Fayette Ave.
Mamaroneck, NY 10453
Comic

**Archive of Contemporary
Music**
110 Chambers St.
New York, NY 10007
Robert George, Director

Arena U.S.A., Inc.
Subsidiary of Adidas
28 Engelhard Dr.
Cranbury, NJ 08512
Peter Tannenbaum, Vice-
President of Manufacturing
Manufactures sports apparel

Arlas, Jimmy
U.S. Tennis Association
1212 Ave. of the Americas
New York, NY 10036
Tennis player

Arista Records, Inc.
6 W. 57th St.
New York, NY 10019
Clive Davis, President
Record label

(Los Angeles Office)
8370 Wilshire Blvd.
Beverly Hills, CA 90211

Arkin, Adam
1999 Ave. of the Stars, #2850
Los Angeles, CA 90067
Actor

Arkin, Alan
21 E. 40th St., #1705
New York, NY 10076
Actor
birthdate 3/26/34

Arkoff, Samuel Z.
Arkoff International Pictures
4000 Warner Blvd., #92
Burbank, CA 91522-0001
Motion picture executive, producer

Arledge, Roone
ABC
47 W. 66th St., 5th Fl.
New York, NY 10023
Television executive

Armani, Giorgio
650 Fifth Ave.
New York, NY 10019
Fashion designer

**Armenian Church Youth
   Organization of America**
630 2nd Ave.
New York, NY 10016
Charles H. Shoshan, III,
   Chairman

Armey, Richard K.
301 Cannon House Office
   Bldg.
Washington, DC 20515-4326
*Representative from Texas,
   Republican
Twenty-sixth District*

Armitage, Karole
225 Lafayette St., #1102
New York, NY 10012
Dancer, choreographer

Armstrong, Bruce
New England Patriots
Foxboro Stadium, Rte. 1
Foxboro, MA 02035
Football player

Armstrong, Charles G.
Seattle Mariners
100 S. King St., #300
Seattle, WA 98104-2842
Professional baseball executive

Armstrong, Curtis
10100 Santa Monica Blvd.,
   25th Fl.
Los Angeles, CA 90067
Actor

Armstrong, Vanessa Bell
c/o Jive
6777 Hollywood Blvd., 6th Fl.
Hollywood, CA 90028
Singer

Arnold, Eddy
Gerard W. Purcell Association
210 E. 51st St.
New York, NY 10022-6501
Singer
birthdate 5/15/18

Arnold, Tom
ABC Entertainment
2040 Ave. of the Stars
Los Angeles, CA 90067
Actor, comedian, producer

Arquette, Patricia
232 N. Canon Dr.
Beverly Hills, CA 90210
Actress

Arquette, Rosanna
4000 Warner Blvd.
Burbank, CA 91522-0001
Actress
birthdate 8/10/59

Arron, Judith Hagerty
Carnegie Hall Corp.
881 7th Ave.
New York, NY 10019-3210
Concert hall executive

Arsenal
c/o Touch & Go
P.O. Box 25520
Chicago, IL 60625
Recording artists

Art Dreco Institute
1709 Sanchez
San Francisco, CA 94131
Paul Drexler, Director
*Total disregard for public taste
and fashion*

Arthur, Beatrice
846 N. Cahuenga Blvd.
Los Angeles, CA 90038
Actress
birthdate 5/13/26

Arthur, Rebeca
9255 Sunset Blvd., #515
Los Angeles, CA 90069
Actress

**Artistic Roller Skating
Federation**
P.O. Box 6579
Lincoln, NE 68506
George Pickard, Executive
Director

Artner, Alan Gustave
Chicago Tribune Co.
435 N. Michigan Ave.
P.O. Box 25340
Chicago, IL 60625-0340
Art critic, journalist

Arum, Robert
3900 Paradise Rd.
Las Vegas, NV 89109-0931
Lawyer, sports events promoter

**Asbestos Information
Association/North America**
1745 Jefferson Davis Hwy.,
#406
Arlington, VA 22202
B. J. Pigg, President

Ash, Mary Kay Wagner
Mary Kay Cosmetics, Inc.
8787 N. Stemmons Fwy.
Dallas, TX 75247-3713
*Pink Cadillac cosmetics
entrepreneur*

Ashford, Evelyn
818 Plantation Lane
Walnut, CA 91789
Track and field athlete

**Ashkenazy, Vladimir
Davidovich**
Royal Philharmonic Orchestra
16 Clerkenwell Green
London EC1R 0DP England
Concert pianist, conductor

Ashley, Elizabeth
232 N. Canon Dr.
Beverly Hills, CA 90210
Actress
birthdate 8/30/41

Ashton, Alan C.
Wordperfect Corp.
1555 N. Technology Way
Orem, UT 84057-2399
*Computer software company
executive*

Ashton, John
232 N. Canon Dr.
Beverly Hills, CA 90210
Actor

Ask a Silly Question
P.O. Box 1950
Hollywood, CA 90078
Kathleen Conner, President
Research firm

Asleep at the Wheel
c/o Buddy Lee
38 Music Sq. E., #300
Nashville, TN 37203
Country and western group

Asner, Ed
10100 Santa Monica Blvd.,
   #700
Los Angeles, CA 90067-4011
Actor
birthdate 11/15/29

Asphalt Ballet
c/o Virgin
338 N. Foothill Rd.
Beverly Hills, CA 90210
Rock group

ASPIRE
Association of Special People
   Inspired to Riding
   Excellence
R.D. 4, Box 115
Malvern, PA 19355
Dottie Heffner, Executive
   Officer
Horseback riding for the physically
   challenged

al-Assad, Lieutenant General
   Hafiz
Office of the President
Damascus, Syria
President of Syria

Assante, Armand
335 N. Maple Dr.
Beverly Hills, CA 90210
Actor
birthdate 10/4/49

Assistance Dogs of America
8806 State Rte. 64
Swanton, OH 43558
Pat Thomasson, Director
Dogs for people with mobility
   impairments

Associated Corset and
   Brassiere Manufacturers
475 5th Ave., #1908
New York, NY 10017
Jack Glauberman, Executive
   Director

Associated Press
50 Rockefeller Plaza
New York, NY 10020
Susan Clark, Administrative
   Assistant

Association, The
c/o Variety Artists
   International
15490 Ventura Blvd., #210
Sherman Oaks, CA 91403
Recording artists

Association for Children for
   Enforcement of Support
723 Phillips Ave., #216
Toledo, OH 43612
Geraldine Jensen, President
Enforcement of child support
   awards

Association for Conservation
   Information
c/o Bob Campbell
P.O. Box 12559
Charleston, SC 29412

Association for Death
   Education and Counseling
638 Prospect Ave.
Hartford, CT 06105-4298
M. Suzanne C. Berry,
   Managing Director

Association for Gravestone Studies
c/o Miranda Levin
30 Elm St.
Worcester, MA 01609

Association for Informal Logic and Critical Thinking
Baker University
Philosophy and Religion Department
Baldwin City, KS 66006
Dr. Donald Hatcher, Treasurer

Association for Recognizing the Life of Stillborns
11128 W. Frost Ave.
Littleton, CO 80127
Frank J. Pavlak, Executive Officer

Association for the Sexually Harassed
P.O. Box 27235
Philadelphia, PA 19118
Cheryl Gomez-Preston, Executive Director

Association for the Study of Dada and Surrealism
c/o George H. Bauer
University of Southern California
Department of French and Italian
Taper 126, University Park
Los Angeles, CA 90089

Association for the Study of Play, The
c/o Garry E. Chick, Ph.D.
University of Illinois
104 Huff Hall
1206 S. 4th St.
Champaign, IL 61820
Studies the effects of play on children

Association for Voluntary Surgical Contraception
79 Madison Ave.
New York, NY 10016
Hugo Hoogenboom, Executive Director

Association of Administrators of the Interstate Compact on the Placement of Children
c/o American Public Welfare Association
810 1st St. NE, #500
Washington, DC 20005
Tim Hickey, President
Helps kids get adopted or placed in good foster care, even if it is across state lines

Association of Alternate Postal Systems
P.O. Box 324
Millburn, NJ 07041
Joy Rudy, Executive Director

Association of American Editorial Cartoonists
4101 Lake Boone Tr., #201
Raleigh, NC 27607
Sally Nicholson, General Manager

Association of Author's Representatives
10 Astor Pl., 3rd Fl.
New York, NY 10013
Ginger Knowlton, Contact

Association of Battery Recyclers
Sanders Lead Co. Corp.
Sanders Rd.
P.O. Drawer 707
Troy, AL 36081
N. Kenneth Campbell, Executive Secretary

Association of Bridal Consultants
200 Chestnutland Rd.
New Milford, CT 06776-2521
Gerard I. Monaghan, President

Association of Child Advocates
1625 K St., NW, #510
Washington, DC 20006
Eve Brooks, President
Lawyers for kids

Association of Clandestine Radio Enthusiasts
P.O. Box 11201
Shawnee Mission, KS 66207
Kirk Baxter, Executive Officer
Pirate radio listeners

Association of Collegiate Entrepreneurs
342 Madison Ave., #1104
New York, NY 10173
Edward Michitsch, Contact

Association of Comedy Artists, The
P.O. Box 1796
New York, NY 10025
Barbara Contardi, President

Association of Concert Bands
3020 E. Majestic Ridge
Las Cruces, NM 88001
Dr. Donald M. Hardisty, Executive Administrator

Association of Conservation Engineers
c/o Terry N. Boyd
Alabama Department of Conservation
64 N. Union St.
Montgomery, AL 36130

Association of Environmental and Resource Economists
1616 P St. NW, #507
Washington, DC 20036
Paul R. Portney, Secretary

Association of Film Commissioners International
c/o Utah Film Commission
324 S. State St., 5th Fl.
Salt Lake City, UT 84111
Leigh Von der Esch, President

Association of Foreign Trade Representatives
P.O. Box 300
New York, NY 10024
John J. McCabe, Executive Director

Association of Former Agents of the U.S. Secret Service
P.O. Box 11681
Alexandria, VA 22312
P. Hamilton Brown, Executive Secretary

Association of Image Consultants International
509 Madison Ave., #1400
New York, NY 10022
Janet F. Babcock, President

Association of Importers/ Manufacturers for Muzzleloading
c/o Butch Winter
P.O. Box 684
Union City, TN 38261

Association of Insolvency Accountants
31332 Via Colinas, #112
Westlake Village, CA 91362
Peter J. Gibbon, President

Association of Professional Ball Players of America
12062 Valley View St., #211
Garden Grove, CA 92645
Charles Stevens, Secretary-Treasurer

Association of Railway Museums
P.O. Box 79
Clifton Forge, VA 24422
Thomas W. Dixon, Jr., President

Association of Representatives of Professional Athletes
P.O. Box 90053
World Way Postal Center
Los Angeles, CA 90009
Richard S. Brinkman, Administrator

Association of State Wetland Managers
P.O. Box 2463
Berne, NY 12023
Jon Kusler, Executive Director

Association of Talent Agents
9255 Sunset Boulevard, #318
Los Angeles, CA 90069
Chester L. Migden, Executive Director

Association of Ukrainian Sports Clubs in North America
680 Sanford Ave.
Newark, NJ 07106
Alexander Napora, Secretary

Astin, John
P.O. Box 49698
Los Angeles, CA 90049-0698
Actor, director, writer, TV's Mr. Addams
birthdate 3/30/30

Astin, Sean
9830 Wilshire Blvd.
Beverly Hills, CA 90212
Actor

Astroturf Industries, Inc.
Subsidiary of Balsam Corp.
809 Kenner St.
Dalton, GA 30720
E. M. Milner, President
Manufactures astroturf

Atari Corporation
1196 Borregas Ave.
Sunnyvale, CA 94086
Sam Tramiel, CEO
Video game manufacturer

Atari Explorer
Jainschigg Communications
2905 Broadway, #2
Long Island City, NY 11106
John Jainschigg, Editor
Game magazine

Atco/East West America
75 Rockefeller Plaza
New York, NY 10019
Sylvia Rhone, Chairperson/ CEO
Record label

ATEC
115 Post St.
Santa Cruz, CA 95060
Jack Shepard, CEO
Baseball and softball equipment

Athletic and Educational Opportunities/International Center
P.O. Box 31113
Chicago, IL 60631
Michael Jedson, President

Athletics Congress of the U.S.A., The
200 Jenkins Ct.
610 Old York Rd.
Jenkintown, PA 19046
Frank Greensberg, President
Track and field

Atkins, Chet
CGP Entertainment
1013 17th Ave. S.
Nashville, TN 37212
Record company executive,
guitarist
birthdate 6/20/24

Atlanta Braves
P.O. Box 4064
Atlanta, GA 30302
Professional baseball team

Atlanta Falcons
Suwanee Rd.
Suwanee, GA 30174
Professional football team

Atlanta Hawks
1 CNN Center
Atlanta, GA 30303
Professional basketball team

Atlanta Rhythm Section
c/o Variety Artists
15490 Ventura Blvd., #210
Sherman Oaks, CA 91403
Recording artists

Atlantic Records
75 Rockefeller Plaza
New York, NY 10019
Ahmet M. Ertegun,
   Chairman/CEO
Record company

(Los Angeles Office)
9229 Sunset Blvd., #900
Los Angeles, CA 90069

(Nashville Office)
1812 Broadway
Nashville, TN 37203

Attenborough, Sir Richard
Old Friars
Richmond Green Surrey
England
Actor, producer, director
birthdate 8/29/23

Atwater, Stephen Dennis
Denver Broncos
13655 Broncos Pkwy.
Englewood, CO 80112
Football player

Atwood, Margaret Eleanor
Oxford University Press
70 Wynford Dr.
Don Mills, ON Canada
   M3C 1J9
Author

Audio Two
c/o Atlantic
75 Rockefeller Plaza
New York, NY 10019
Recording artists

Audubon Naturalist Society of
   the Central Atlantic States
8940 Jones Mill Rd.
Chevy Chase, MD 20815
Ken Nicholls, Executive
   Director

Auerbach, Red
(Arnold Jacob)
Boston Celtics
151 Merrimac, 5th Fl.
Boston, MA 02114
Basketball team executive

Aufzien, Alan L.
NJ Nets
Meadowlands Arena
East Rutherford, NJ 07073
Sports team executive

August, Bille
Danish Govt. Film Office
Vestergade 27
1456 Copenhagen, K Denmark
Film director

Austin Athletic Equipment Corporation
705 Bedford Ave., Box 423
Bellmore, NY 11710
Jonathan Austin, President
Sports equipment, including AMF, Playworld, and Curvemaster lines

Austin, Patti
9000 Sunset Blvd., #1200
Los Angeles, CA 90069
Singer
birthdate 8/10/48

Austin, Timothy
c/o U.S. Olympic Committee
1750 E. Boulder St.
Colorado Springs, CO 80909
Boxer

Austin, Tracy Ann
c/o Advantage International
1025 Thomas Jefferson, NW
Washington, DC 20007
Tennis player

Austrian, Neil R.
National Football League
410 Park Ave.
New York, NY 10022-4407
Football league executive

Authors League of America
330 W. 42nd St., 29th Fl.
New York, NY 10036
Helen A. Stephenson, Contact

Auto & Cherokee
c/o Morgan Creek
1875 Century Park E., #600
Los Angeles, CA 90067
Musicians

Automatic Musical Instrument Collectors Association
AMICA
919 Lantern Glow Trail
Dayton, OH 45431
Paper-roll instrument association

Automotive Dismantlers and Recyclers Association
3975 Fair Ridge Dr., #20
Terrace Level North
Fairfax, VA 22033-2906
William P. Steinkuller,
Executive Vice-President

Automotive Hall of Fame
P.O. Box 1727
Midland, MI 48641
Donald N. Richetti, President

Autry, Gene
P.O. Box 710
Los Angeles, CA 90078
Actor, radio entertainer, broadcasting executive, baseball team executive
birthdate 9/29/07

Autumn Cathedral
c/o Epithet
P.O. Box 6367
Stanford, CA 94309
Rock group

Avalon, Frankie
5513 S. Rim St.
Westlake Village, CA 91362
Singer
birthdate 9/18/39

Avedon, Richard
407 E. 75th St.
New York, NY 10021
Photographer

Aversion
c/o Restless
1616 Vista Del Mar
Hollywood, CA 90028
Recording artists

Avery, Steven Thomas
Atlanta Braves
P.O. Box 4064
Atlanta, GA 30302
Baseball player

Avi
(Avi Wortis)
McIntosh & Otis
310 Madison Ave.
New York, NY 10017-6006
Author

Avildsen, John
2423 Briarcrest Rd.
Beverly Hills, CA 90210-1819
Film director

Awana Clubs International
1 E. Bode Rd.
Streamwood, IL 60107
Arthur Rorheim, President
Bible study, Christian leadership

Awtrey, Jim L.
PGA
100 Ave. of Champions
Palm Beach Gardens, FL
    33410
Sport association executive

Ax, Emmanual
173 Riverside Dr., #12G
New York, NY 10024
Pianist
birthdate 6/8/49

Axton, Hoyt
P.O. Box 1077
Hendersonville, TN 37077-
    1077
Singer, composer
birthdate 3/25/38

Aykroyd, Dan
9830 Wilshire Blvd.
Beverly Hills, CA 90212-1825
Actor, writer
birthdate 7/1/52

Aylwin, Patricio
Oficina de Presidente
Palacio de la Moneda
Santiago, Chile
President of Chile

Azinger, Paul
PGA Tour
112 TPC Blvd.
Ponte Vedra Beach, FL 32082
Golfer

Aziz, King Fahd Ibn Abdul
Royal Diwan
Riyadh, Saudi Arabia
Ruler of Saudi Arabia

B

If you want to know your true opinion of someone, watch the effect produced in you by the first sight of a letter from him.

—SCHOPENHAUER

B Angie B
c/o Bust It Productions
80 Swan Way, #130
Oakland, CA 94612
Rock group

B Side
P.O. Box 1860
Burlington, NJ 08016
Music magazine

B-52's Addicts Anonymous
P.O. Box 506
Canal Street Station
New York, NY 10013
Fan club

B-52's, The
P.O. Box 506
Canal Street Station
New York, NY 10013
Rock group

B.M.X. Products
1250 Avenida a Caso, Suite H
Camarillo, CA 93010
Skip Hess, President
Manufactures bicycles, including the Mongoose

Babangida, General Ibrahim Badamasi
Office of the President
Dodan Barracks
Ikoyi, Lagos
Nigeria
President of Nigeria

Babbitt, Bruce
Department of the Interior
C Street between 18th & 19th
Streets, NW
Washington, DC 20240
Secretary of the Interior

Babe Ruth Baseball/Softball
P.O. Box 5000
1770 Brunswick Pike
Trenton, NJ 08638
Ronald Tellefsen, CEO

Babylon Minstrels
c/o Hollywood Records
500 S. Buena Vista, Animation
Bldg.
Burbank, CA 91505
Recording artists

**Bacall, Lauren
(Betty Joan Perske)**
1350 Ave. of the Americas
New York, NY 10019-4701
Actress
birthdate 9/16/24

Bacchus of the U.S.
National Headquarters
P.O. Box 100430
Denver, CO 80250
Drew Hunter, Executive
  Director
*Anti-alcohol education to college
  students*

Bacchus, Jim
432 Cannon House Office
  Bldg.
Washington, DC 20515-0915
*Representative from Florida,
  Democrat
Fifteenth District*

Bach, Richard
1350 Ave. of the Americas
New York, NY 10019
Author

Bacharach, Burt
c/o Whinney
1875 Century Pk. E.
Los Angeles, CA 90067
Composer, conductor

**Bachrach Rasin Sporting
  Goods, Inc.**
802 Gleneagles Court
Towson, MD 21204
Frederick W. Whitridge,
  President
Sporting goods and equipment

Bachus, Spencer T. III
216 Cannon House Office
  Bldg.
Washington, DC 20515-0106
*Representative from Alabama,
  Republican
Sixth District*

Back to the Future
Universal Cartoon Studios
100 Universal City Plaza
Universal City, CA 91608
Animated series

Bacon, Kevin
9830 Wilshire Blvd.
Beverly Hills, CA 90212
Actor
birthday 7/8/58

Bad 4 Good
c/o Atlantic
9229 Sunset Blvd., #900
Los Angeles, CA 90069
Recording artists

Bad Brains
151 El Camino
Beverly Hills, CA 90212
Recording artists

Bad Company
c/o Atco
9229 Sunset Blvd.
Los Angeles, CA 90069
Recording artists

BAD II
c/o Columbia
2100 Colorado Blvd.
Santa Monica, CA 90404
Recording artists

Bad Religion
c/o Epitaph
6201 Sunset Blvd., #111
Hollywood, CA 90028
Rock group

Badd, Johnny B.
P.O. Box 105366
Atlanta, GA 30348
Professional wrestler

Badfinger
c/o Nationwide Entertaiment
  Services
7770 Regents Rd., #113-905
San Diego, CA 92122
Rock group

Badlees, The
c/o Media Five Entertainment
400 Northampton St., #600
Easton, PA 18042
Recording artists

Baerga, Carlos Obed Ortiz
Cleveland Indians
Cleveland Stadium
Cleveland, OH 44114
Baseball player

Baesler, Scotty
508 Cannon House Office
   Bldg.
Washington, DC 21505-1706
Representative from Kentucky,
   Democrat
Sixth District

Baez, Joan Chandos
P.O. Box 1026
Menlo Park, CA 94026-1026
Folk singer
birthdate 1/9/41

Bagwell, Wendy
c/o Word
3319 W. End Ave., #200
Nashville, TN 37203
Singer

Baha Men
c/o Atlantic
75 Rockefeller Plaza
New York, NY 10019
Recording artists

Bailey, F. Lee
1400 Centre Park Blvd., #909
W. Palm Beach, FL 33401
Star lawyer

Bailey, John
1782 N. Orange Dr.
Hollywood, CA 90028
Cinematographer

Baines, Harold Douglass
Baltimore Orioles
401 W. Camden St.
Baltimore, MD 21218
Baseball player

Baio, Scott
c/o Hargrove Prods.
100 Universal City Plaza,
   #507-3E
Universal City, CA 91608
Actor
birthdate 9/22/61

Bair, Sheila Colleen
Commodity Futures Trading
   Commission
2033 K St. NW
Washington, DC 20581
Commissioner

Baker Street Irregulars
34 Pierson Ave.
Norwood, NJ 07648
Thomas L. Stix, Jr., Wiggins
Sherlock Holmes fans

Baker, Anita
All Baker's Music
804 N. Crescent Dr.
Beverly Hills, CA 90210
Singer
birthdate 1/26/57

Baker, Bill
1724 Longworth House Office
   Bldg.
Washington, DC 20515-0510
Representative from California,
   Republican
Tenth District

Baker, Dusty
San Francisco Giants
Candlestick Park
San Francisco, CA 94124
Baseball team manager

Baker, Ginger
c/o Axiom/Island
8920 Sunset Blvd., 2nd Fl.
Los Angeles, CA 90069
Musician

Baker, Herman
NJ Medical School
Maitland GB 159
65 Bergen St.
Newark, NJ 07107
Vitaminologist

Baker, Howard
801 Pennsylvania Ave. NW,
#800
Washington, DC 20004
Former senator, lawyer

Baker, James Addison III
555 13th St. NW, #500
East Washington, DC 20004
Lawyer, former government official

Baker, Kathy
8942 Wilshire Blvd.
Beverly Hills, CA 90211
Actress

Baker, Richard H.
434 Cannon House Office
Bldg.
Washington, DC 20515-1806
*Representative from Louisiana,
Republican
Sixth District*

Baker, Russell
The New York Times
229 W. 43rd St.
New York, NY 10036-3913
Columnist, author

Bakshi, Ralph
c/o Gang, Tyre, Ramer and
Brown
6400 Sunset Blvd.
Los Angeles, CA 90028-7392
Producer, director

Bakula, Scott
9560 Wilshire Blvd., 5th Fl.
Beverly Hills, CA 90212
Actor
birthdate 10/9

Baldridge, Letitia
P.O. Box 32287
Washington, DC 20008-0587
*Writer, management-training
consultant*

Baldwin, Alec
9830 Wilshire Blvd.
Beverly Hills, CA 90212
Actor
birthdate 4/3/58

Baldwin, Daniel
151 E. Camino Dr.
Beverly Hills, CA 90212
Actor

Baldwin, Stephen
Box 447
Camillus, NY 13031-0447
Actor

Baldwin, William
c/o Bloom
9200 Sunset Blvd., #710
Los Angeles, CA 90069
Actor
birthdate 1963

Balin, Marty
(Martyn Jerel Buchwald)
P.O. Box 347008
San Francisco, CA 94134
Founder of Jefferson Airplane

Balin, Trace
c/o Word
5221 N. O'Connor Blvd.,
#1000
Irving, TX 75039
Singer

Ball, Jerry Lee
Detroit Lions
1200 Featherstone Rd.
Pontiac, MI 48057
Football player

Ballard, Robert
Woods Hole Oceanographic
Water St.
Woods Hole, MA 02543
Marine scientist

Ballenger, Cass
2238 Rayburn House Office
Bldg.
Washington, DC 20515-3310
*Representative from North
Carolina, Republican
Tenth District*

Ballesteros, Severiano
Fairway SA
Pasaje de Pena 2-4
39008 Santander Spain
Golfer

Balloon Federation of America
P.O. Box 400
Indianola, IA 50125
Air balloon enthusiasts

BALLS
c/o Original Sound Records
7120 Sunset Blvd.
Hollywood, CA 90046
Recording artists

Balog, James Dennis
667 Walden Circle
Boulder, CO 80303
Photographer

Baltimore Orioles
401 W. Camden St.
Baltimore, MD 21202
Professional baseball team

Balukas, Jean
Billiard Congress
9 S. Linn St.
Iowa City, IA 52240-3921
Pocket billiard player

Bananarama
c/o London Records
825 8th Ave., 24th Fl.
New York, NY 10019
Rock group

Bancroft, Anne
P.O. Box 900
Beverly Hills, CA 90213
Actress
birthdate 9/17/31

Band AKA, The
151 El Camino
Beverly Hills, CA 90212
Rock group

Band of Susans
c/o Restless
1616 Vista Del Mar
Hollywood, CA 90028
Recording artists

Banda, Hastings Kamuzu
Office of the President
Private Bag 388
Capital City, Lilongwe 3
Malawi
President of Malawi

Banderas
c/o London
825 8th Ave., 24th Fl.
New York, NY 10019
Recording artists

Bands of America
P.O. Box 665
Arlington Heights, IL 60006
L. Scott McCormick, Executive
Director
School band association

Banking Law Institute
22 W. 21st St.
New York, NY 10010
James F. Slabe, Executive Vice-
President

Banks, Ernie
New World Van Lines
14322 Commerce Dr.
Garden Grove, CA 92643-4946
*Business executive, former baseball
player*

Banner, Bob
1875 Century Park E., #2250
Los Angeles, CA 90067
Television producer

Barbera, Joseph
3400 Cahuenga Blvd. W.
Los Angeles, CA 90068-4301
Motion picture and TV producer,
  cartoonist

Barbie and Ken
5150 Rosecrans Ave.
Hawthorne, CA 90250
Famous doll and famous doll
  boyfriend

Barca, Peter W.
1719 Longworth House Office
  Bldg.
Washington, DC 20515-4901
Representative from Wisconsin,
  Democrat
First District

Barcia, James A.
1717 Longworth House Office
  Bldg.
Washington, DC 20515-2205
Representative from Michigan,
  Democrat
Fifth District

Bare, Bobby
(Robert Joseph)
P.O. Box 2422
Hendersonville, TN 37077
Singer, songwriter

Barenboim, Daniel
220 S. Michigan Ave.
Chicago, IL 60604
Conductor, pianist

Barger, Carl
Florida Marlins
100 NE 3rd Ave., 3rd Fl.
Fort Lauderdale, FL 33301
Sports team executive

Barker, Bob
5730 Wilshire Blvd., #475W
Los Angeles, CA 90036-3602
Television personality
birthdate 12/12/23

Barkin, Ellen
3100 N. Damon Way
Burbank, CA 91505-1015
Actress
birthdate 4/16/55

Barkley, Charles
Phoenix Suns
2910 N. Central Ave.
Phoenix, AZ 85012
Basketball player

Barkley, Ivan
c/o World Boxing Association
1 S. Calvert St.
Baltimore, MD 21202
Boxer

Barlow, Thomas J.
1533 Longworth House Office
  Bldg.
Washington, DC 20515-1701
Representative from Kentucky,
  Democrat
First District

Barnes, Jack Whitter
Socialist Workers Party
406 West St.
New York, NY 10014-2526
National secretary

Barnet, Will
15 Gramercy Park
New York, NY 10003
Artist, educator

Barney
c/o Lyons Group
300 East Bethany Rd.
P.O. Box 8000
Allen, TX 75002
The purple dinosaur

Barrett, Rona
P.O. Box 1410
Beverly Hills, CA 90213
Columnist

Barrett, Thomas M.
313 Cannon House Office
Bldg.
Washington, DC 20515-4905
Representative from Wisconsin,
Democrat
Fifth District

Barrow, Dame Nita
Government House
Bridgetown, Barbados
Governor General of Barbados

Barrowman, Mike
U.S. Olympic Committee
1750 E. Boulder St.
Colorado Springs, CO 80909
Swimmer

Barrows, Sidney Biddle
210 W. 7th St.
New York, NY 10023
Ex–Mayflower Madam

Barry All the Time
521 Pulaski Blvd.
Bellingham, MA 02019
Barry Manilow fan club

Barry Gibb Record
99 Tindall Rd.
Middletown, NJ 07748
Fan club

Barry, Dave
Miami Herald
1 Herald Plaza
Miami, FL 33132-1609
Author, humorist

Barry, Rick
Turner Sports
1050 Techwood Dr. NW
Atlanta, GA 30318-5695
Broadcaster, former basketball
player

Barrymore, Drew
9560 Wilshire Blvd., 5th Fl.
Beverly Hills, CA 90212
Actress

Bartlett, Roscoe G.
312 Cannon House Office
Bldg.
Washington, DC 20515-2006
Representative from Maryland,
Republican
Sixth District

Barton, Greg
U.S. Olympic Committee
1750 E. Boulder St.
Colorado Springs, CO 80909
Kayak racer

Barton, Joe
1514 Longworth House Office
Bldg.
Washington, DC 20515-4306
Representative from Texas,
Republican
Sixth District

Baryshnikov, Mikhail
c/o Edgar Vincent
124 E. 40th St.
New York, NY 10016
Actor, dancer, choreographer
birthdate 1/28/48

Baseball Writers Association of
America
36 Brookfield Rd.
Ft. Salonga, NY 11768
Jack Lang, Executive Secretary

Bashir, Brigadier Omar
Hassam Ahmed
Revolutionary Command
Council
Khartoum, Sudan
Prime Minister of the Sudan

Basinger, Kim
9830 Wilshire Blvd.
Beverly Hills, CA 90212
Actress
birthdate 12/8/53

Baskin-Robbins USA Co.
P.O. Box 1200
Glendale, CA 91209
Jim Earnhardt, President
"31 flavors" ice cream co.

Bass, Ronald
9830 Wilshire Blvd.
Beverly Hills, CA 90212
Screenwriter

Bass, Saul
7039 W. Sunset Blvd.
Los Angeles, CA 90028
Graphic designer, filmmaker

Bass-O-Matic
c/o Virgin
338 N. Foothill Rd.
Beverly Hills, CA 90210
Rock group

Bassett, Angela
9150 Wilshire Blvd., #175
Beverly Hills, CA 90212
Actress

Bateman, Herbert H.
2350 Rayburn House Office
  Bldg.
Washington, DC 20515-4601
Representative from Virginia,
  Republican
First District

Bateman, Jason
8942 Wilshire Blvd.
Beverly Hills, CA 90211
Actor
birthdate 1/14/69

Bates, Alan
Prince of Wales Theatre
Coventry St.
London W1V 7FE England
Actor
birthdate 2/17/34

Bates, Kathy
c/o S. Smith
121 N. San Vicente Blvd.
Beverly Hills, CA 90211
Actress

Bates, Michael
U.S. Olympic Committee
1750 E. Boulder St.
Colorado Springs, CO 80909
Track and field medalist

Batman
Warner Bros. Animation, Inc.
15303 Ventura Blvd., #1100
Sherman Oaks, CA 91403
Animated series

Batres, Eduardo
MetroLight Studios
5724 W. 3rd St., #400
Los Angeles, CA 90036-3078
Computer model builder, animator

Bats, Judy
151 El Camino
Beverly Hills, CA 90212
Singer

Batterers Anonymous
8485 Tamarind, #D
Fontana, CA 92335
Jerry M. Goffman, Ph.D.,
  Founder

Battle, Kathleen
165 W. 57th St.
New York, NY 10019
Soprano

Baucus, Max S.
511 Senate Hart Office Bldg.
Washington, DC 20510-2602
Senator from Montana, Democrat

Bausch & Lomb
42 East Ave.
P.O. Box 743
Rochester, NY 14603
Norman D. Salik, Vice-
President public relations/
promotions, eyewear
division
*Sunglass manufacturer, including
Ray-Bans*

Bavasi, Peter Joseph
Telerate Sports, Inc.
600 Plaza Two
Harborside, NJ 07311
Baseball executive

Baxter, Meredith
10100 Santa Monica Blvd.,
16th Fl.
Los Angeles, CA 90067
Actress
birthdate 6/21/47

Bay City Rollers
31 St. Leonards Rd.
Bexhill-on-Sea, East Sussex
TN40 1HP England
Rock group

Bayh, B. Evan III
Room 206, Statehouse
Indianapolis, IN 46204
Governor of Indiana

Baylor, Don Edward
Colorado Rockies
1700 Broadway, #2100
Denver, CO 80290
Baseball manager

Baylor, Elgin
L.A. Clippers
3939 S. Figueroa St.
Los Angeles, CA 90037-1207
Baseball team executive

Baywatch
5433 Beethoven St.
Los Angeles, CA 90066
TV series

Beach Boys
101 Mesa Lane
Santa Barbara, CA 93109
Perennial pop group

Beach, "Sexy" Sonny
1692 Sprinter St., NW
Atlanta, GA 30318
Professional wrestler

Bean, Orson
9255 Sunset Blvd., #515
Los Angeles, CA 90069
Actor
birthdate 7/22/28

Bear Essential News for Kids
Garret Communications, Inc.
209 E. Baseline Rd.
Tempe, AZ 85283
Terry Garrett, Publisher
*Education and entertainment
magazine*

Beastie Boys, The
1750 N. Vine St.
Hollywood, CA 90028
Rappers

Beat Fantastic, The
17 Gosfield St.
London W1P 7HE England
Recording artists

Beat Farmers
15490 Ventura Blvd., #210
Sherman Oaks, CA 91403
Recording artists

**Beatles Fan Club: Good Day
Sunshine**
397 Edgewood Ave.
New Haven, CT 06511

Beatnik Pop
9724 Washington Blvd., #200
Culver City, CA 90232
Rock group

Beats International
1700 Broadway, 5th Fl.
New York, NY 10019
Recording artists

Beats, The
1304 Fletcher Rd.
Tifton, GA 31794
Recording artists

Beatty, Warren
9830 Wilshire Blvd.
Beverly Hills, CA 90212
Actor, producer, director
birthdate 3/30/37

Beau, Si
8174 Melrose Ave.
Los Angeles, CA 90046
Tailor to the stars

Beaumont, Jim & the Skyliners
141 Dunbar Ave.
Fords, NJ 08863
Rock group

Beauties, The
9720 Wilshire Blvd., 4th Fl.
Beverly Hills, CA 90212
Recording artists

Beautiful South, The
322 King St.
Hammersmith, London
W6 ORR England
Recording artists

Beauty Without Cruelty
175 W. 12th St., #16-G
New York, NY 10011
Dr. Ethel Thurston,
  Chairwoman
*Cosmetics group that opposes
  animal testing*

Beavis and Butt-head
MTV
1515 Broadway
New York, NY 10036
Animated series

Becerra, Xavier
1710 Longworth House Office
  Bldg.
Washington, DC 20515-0530
*Representative from California,
  Democrat
Thirtieth District*

Beck, Marilyn
P.O. Box 11079
Beverly Hills, CA 90213-4579
Columnist

Beck, Rodney
San Francisco Giants
Candlestick Park
San Francisco, CA 94124
Baseball player

Becker, Boris
c/o Tom Betz
GCB Lustig 525 Pembroke 1st
  Bldg.
281 Independence Blvd.
Virginia Beach, VA 23462-2986
Tennis player

Becket
5125 Wisconsin Ave., #14
Washington, DC 20016
Recording artists

Bedelia, Bonnie
Janner, Pariser and Meschures
760 N. La Cienega Blvd.
Los Angeles, CA 90069
Actress
birthdate 3/25/48

Bedford, Brian
c/o STE
888 Seventh Ave.
New York, NY 10019
Actor

Bedlam
P.O. Box 128037
Nashville, TN 37212
Recording artists

Bedlam Rovers
P.O. Box 5187
Berkeley, CA 94705
Recording artists

Bednar, Rudy Gerard
ABC News
157 Columbus Ave., 4th Fl.
New York, NY 10023
Senior producer ABC News

Bee Gees
(Maurice, Barry and Robin
Gibb)
P.O. Box 8179
Miami, FL 33139
Pop group

Beene, Geoffrey
550 7th Ave.
New York, NY 10018-3202
Fashion designer

Beer Can Collectors of
America
747 Merus Ct.
Fenton, MO 63026
Tobi Harms, Contact

Beer Institute
1225 Eye Street NW, #825
Washington, DC 20005
Philip C. Katz, President

Beilenson, Anthony C.
2465 Rayburn House Office
Bldg.
Washington, DC 20515-0524
Representative from California,
Democrat
Twenty-fourth District

Bel-Vistas
1 Franklin Park N.
Buffalo, NY 14202
Rock group

Belafonte, Shari
15301 Ventura Blvd., #345
Sherman Oaks, CA 91403
Actress

Belfour, Ed
Chicago Blackhawks
1800 W. Madison St.
Chicago, IL 60612
Hockey player

Believe the Children
P.O. Box 77
Hermosa Beach, CA 90254
Leslie Floberg, President
Organization for parents of
physically, emotionally or
sexually abused children

Believer
200 W. 57th St., #910
New York, NY 10019
Recording artists

Bell Bicycle, Inc.
Subsidiary of Echelon Sports
Corp.
15301 Shoemaker Ave.
Norwalk, CA 90650
Phil Mathews, President/CEO
Wholesaler of bicycle helmets

Bell, Eddy & Valerie
142 8th Ave., N
Nashville, TN 37203
Singing duo

Bell, George Antonio
Chicago White Sox
324 W. 35th St.
Chicago, IL 60616
Baseball player

Bell, Jay Stuart
Pittsburgh Pirates
Three Rivers Stadium
Pittsburgh, PA 15212
Baseball player

Bellamy Brothers
c/o MCA
70 Universal Plaza
Universal City, CA 91608
Country and western singers

Belle, Albert Jojuan
Cleveland Indians
Cleveland Stadium
Cleveland, OH 44114
Baseball player

Bellen, Sixto Duran
Office of the President
Palacio Nacional
Garcia Moreno 1043
Quito, Ecuador
President of Ecuador

Bellisario, Donald P.
8439 Sunset Blvd., #402
Los Angeles, CA 90069
TV producer

Bellow, Saul
Committee Social Thought
University of Chicago
1126 E. 59th St.
Chicago, IL 60637-1539
Author

Bellson, Louie
Associated Booking Corp.
1995 Broadway
New York, NY 10023-5882
Drummer

Belltower
c/o Atlantic Records
75 Rockefeller Plaza
New York, NY 10019
Recording artists

Belmonts
141 Dunbar Ave.
Fords, NJ 08863
Rock group

Beloved, The
c/o Atlantic Records
75 Rockefeller Plaza
New York, NY 10019
Recording artists

Belushi, Jim
9830 Wilshire Blvd.
Beverly Hills, CA 90212-1825
Actor
birthdate 6/15/54

Bemshi
325-331 Lafayette St., 2nd Fl.
New York, NY 10012
Recording artists

**Ben and Jerry's Homemade
Ice Cream**
P.O. Box 240
Waterbury, VT 05676
Ben Cohn, Jerry Greenfield,
owners

**Benatar, Pat
(Andrejewski)**
Gold Mountain Management
2575 Cahuenga Blvd., #470
Los Angeles, CA 90068
Singer
birthdate 1/10/53

Bench, Johnny
P.O. Box 5367
Cincinnati, OH 45201
Former baseball player

Benchley, Peter
c/o ICM
40 W. 57th St.
New York, NY 10019
Author

Bendik
2100 Colorado Blvd.
Santa Monica, CA 90404
Recording artists

Bening, Annette
232 N. Canon Dr.
Beverly Hills, CA 90210
Actress
born 1958

Bennet, Cornelius
Buffalo Bills
1 Bills Dr.
Orchard Park, NY 14127-2296
Football player

Bennett, Harve
4000 Warner Blvd.
Burbank, CA 91522
"Star Trek" producer, writer

Bennett, Robert F.
241 Senate Dirksen Office
Bldg.
Washington, DC 20510-4403
Senator from Utah, Republican

Bennett, Tony
(Anthony Dominick
Benedetto)
101 W. 55th St.
New York, NY 10019-5343
Entertainer
birthdate 8/3/26

Benoit, David
9000 Sunset Blvd., #1200
Los Angeles, CA 90069
Musician

Benson, George
648 N. Robertson Blvd.
Los Angeles, CA 90069
Musician
birthdate 3/22/43

Benson, Robby
9150 Wilshire Blvd., #205
Beverly Hills, CA 90212
Actor, director, writer, composer,
producer
birthdate 1/21/55

Bentely
315 Bainbridge St., #2
Brooklyn, NY 11233
Recording artists

Bentley, Eric
194 Riverside Dr.
New York, NY 10025
Author

Bentley, Helen Delich
1610 Longworth House Office
Bldg.
Washington, DC 20515-2002
Representative from Maryland,
Republican
Second District

Benton, Robert
40 W. 5th St., 18th Fl.
New York, NY 10019-4001
Film director

Bentsen, Lloyd
Department of the Treasury
1500 Pennsylvania Ave., NW
Washington, DC 20220
Secretary of the Treasury

Beowulf
1616 Vista Del Mar
Hollywood, CA 90028
Recording artists

Bereaved Parents
P.O. Box 3147
Scottsdale, AZ 85271
Lewis Bove, President
Parents of children who have died
during autoerotic asphyxiation

Berenger, Tom
c/o Bill Truesch
853 7th Ave.
New York, NY 10019-5215
Actor
birthdate 5/31/50

Berenstain, Janice
Berenstain, Stanley
Sterling Lord
1 Madison Ave.
New York, NY 10010
Authors, illustrators

Beresford, Bruce
c/o Williams
55 Victoria St.
Potts Point NSW 2011
Australia
Film director

Bereuter, Doug
2348 Rayburn House Office
Bldg.
Washington, DC 20515-2701
Representative from Nebraska,
Republican
First District

Bergen, Candice
4000 Warner Blvd.
Burbank, CA 91522
Actress
birthdate 5/9/46

Bergman, Alan
Bergman, Marilyn
888 7th Ave., #2501
New York, NY 10016
Writers, lyricists

Bergman, Ingmar
Box 73
S-620
35 Farosund, Sweden
Film writer, director

Berisha, Sali
Office of the President
Tirana, Albania
President of Albania

Berle, Milton
151 El Camino
Beverly Hills, CA 90212-2775
Comedian
birthdate 7/12/08

Berman, Howard L.
2201 Rayburn House Office
Bldg.
Washington, DC 20515-0526
Representative from California,
Democrat
Twenty-sixth District

Bernard Shaw Society, The
Box 1159
Madison Square Station
New York, NY 1019-1159
Douglas Laurie, Secretary

Bernard, Crystal
151 El Camino
Beverly Hills, CA 90212
Actress

Bernhard, Sandra
10100 Santa Monica Blvd.,
#1600
Los Angeles, CA 90067
Actress, singer, comedienne

Bernsen, Corbin
8942 Wilshire Blvd.
Beverly Hills, CA 90211
Actor
birthdate 9/7/54

Bernstein, Elmer
3815 W. Olive Ave., #201
Burbank, CA 91505
Composer, conductor

Berra, Yogi
(Lawrence Peter)
P.O. Box 288
Houston, TX 77001-0288
Baseball personality, former coach
and player

Berry, Bertice
Twentieth Television
P.O. Box 900
Beverly Hills, CA 90213
Talk show host

Berry, Chuck
(Charles Edward Anderson
Berry)
Berry Park, 691 Buckner Rd.
Wentzville, MO 63385
Singer, composer
birthdate 10/18/26

Berry, Halle
8942 Wilshire Blvd.
Beverly Hills, CA 90211
Actress

Bertinelli, Valerie
12700 Ventura Blvd., #100
Studio City, CA 91604
Actress
birthdate 4/23/60

Bertolucci, Bernardo
Via de Babuino, #51
I-00184 Rome Italy
Film director

Best Kissers in the World
89 5th Ave., 8th Fl.
New York, NY 10023
Recording artists

Better Boys Foundation
845 W. Washington St.
Chicago, IL 60607
Gary Mayberry, Executive Vice-
  President
*Official children's charity of the
  NFL*

Betts, Dicky
(Richard Forrest Betts)
304 E. 65th St., #5A
New York, NY 10021-6783
Guitarist, songwriter, vocalist

Beverly Hills, 90210
Spelling Television
5700 Wilshire Blvd.
Los Angeles, CA 90036
TV series

Beverly Hills, 90210 Magazine
Welsh Publishing Group
300 Madison Ave.
New York, NY 10017
Fan magazine

Bevill, Tom
2302 Rayburn House Office
  Bldg.
Washington, DC 20515-0104
*Representative from Alabama,
  Democrat*
Fourth District

Bewitched
P.O. Box 25581
Chicago, IL 60625
Recording artists

Beyond Beef
1130 17th St. NW, #300
Washington, DC 20036
Howard Lyman, Executive
  Director
*Works to decrease the worldwide
  consumption of beef*

Bailik, Mayim
8942 Wilshire Blvd.
Beverly Hills, CA 90211
Blossom *actress*

Bic Pen Corporation
500 Bic Dr.
Milford, CT 06460
Bruno Bich, President
Ballpoint pen manufacturer

Bicycle Face
133½ E. Franklin St.
Chapel Hill, NC 27514
Recording artists

Biddle, Adrian
127 Charing Cross Rd.
London WC2 England
Cinematographer

Biden, Joseph R.
221 Senate Russell Bldg.
Washington, DC 20510-0802
Senator from Delaware, Democrat

Big Audio Dynamite
1775 Broadway, 7th Fl.
New York, NY 10019
Recording artists

Big Dipper
Laufer Publishing Co.
3500 W. Olive Ave., #850
Burbank, CA 91505
Fan magazine

Big Brother Jake
NorthStar Entertainment
Group
1000 Centerville Turnpike
Virginia Beach, VA 23463
TV series

Big Brothers/Big Sisters of America
230 N. 13th St.
Philadelphia, PA 19107
Thomas M. McKenna,
Executive Director
Adult support for kids without both parents

Big Island Rainforest Action Group
P.O. Box 341
Kurtistown, HI 96760

Big Little Book Collector's Club of America
P.O. Box 1242
Danville, CA 94526
Lawrence F. Lowery, President

Big Thicket Association
Box 198–Hwy. 770
Saratoga, TX 77585
Sunan Rosser, Director

Bike Athletic Co.
Susidiary of Kazmaier
International
P.O. Box 666
Knoxville, TN 37901
James R. Corbett, President
Manufactures and distributes sports clothing and protective equipment

Bilbray, James H.
2431 Rayburn House Office
Bldg.
Washington, DC 20515-2801
Representative from Nevada, Democrat
First District

Bilirakis, Michael
2240 Rayburn House Office
Bldg.
Washington, DC 20515-0909
Representative from Florida, Republican
Ninth District

Bill, Tony
73 Market St.
Venice, CA 90291
Actor, producer, director

Billboard
BPI Communications
Publication
49 Music Square W.
Nashville, TN 37203
Ken Schlager, Editor
Professional entertainment publication

Billiard Congress of America
1700 S. 1st Ave., #25A
Iowa City, IA 52240
Mark Cord, Executive Vice-
President

Billy "Crash" Craddock Fan Club
c/o Leola Butcher
P.O. Box 1585
Mt. Vernon, IL 62864

Billy Barty Foundation
929 W. Olive Ave., #C
Burbank, CA 91506
Carlton L. Russell, Executive
Director
Medical, educational, vocational, etc. support for people less than 4'10" tall

Bilt, Carl
Statsradsbereduingen
10333 Stockholm, Sweden
Prime Minister of Sweden

Bing Records
947 Steiner St.
San Francisco, CA 94117
Kathy McBride, Contact
Independent record label

Bingaman, Jeff
110 Senate Hart Office Bldg.
Washington, DC 20510-3102
Senator from New Mexico,
  Democrat

Binney & Smith, Inc.
P.O. Box 431
Easton, PA 18044
Richard Guren, CEO
Manufactures Crayola crayons

Biondi, Matt
U.S. Olympic Committee
1750 E. Boulder St.
Colorado Springs, CO 80909
Swimmer, diver

Birch, Thora
151 El Camino
Beverly Hills, CA 90212
Actress

Bird, Larry
c/o Boston Celtics
North Station
Boston, MA 02114
Basketball executive

Birmingham, Stephen
Brandt & Brandt
1501 Broadway
New York, NY 10036
Writer

Bishop, Joey
(Joseph Abraham Gottlieb)
151 El Camino
Beverly Hills, CA 90212-2775
Comedian
birthdate 2/3/18

Bishop, Sanford D., Jr.
1632 Longworth House Office
  Bldg.
Washington, DC 20515-1002
Representative from Georgia,
  Democrat
Second District

Bishop, Stephen
10100 Santa Monica Blvd.,
  16th Fl.
Los Angeles, CA 90067
Singer, songwriter

Bisset, Jacqueline
8942 Wilshire Blvd.
Beverly Hills, CA 90212
Actress
birthdate 9/13/44

Bissett, Josie
8942 Wilshire Blvd.
Beverly Hills, CA 90211
Actress

Biya, Paul
Office of the President
Yaounde, Cameroon
President of Cameroon

Blab!
Kitchen Sink Press
2 Swamp Rd.
Princeton, WI 54968
Comics magazine

Black Beat
Sterling's Magazines, Inc.
355 Lexington Ave., 13th Fl.
New York, NY 10017
Black music magazine

Black Crowes, The
75 Rockefeller Plaza, 20th Fl.
New York, NY 10019
Rock group

**Black Entertainment and
Sports Lawyers Association**
P.O. Box 508067
Chicago, IL 60650
Maisha Mayo, Executive
   Director

Black, Clint
30 Music Square W.
Nashville, TN 37203
Singer, musician
born 1962

Black, Craig
Classics on Tape
P.O. Box 969
Ashland, OR 97520
Audio book co.

Black, Shirley Temple
8949 Wilshire Blvd.
Beverly Hills, CA 90211
Ambassador, former actress
birthdate 4/23/28

Blackman, Rolando Antonio
NY Knicks
Madison Square Garden
Two Pennsylvania Plaza
New York, NY 10121-0091
Basketball player

Blackwell, Lucien E.
410 Canon House Office Bldg.
Washington, DC 20515-3802
*Representative from Pennsylvania,
   Democrat*
Second District

Blades, Ruben
c/o David Maldonado
1674 Broadway, #703
New York, NY 10019
Singer, songwriter, composer

Blair, Bonnie
Advantage Intl. Mgmt., Inc.
1025 Thomas Jefferson St. NW
Washington, DC 20007
*Speedskater, won most gold medals
   in Winter Olympics*

Blake, Michael
9200 Sunset Blvd., #402
Los Angeles, CA 90069
Writer

**Blake, Robert
(Michael Gubitosi)**
Mickey Productions
11604 Dilling
N. Hollywood, CA 91604
Actor
birthdate 9/18/33

Blass, Bill
550 7th Ave.
New York, NY 10018-3203
Designer

Blast
Ashley Communications
19431 Business Center Dr.,
   #27
Northridge, CA 91324
Heavy metal magazine

Blasters, The
2667 N. Beverly Glen
Los Angeles, CA 90077
Rock group

Blatty, William Peter
151 El Camino
Beverly Hills, CA 90212-2775
Writer

Blauser, Jeffrey Michael
Atlanta Braves
P.O. Box 4064
Atlanta, GA 30302
Baseball player

Bliley, Thomas Jr.
2241 Rayburn House Office
   Bldg.
Washington, DC 20515-4607
*Representative from Virginia,
   Republican*
Seventh District

Blind Outdoor Leisure Development
533 E. Main
Aspen, CO 81611
Peter Maines, Director

Block, Lawrence
Knox Burger Associates
39½ Washington Square S.
New York, NY 10012
Author

Blockbuster Entertainment Corporation
901 E. Olas Blvd.
Ft. Lauderdale, FL 33301
H. Wayne Huizenga,
Chairman and CEO
U.S. leader in video rentals

Blood, Sweat & Tears
9200 Sunset Blvd., #822
Los Angeles, CA 90069
Rock group

Blood Times
Retro Rock
44 E. 5th St.
Brooklyn, NY 11218
Louis Paul, Editor
Magazine on horror and terror films

Bloodworth-Thomason, Linda
Mozark Productions
4024 Radford Ave.
Studio City, CA 91604
TV producer, writer

Blossom
Witt/Thomas Productions
1438 N. Gower St.
Hollywood, CA 90028
TV series

Blume, Judy
c/o Harold Ober
425 Madison Ave.
New York, NY 10017-1110
Young adult and children's author

Blute, Peter I.
1029 Longworth House Office Bldg.
Washington, DC 20515-2103
Representative from Massachusetts, Republican Third District

BMG Music/RCA
1133 Ave. of the Americas
New York, NY 10036
Michael Dornemann,
Chairman/CEO
Record company

(Los Angeles Office)
6363 Sunset Blvd.
Hollywood, CA 90028

(Nashville Office)
1 Music Square W.
Nashville, TN 37203

Bochco, Steven
Fox Studios
10201 W. Pico Blvd.
Los Angeles, CA 90064-2651
TV producer, writer
birthdate 12/16/43

Boehlert, Sherwood L.
1127 Longworth House Office Bldg.
Washington, DC 20515-3223
Representative from New York, Republican Twenty-third District

Boehner, John A.
1020 Longworth House Office Bldg.
Washington, DC 20515-3508
Representative from Ohio, Republican Eighth District

Bogart, Paul
760 N. La Cienega Blvd.
W. Hollywood, CA 90069-5204
Film director

Bogdanovich, Peter
c/o William Peiffer
2040 Ave. of the Stars
Los Angeles, CA 90067
Film director, writer, producer
birthdate 7/30/39

Boggs, Gil
American Ballet Theatre
890 Broadway
New York, NY 10003-1211
Ballet dancer

Boggs, Wade Anthony
NY Yankees
Yankee Stadium
Bronx, NY 10451
Baseball player

Bogguss, Suzy
Gurley & Co.
1101 17th Ave. S.
Nashville, TN 37212
Country music singer, songwriter

Boitano, Brian
c/o Leigh Steinberg
2737 Dunleer Place
Los Angeles, CA 90064
Figure skater

Bolger, James Brendan
Prime Minister's Office
Parliament Buildings
Wellington, New Zealand
Prime Minister of New Zealand

Bolton, Michael
8980 Wilshire Blvd.
Beverly Hills, CA 90212
Singer, songwriter

Bombeck, Erma
Universal Press Syndicate
4900 Main St.
Kansas City, MO 64112-2644
Author, columnist

Bomp
(Who Put the Bomp)
Box 7112
Burbank, CA 91510
Music magazine

Bon Jovi, Jon
c/o Mercury
825 8th Ave.
New York, NY 10019
Rock singer, composer
birthdate 3/2/61

Bond, Christopher S.
293 Senate Russell Office
   Bldg.
Washington, DC 20510-2503
Senator from Missouri,
   Republican

Bond, Julian
6002 34th Pl. NW
Washington, DC 20015-1607
Civil rights leader

Bonds, Barry Lamar
San Francisco Giants
Candlestick Park
San Francisco, CA 94124
Baseball player

Bongo, Omar (Albert-Bernard)
Presidence de la Republique
Boite Postale 546
Libreville, Gabon
President of Gabon

Bonilla, Bobby
NY Mets
Shea Stadium
Roosevelt Ave. and 126th St.
Flushing, NY 11368
Baseball player

Bonilla, Henry
1529 Longworth House Office
   Bldg.
Washington, DC 20515-4323
Representative from Texas,
   Republican
Twenty-third District

Bonior, David E.
2207 Rayburn House Office
  Bldg.
Washington, DC 20515-2210
Representative from Michigan,
  Democrat
Ninth District

Bonkers
Walt Disney Television
  Animation
5200 Lankershim Blvd.
N. Hollywood, CA 91601
Animated series

Bono
(Paul Hewson)
c/o Island
14 E. 4th St.
New York, NY 10012
Singer, songwriter

Bono, Sonny Salvatore
P.O. Box 1786
32 E. Tahgutz-McCullum Way
Palm Springs, CA 92262
Singer, composer, mayor
birthdate 2/16/35

Bonsall, Joseph Sloan Jr.
c/o J. Halsey Co., Inc.
3225 S. Norwood Ave.
Tulsa, OK 74135
Singer (Oak Ridge Boys)

Boogie
221 Venetian Ave.
Gulfport, MI 39507
Music magazine

Boomerang! Magazine
Listen & Learn Home Ed.,
  Inc.
123 Townsend, #636
San Francisco, CA 94107
David Strohm, Editor
Audio magazine

Boorman, John
8942 Wilshire Blvd.
Beverly Hills, CA 90212
Film director, producer,
  screenwriter

BOP
c/o Relativity
P.O. Box 10770
Oakland, CA 94610
Recording artists

Bop
Laufer Publishing Co.
3500 W. Olive Ave., #850
Burbank, CA 91505
Julie Laufer, Editor
Fan magazine

Boren, David L.
453 Senate Russell Office
  Bldg.
Washington, DC 20510-3601
Senator from Oklahoma, Democrat

Borg, Bjorn
The Pier House
Strand on Green
Chiswick, London W4 3NN
  England
Tennis player

Borge, Victor
c/o Gutman & Murtha
  Associates
162 W. 56th St.
New York, NY 10019
Pianist, comedian
birthdate 1/3/09

Boring Institute
P.O. Box 40
Maplewood, NJ 07040
Alan Caruba, Founder
Against boredom

Borman, Frank
Patlex Corp.
250 Cotorro Ct.
Las Cruces, NM 88005-6506
Laser patent company executive,
former astronaut

Bornand, Ruth Chaloux
139 4th Ave.
Pelham, NY 10803-1409
Antique music-box specialist

Borski, Robert A.
2161 Rayburn House Office
  Bldg.
Washington, DC 20515-3803
Representative from Pennsylvania,
Democrat
Third District

Bosco, Philip
Select Artist
337 W. 43rd St.
New York, NY 10036
Actor
birthdate 9/26/30

Bossy, Michael
NY Islanders
Nassau Veterans Memorial
  Coliseum
Uniondale, NY 11553
Hockey player

Boston Bruins
150 Causeway St.
Boston, MA 02114
Professional hockey team

Boston Celtics
151 Merrimac St.
Boston, MA 02114
Professional basketball team

Boston Red Sox
24 Yawkey Way
Boston, MA 02215
Professional baseball team

Bostwick, Barry
151 El Camino
Beverly Hills, CA 90212-2775
Actor
birthdate 2/24/46

Boucher, Rick
2245 Russell House Office
  Bldg.
Washington, DC 20515-4609
Representative from Virginia,
Democrat
Ninth District

Bourque, Ray
Boston Bruins
Boston Garden
150 Causeway St.
Boston, MA 02114-1310
Hockey player

Boutsikaris, Dennis
1999 Ave. of the Stars, #2850
Los Angeles, CA 90067
Actor

Bowe, Riddick Lamont
International Boxing
  Federation
134 Evergreen Pl., 9th Fl.
East Orange, NJ 07018
Boxer

Bowie, David
(David Robert Jones)
Duncan Heath Associates
162 Wardour St.
London W1 England
Musician, actor
birthdate 1/8/47

BOX
c/o Wild West
7201 Melrose Ave., #D
Los Angeles, CA 90046
Recording artists

Boxer, Barbara
112 Senate Hart Office Bldg.
Washington, DC 20515-0505
Senator from California, Democrat

Boxleitner, Bruce
151 El Camino
Beverly Hills, CA 90212
Actor
birthdate 5/12/50

Boy Meets World
Touchstone Television
500 S. Buena Vista St.
Burbank, CA 91521
TV series

Boy Scouts of America
1325 W. Walnut Hill Lane
P.O. Box 152079
Irving, TX 75015
Ben H. Love, Chief Scout

Boyle, Lara Flynn
606 N. Larchmont Blvd., #309
Los Angeles, CA 90004
Actress

Boyle, Peter
3100 N. Damon Way
Burbank, CA 91505-1015
Actor
birthdate 10/18/33

Boys and Girls International Floor Hockey
124 E. Michigan
Battle Creek, MI 49017
Don Silver, Contact

Boyz II Men
729 7th Ave., 12th Fl.
New York, NY 10019
Singing group

Bradford, Barbara Taylor
450 Park Ave.
New York, NY 10022-2605
Author, journalist, novelist

Bradlee, Ben
Washington Post
1150 15th St. NW
Washington, DC 20071-0002
Executive Editor

Bradley, Bill
731 Senate Hart Office Bldg.
Washington, DC 20510-3001
Senator from New Jersey, Democrat

Bradshaw, Terry
1925 N. Pearson Lane.
Roanoke, TX 76262-9018
Former football player

Braeden, Eric
9300 Wilshire Blvd., #410
Beverly Hills, CA 90212
Actor

Branagh, Kenneth
83 Berwick St.
London W1V 3PJ England
Actor, director, producer
born 1961

Branca, John
Ziffren, Brittenham, and Branca
2121 Ave. of the Stars, 32nd Fl.
Los Angeles, CA 90067
Music attorney

Brandauer, Klaus Maria
8942 Wilshire Blvd.
Beverly Hills, CA 90212
Actor

Brando, Marlon
Brown, Craft & Co.
11940 San Vicente Blvd.
Los Angeles, CA 90049
Actor
birthdate 4/3/24

Branstad, Terry E.
State Capitol
Des Moines, IA 50319
Governor of Iowa

Brashear, Diane Lee
Indiana University
926 W. Michigan St.
Indianapolis, IN 46202-5203
Marital and sex therapist

Brass Ring Society
7029 NW 12th St.
Oklahoma City, OK 73127
Ray Esposito, President
Dream fulfillment organization

Braun, Lilian Jackson
G. P. Putnam's Sons
200 Madison Ave.
New York, NY 10016
Writer

Bravo Cable Network
150 Crossways Park West
Woodbury, NY 11797

Bread and Roses
78 Throckmorton
Mill Valley, CA 94941
Mimi Farina, Executive
Director
*Free, live entertainment for
prisons, convalescent homes, etc.*

Bream, Julian
c/o Harold Holt Ltd.
31 Sinclair Rd.
London W14 ONS England
Classical guitarist and lutanist

Breathed, Berkeley
Washington Post Writers
Group
1150 15th St. NW
Washington, DC 20071-0002
Cartoonist

Breaux, John B.
516 Senate Hart Office Bldg.
Washington, DC 20510-1803
Senator from Louisiana, Democrat

Brenner, David
c/o Brian Winthrop
1975 Broadway
New York, NY 10023-5882
Comedian
birthdate 2/4/45

Breslin, Jimmy
New York Newsday
2 Park Ave.
New York, NY 10016-5603
Newspaperman, author

Brett, George
P.O. Box 1969
Kansas City, MO 64141
Former baseball player

Brevig, Eric
ILM
P.O. Box 2459
San Rafael, CA 94912-2459
Film special-effects expert

Brewster, Bill K.
1727 Longworth House Office
Bldg.
Washington, DC 20515-3603
*Representative from Oklahoma,
Democrat
Third District*

Bridge Across the Pond
c/o Nancy Rosas
707 Flintlock Dr.
Bel Air, MD 21014
Tom Jones fan club

Bridges, Beau
9830 Wilshire Blvd.
Beverly Hills, CA 90212
Actor
birthdate 12/9/41

Bridges, Jeff
9830 Wilshire Blvd.
Beverly Hills, CA 90212
Actor
birthdate 12/4/49

Bridges, Lloyd
151 El Camino
Beverly Hills, CA 90212
Actor
birthdate 1/15/13

Briggs, Joe Bob
P.O. Box 33
Dallas, TX 75221
Drive-in movie critic

Brightman, Sarah
9830 Wilshire Blvd.
Beverly Hills, CA 90212
Singer

Brinkley, Christie
151 El Camino
Beverly Hills, CA 90212
Model

Brinkley, David
1717 DeSales St. NW
Washington, DC 20036-4407
News commentator

Brisco-Hooks, Valerie
P.O. Box 21053
Long Beach, CA 90801-4053
Track and field athlete

BMI
Broadcast Music, Inc.
320 W. 57th St.
New York, NY 10019
Frances W. Preston, CEO and
   President

Broccoli, Albert
1875 Century Park E., #1160
Los Angeles, CA 90067
James Bond movie producer

Brock, Alice May
69 Commercial St.
Provincetown, MA 02657
Alice of Alice's Restaurant

Brockett, Oscar G.
University of Texas
Austin, TX 78712
Theater educator

Broderick, Matthew
BJRC
19345 W. Olympic Blvd.
Los Angeles, CA 90069
Actor
birthdate 3/21/62

Bronson, Charles
9169 Sunset Blvd.
W. Hollywood, CA 90069-3168
Actor
birthdate 11/3/22

Brooks, Albert
8942 Sunset Blvd.
Beverly Hills, CA 90212
Actor, writer
birthdate 7/22/47

Brooks, Garth
1109 17th Ave. S.
Nashville, TN 37212
Singer
birthdate 2/7/62

Brooks, Jack
2449 Rayburn House Office
   Bldg.
Washington, DC 20515-4309
Representative from Texas,
   Democrat
Ninth District

Brooks, Mel
P.O. Box 900
Beverly Hills, CA 90213-0900
Producer, director, writer, actor
birthdate 6/28/26

Brosnan, Pierce
9830 Wilshire Blvd.
Beverly Hills, CA 90212
Actor
birthdate 5/15/53

Brothers, Dr. Joyce
Westwood One Radio Network
1700 Broadway
New York, NY 10019-5903
TV personality, psychologist

Broun, Heywood Hale
CBS News
555 W. 57th St.
New York, NY 10019-2925
Author, broadcaster

Browder, Glen
1221 Longworth House Office
Bldg.
Washington, DC 20515-0103
Representative from Alabama,
Democrat
Third District

Brower, David Ross
Earth Island
300 Broadway
San Francisco, CA 94133
Conservationist

Brown, Charlie
One Snoopy Place
Santa Rosa, CA 95401
"Peanuts" character

Brown, Corrine
1037 Longworth House Office
Bldg.
Washington, DC 20515-0903
Representative from Florida,
Democrat
Third District

Brown, David
Manhattan Project Ltd.
888 7th Ave.
New York, NY 10106
Motion picture producer, writer

Brown, George E., Jr.
2300 Rayburn House Office
Bldg.
Washington, DC 20515-0542
Representative from California,
Democrat
Forty-second District

Brown, Hank
716 Senate Hart Office Bldg.
Washington, DC 20510-0604
Senator from Colorado,
Republican

Brown, Helen Gurley
The Hearst Corp.
224 W. 57th St.
New York, NY 10019-3203
Writer, editor

Brown, James
Brothers Management
Associates
141 Dunbar Ave.
Fords, NJ 08863
Singer, broadcasting executive
birthdate 6/17/28

Brown, Jerry
(Edmund Gerald, Jr.)
3022 Washington St.
San Francisco, CA 94115
Politician

Brown, Jesse
Department of Veterans
Affairs
810 Vermont Ave., NW
Washington, DC 20420
Secretary of Veterans Affairs

Brown, Robert William
American League
350 Park Ave.
New York, NY 10022-6022
League president

Brown, Ronald H.
Department of Labor
14th Street between
Constitution & E Street, NW
Washington, DC 20230
Secretary of Labor

Brown, Sherrod
1407 Longworth House Office
  Bldg.
Washington, DC 20515-3513
Representative from Ohio,
  Democrat
Thirteenth District

Brown, Timothy Donell
L.A. Raiders
332 Center St.
El Segundo, CA 90245
Football player

Brown, Tina
The New Yorker
20 W. 43rd St.
New York, NY 10036
Magazine editor

Browne, Jackson
RR 1, Box 648
Del Valle, TX 78617
Singer, songwriter

Browne, Leslie
Paul Szilard Productions
2000 Broadway, #2B
New York, NY 10023
Dancer, actress

Browning, Kurt
Canadian Figure Skating
  Association
1600 James Naismith Dr., #403
Gloucester, ON Canada
  K1B 5N4
Figure skater

Brubeck, Dave
Derry Music Co.
601 Montgomery St., #800
San Francisco, CA 94111-2611
Musician

Bruckheimer, Jerry
Hollywood Pictures
Animation 1B
500 S. Buena Vista St.
Burbank, CA 91521-0001
Film producer

Bryan, Richard H.
364 Senate Russell Office
  Bldg.
Washington, DC 20510-2804
Senator from Nevada, Democrat

Bryant, Gay
Mirabella Magazine
200 Madison Ave., 8th Fl.
New York, NY 10016
Magazine editor, writer

Bryant, John
205 Cannon House Office
  Bldg.
Washington, DC 20515-4305
Representative from Texas,
  Democrat
Fifth District

Buchwald, Art
2000 Pennsylvania Ave. NW
Washington, DC 20006-1812
Columnist, writer

Buckingham, Lindsey
3389 Camino De La Cumbre
Sherman Oaks, CA 91423-4512
Musician

Buckley, William F., Jr.
150 E. 35th St.
New York, NY 10016-4168
Magazine editor, writer

Buddy Holly Memorial Society
3806 55th St.
Lubbock, TX 79413

Buffalo Bill Memorial
  Association
P.O. Box 1000
Cody, WY 82414
Peter H. Hassrick, Director

Buffalo Bills
1 Bills Dr.
Orchard Park, NY 14127
Professional football team

Buffalo, Inc.
North 724 Madelia
Spokane, WA 99202
Peter Lindstrom, President
Manufacturers of Fruit of the
  Loom products

Buffalo Sabres
Memorial Auditorium
Buffalo, NY 14202
Professional hockey team

Buffett, Jimmy
c/o Frontline Management
80 Universal City Plaza, 4th Fl.
Universal City, CA 91608
Singer, songwriter

Bufman, Zev
1 Blockbuster Plaza
Miami, FL 33133-6030
Stage producer, theater chain
  executive

Bugliosi, Vincent T.
8530 Wilshire Blvd., #404
Beverly Hills, CA 90211
Lawyer, author

Bugs Bunny and Tweety Show,
  The
Warner Bros. Animation
15303 Ventura Blvd., #1100
Sherman Oaks, CA 91403
Animated series

Bullwinkle, Rocky, Boris,
  Natasha, Dudley Do-Right,
  Snidely Whiplash, etc.
8214 Sunset Blvd.
Hollywood, CA 90046
Characters from the Rocky and
  Bullwinkle Show

Bumpers, Dale L.
229 Senate Dirksen Office
  Bldg.
Washington, DC 20510-0401
Senator from Arkansas, Democrat

Bunning, Jim
2437 Rayburn House Office
  Bldg.
Washington, DC 20515-1704
Representative from Kentucky,
  Republican
Fourth District

Bure, Pavel
Vancouver Canucks
100 N. Renfrew St.
Vancouver, BC U5K 3N7
  Canada
Hockey player

Burger King
17777 Old Cutler Rd.
Miami, FL 33157
Barry J. Gibbons, CEO
Fast-food chain

Burgess, Greg
U.S. Olympic Committee
1750 E. Boulder St.
Colorado Springs, CO 80909
Swimmer

Burke, Chris
c/o Abrams
420 Madison Ave.
New York, NY 10017
Actor

Burlesque Historical Society
c/o Exotic World
29053 Wild Rd.
Helendale, CA 92342
Dixie Evans, Executive Officer

Burnett, Carol
8942 Wilshire Blvd., 2d Fl.
Beverly Hills, CA 90212
Actor, comedian, singer
birthdate 4/26/33

Burnette, Olivia
151 El Camino
Beverly Hills, CA 90212
Actress

Burns, Conrad
183 Senate Dirksen Office
  Bldg.
Washington, DC 20510-2603
Senator from Montana,
  Republican

Burns, George
c/o Irving Fine
1100 Alta Loma Rd.
Woodland Hills, CA 90069-
  2455
Actor, comedian
birthdate 1/20/1896

Burns, Ken
Maple Grove Rd.
Walpole, NH 03608
Filmmaker, historian

Burrows, James
Paramount TV
5555 Melrose Ave.
Los Angeles, CA 90038
TV producer

Burton, Dan
2411 Rayburn House Office
  Bldg.
Washington, DC 20515-1406
Representative from Indiana,
  Republican
Sixth District

Burton, Levar
Peaceful Warrior Productions
13601 Ventura Blvd., #209
Sherman Oaks, CA 91423
Actor
birthdate 2/16/57

Burton, Tim
151 El Camino
Beverly Hills, CA 90212
Film director

Buscaglia, Leo
Box 599
Glenbrook, NV 89413
Author

Busey, Gary
12424 Wilshire Blvd., #840
Los Angeles, CA 90025-1042
Actor
birthdate 6/29/44

Bush, George Herbert Walker
10000 Memorial Dr.
Houston, TX 77024
Former President

Business Espionage Controls
  and Countermeasures
  Association
P.O. Box 55582
Seattle, WA 98155
William Johnson, Executive
  Director

Buster Brown Apparel
2001 Wheeler Ave.
Chattanooga, TN 37406
Kent C. Robinson, CEO
Children's clothing co.

Butcher, Susan Howlet
Trail Breaker Kennel
1 Eureka
Manley Hot Springs, AK
  99756-9999
Sled dog racer

Butler, Kevin Gregory
Chicago Bears
Halas Hall
250 Washington Rd.
Lake Forest, IL 60045-2499
Football player

Button, Dick
250 W. 57th St., #1818
New York, NY 10107-1818
Commentator, producer, former
  figure skater

Buyer, Stephen E.
1419 Longworth House Office
  Bldg.
Washington, DC 20515-1405
Representative from Indiana,
  Republican
Fifth District

Buyoya, Major Pierre
Office of the President and
  National Defense
Bujumbura, Burundi
President of Burundi

Buzzi, Ruth
6310 San Vicente Blvd., #407
Los Angeles, CA 90048
Actress
birthdate 7/24/36

Byrd, Chris
U.S. Olympic Committee
1750 E. Boulder St.
Colorado Springs, CO 80909
Boxer

Byrd, Robert C.
311 Senate Hart Office Bldg.
Washington, DC 20515-4801
Senator from West Virginia,
  Democrat

Byrne, Leslie L.
1609 Longworth House Office
  Bldg.
Washington, DC 20515-4611
Representative from Virginia,
  Democrat
Eleventh District

C

A telephone call from a friend is a joy—unless you're in the middle of a meal, having a bath or on the point of going out to an engagement for which you are already late. A letter sender in effect is saying, "I am setting aside some of my time for you alone; I'm thinking of you. This is more important to me than any other thing that I am doing."

—JOHN GREENALL, *Daily Telegraph*

C-Span
Cable Satellite Public Affairs
  Network
400 N. Capitol St. NW, #650
Washington, DC 20001

C.H.U.C.K.
(Committee to Halt Useless
  College Killings)
P.O. Box 188
Sayville, NY 11782
Eileen Stevens, President
Anti-hazing organization

Caan, James
c/o Nugit & Licker
11999 San Vicente Blvd., #460
Los Angeles, CA 90049-7110
Actor
birthdate 3/26/39

Cadaco Inc.
4300 W. 47th St.
Chicago, IL 60632
Wayman Wittman, President
Manufactures board games

Caen, Herb
Chronicle Publishing Co.
901 Mission St.
San Francisco, CA 94103-2988
Newspaper columnist, author

Caesar, Sid
Orland & Orland
9200 Sunset Blvd., #715
Los Angeles, CA 90069
Actor, comedian
birthdate 9/8/22

Cage, Nicholas
(Coppola)
8942 Wilshire Blvd.
Beverly Hills, CA 90211
Actor
birthdate 1/7/64

Cain, Dean
9320 Wilshire Blvd., 3rd Fl.
Beverly Hills, CA 90212
Actor

Caine, Michael
c/o Jerry Pam
118 S. Beverly Dr.
Beverly Hills, CA 90212
Actor
birthdate 3/14/33

Calcevecchia, Mark
PGA
100 Ave. of the Champions
Palm Beach Gardens, FL
  33410
Golfer

Caldwell, Sarah
Opera Co. Boston, Inc.
P.O. Box 50
Newton, MA 02258-0001
Opera producer, conductor, etc.
birthdate 3/6/24

Calgary Flames
P.O. Box 1540
Calgary, Alberta T2P 3B9
  Canada
Professional hockey team

California Angels
Anaheim Stadium
Anaheim, CA 92803
Professional baseball team

Call, Brandon
9744 Wilshire Blvd., #308
Beverly Hills, CA 90212
Actor

Callahan, Sonny
2418 Rayburn House Office
  Bldg.
Washington, DC 20515-0101
Representative from Alabama,
  Republican
First District

Callejas, Rafael Leonardo
Casa Presidencial
6a Avda, la Calle
Tegucigalpa, Honduras
President of Honduras

Calliope
Cobblestone Publishing, Inc.
7 School St.
Peterborough, NH 03458
Caroline Yoder, Editor
History magazine

Calorie Control Council
5775 Peachtree-Dunwoody Rd.,
  #500G
Atlanta, GA 30342
Robert C. Gelardi, Executive
  Director

Calvert, Ken
1523 Longworth House Office
  Bldg.
Washington, DC 20515-0543
Representative from California,
  Republican
Forty-third District

Cameron, Candace
c/o Full House
4000 Warner Blvd.
Burbank, CA 91522
Actress

Camp, Dave
137 Cannon House Office
  Bldg.
Washington, DC 20515-2204
Representative from Michigan,
  Republican
Fourth District

Campaore, Blaise
Office of the President
Ouagadougou, Burkina Faso
Chairman of the Popular Front

Campbell, Ben Nighthorse
380 Senate Russell Office
  Bldg.
Washington, DC 20510-0605
Senator from Colorado, Democrat

Campbell, Carroll A., Jr.
State House
Columbia, SC 29211
Governor of South Carolina

Canady, Charles T.
1107 Longworth House Office
  Bldg.
Washington, DC 20515-0912
Representative from Florida,
  Republican
Twelfth District

Cantwell, Maria
1520 Longworth House Office
  Bldg.
Washington, DC 20515-4701
Representative from Washington,
  Democrat
First District

Caperton, Gaston
State Capitol
Charleston, WV 25305
Governor of West Virginia

Capitol Records
1750 N. Vine St.
Hollywood, CA 90028
Hale Milgram, President/
  Capitol
Joe Smith, President/CEO
  Capitol-EMI Music
Record label

(New York Office)
810 7th Ave., 4th Fl.
New York, NY 10019

Capriati, Jennifer
c/o International
  Management Group
One Erieview Plaza, #1300
Cleveland, OH 44114
Tennis player

Captain America
Marvel Entertainment Group
387 Park Ave. S.
New York, NY 10016
Comic

Car'toons
Petersen Publishing Co.
8490 Sunset Blvd.
Los Angeles, CA 90069
Automobile comic

Cardenes, Andres Jorge
c/o American International
  Artists
515 E. 89th St., #6B
New York, NY 10028
Violinist

Cardin, Benjamin L.
227 Cannon House Office
  Bldg.
Washington, DC 20515-2003
Representative from Maryland,
  Democrat
Third District

Career Success
Target Marketing, Inc.
115 Blue Jay Dr.
Liberty, MO 64068
Vocational and technical
  information

Carey, Mariah
51 West 52nd St.
New York, NY 10019
Singer

Caricaturists Society of
  America
P.O. Box 07098
Brooklyn, NY 11207
Joseph Kaliff, President

Carlson, Arne
State Capitol
St. Paul, MN 55155
Governor of Minnesota

Carnahan, Mel
State Capitol
Jefferson City, MO 65101
Governor of Missouri

Carpenter, Richard
P.O. Box 1084
Downey, CA 90240
Composer, arranger

Carper, Tom
Legislative Hall
Dover, DE 19901
Governor of Delaware

Carr, Bob
2347 Rayburn House Office
   Bldg.
Washington, DC 20515-2208
Representative from Michigan,
   Democrat
Eighth District

Carr, Vikki
(Florencia Bisenta De Casillas
   Martinez Cardona)
P.O. Box 5126
Beverly Hills, CA 90209
Singer
birthdate 7/19/41

Carter Family Fan Club
P.O. Box 1371
Hendersonville, TN 37077

Carteris, Gabrielle
15301 Ventura Blvd., #345
Sherman Oaks, CA 91403
Actress

Cartoonists Guild of New
   York
11 W. 20th St., 9/8th Fl.
New York, NY 10011
Erica Meinhardt, Executive
   Director

Caruso, David
c/o Rowlins/Wright
3340 Barham Blvd.
Los Angeles, CA 90068
Actor

Carvey, Dana
40 W. 57th St.
New York, NY 10019
Actor, comedian, Garth
birthdate 6/6/55

Case Closed
Four Point Entertainment
3575 Cahuenga Blvd., #600
Los Angeles, CA 90068
TV series

Casey, Robert P.
State Capitol
Harrisburg, PA 17120
Governor of Pennsylvania

Cash, Johnny
House of Cash, Inc.
P.O. Box 508
Hendersonville, TN 37077
Singer
birthdate 2/26/32

Cash, June Carter
House of Cash, Inc.
P.O. Box 508
Hendersonville, TN 37077
Singer

Cashbox
6464 Sunset Blvd., #605
Hollywood, CA 90028
George Albert, Publisher
Music magazine

Casino and Theme Party
   Operators Association
2120G S. Highland Dr.
Las Vegas, NV 89102
Marty Wolf, President

Casket Manufacturers
   Association of America
708 Church
Evanston, IL 60201
George W. Leuke, Executive
   Director

Caso, Mark
10600 Holman, #1
Los Angeles, CA 90024
Actor, Ninja Turtle

Casper
Harvey Comics Entertainment,
   Inc.
100 Wilshire Blvd., #500
Santa Monica, CA 90401
Comic

Cassidy Class
667 Center Ave.
Martinez, CA 94553
*David, Shaun, and Shirley Jones
fan club*

Cassidy, David
8721 Sunset, PH7
Los Angeles, CA 90069
Actor, singer
birthdate 4/12/50

Castle, Michael N.
1205 Longworth House Office
Bldg.
Washington, DC 20515-0801
*Representative from Delaware,
Republican At Large*

Castro (Ruz), Fidel
Palacio del Gobierno
Havana, Cuba
*Head of State and President of
Council of State*

Catalina, Inc.
Subsidiary of Kayser/Roth Inc.
6040 Bandini Blvd.
Los Angeles, CA 90040
John E. Watte, Jr., President
*Manufactures gymnastic apparel,
water sports apparel and
swimsuits*

Caterpillar Club
P.O. Box 1328
Trenton, NJ 08607-1328
Richard A. Switlik, Sr.,
President
*Honorary club for airmen and
individuals who successfully
used a parachute to save their
lives*

**Catholic Commission on
Intellectual and Cultural
Affairs**
LaSalle University
1900 W. Olney Ave.
Box 673
Philadelphia, PA 19141-1199
Brother Daniel Burke,
Executive Director

Catholic Guardian Society
1011 1st Ave.
New York, NY 10022
James P. O'Neill, Executive
Director
*Cares for dependent, neglected and
delinquent children*

**CBN
Christian Broadcasting
Network**
1000 Centerville Turnpike
Virginia Beach, VA 23463

CBS Inc.
Los Angeles
7800 Beverly Blvd.
Los Angeles, CA 90036
TV network

(New York Office)
51 W. 52nd St.
New York, NY 10019

CBS Records Inc.
51 W. 52nd St.
New York, NY 10019
Walter Yetnikoff, President &
CEO
Record company

**CD Review Digest—Jazz,
Popular, etc.**
Peri Press
Hemlock Ridge, P.O. Box 348
Voorheesville, NY 12186
Janet Grimes, Editor
Music publication

Cellular Telecommunications Industry Association
1133 21st NW, 3rd Fl.
Washington, DC 20036
Thomas E. Wheeler, President & CEO

Cemetery Dance
Box 858
Edgewood, MD 21040
Horror magazine

Center for Academic Ethics
c/o Dr. Arthur Brown
Wayne State University
311 Education Bldg.
Detroit, MI 48202

Center for Auto Safety
2001 S St. NW, #410
Washington, DC 20009-1160
Clarence M. Ditlow, III, Director

Center for Constitutional Rights
666 Broadway, 7th Fl.
New York, NY 10012
Miriam Thompson, Executive Director

Center for Family Business
5862 Mayfield Rd.
P.O. Box 24268
Cleveland, OH 44124
Leon A. Danco, Ph.D., President

Center for Holistic Resource Management
P.O. Box 7128
Albuquerque, NM 87194
Shannon Horst, President

Center for Lesbian and Gay Studies
CUNY Graduate Center
33 W. 42nd St.
New York, NY 10036
Martin Duberman, Executive Officer

Center for Marine Conservation
1725 DeSales St. NW, #500
Washington, DC 20036
Roger E. McManus, President

Center for Plant Conservation
Botanical Gardens
P.O. Box 299
St. Louis, MO 63166
Donald Falk, Executive Director

Center for Surrogate Parenting
8383 Wilshire Blvd., #750
Beverly Hills, CA 90211
William Handle, President

Center for the Study of Law and Politics
2962 Fillmore St.
San Francisco, CA 94123
Walter McGuire, President
Environmental law

Chafee, John H.
567 Senate Dirksen Office Bldg.
Washington, DC 20510-3902
Senator from Rhode Island, Republican

Champion Products Inc.
Subsidiary of SaraLee Corp.
P.O. Box 850
3141 Monroe Ave.
Rochester, NY 14603
Roger Holland, CEO
Manufactures sports apparel

Chapman, Jim
2417 Rayburn House Office Bldg.
Washington, DC 20515-4301
Representative from Texas, Democrat
First District

Chapman, Tracy
9229 W. Sunset Blvd., #718
West Hollywood, CA 90069
Singer, songwriter

**Charles Darwin Foundation
for the Galapagos Isles**
National Zoological Park
Washington, DC 20008
Craig MacFarland, President

**Charles, Ray
(Ray Charles Robinson)**
2107 W. Washington Blvd.,
#200
Los Angeles, CA 90018
Musician, singer, composer
birthdate 9/23/30

Charley Pride Fan Club
P.O. Box 670507
Dallas, TX 75367

Charlie Daniels Band
Rte. 6, Box 156A
Lebanon, TN 37087
Country band

Charlotte Hornets
Hive Drive
Charlotte, NC 28217
Professional basketball team

Cheap Trick
315 W. Gorham St.
Madison, WI 53703
Rock group

Cheap Trick International
P.O. Box 4321
Madison, WI 53711
Fan club

**Chemical Manufacturer's
Association**
2501 M St. NW
Washington, DC 20037
Charles W. Van Vlack,
Secretary and Vice-President

Cher
P.O. Box 690
Beverly Hills, CA 90213
Actress, singer
birthdate 5/20/46

Cher'd Interest
c/o Linda Huston
5807 Hornet Dr.
Orlando, FL 32808
Cher Fan Club

Chicago
80 Universal City Plaza, #400
Universal City, CA 91608
Rock group

Chicago Bears
250 N. Washington Rd.
Lake Forest, IL 60045
Professional football team

Chicago Black Hawks
1800 W. Madison St.
Chicago, IL 60612
Professional hockey team

Chicago Bulls
980 N. Michigan Ave.
Chicago, IL 60611
Professional basketball team

Chicago Cubs
Wrigley Field
Chicago, IL 60613
Professional baseball team

Chicago White Sox
333 W. 35th St.
Chicago, IL 60616
Professional baseball team

**Chihuahuan Desert Research
Institute**
Box 1334
Alpine, TX 79831
Dennis J. Miller, Executive
Director

Child Abuse Institute of Research
P.O. Box 1217
Cincinnati, OH 45201
Lou Torok, Founder and Director

Child Abuse Listening and Mediation
P.O. Box 90754
Santa Barbara, CA 93190
Carol Brenner, Contact

Child Find of America
P.O. Box 277
New Paltz, NY 12561
Carolyn Zogg, Executive Director
Brings missing children home

Child Help USA Inc.
6463 Independence Ave.
Woodland Hills, CA 91370
Sara O'Meara, Board Chairperson
Research, prevention and treatment of child abuse

Child Keyppers' International
P.O. Box 6292
Lake Worth, FL 33466
JoAnn Currier, Executive Officer
Sponsors identification program for children

Child Reach
155 Plan Way, L024
Warwick, RI 02886
Kenneth H. Phillips, President
U.S. Branch of Foster Parents Plan, supports needy children worldwide

Child Support Resistance
P.O. Box 46666
Cincinnati, OH 45246
Robert M. Evenson, Director
Opposes child support laws and their enforcement

Child Trends
2100 M St., NW
Washington, DC 20037
Nicholas Zill, Ph.D., Executive Officer
Works to improve statistical and research information re: kids and their families

Child Welfare Institute
1365 Peachtree St., NE, #700
Atlanta, GA 30309
Thomas D. Morton, Executive Director
Individuals interested in child welfare issues

Child Welfare League of America
440 1st St. NW, #310
Washington, DC 20001
David S. Liederman, Executive Director
Works to improve care and services for abused, dependent or neglected children

Children Before Dogs
565 West End Ave.
New York, NY 10024
Fran Lee, Director
Organization that believes that unchecked dog waste in urban areas affects the health of children

Children Inc.
P.O. Box 5381
1000 Westover Rd.
Richmond, VA 23220
Jeanne Clarke, President
International child assistance organization

Children of Alcoholic Parents
23425 N.W. Hwy.
Southfield, MI 48075
Support group

Children of the Americas
c/o W.O. Mills III
P.O. Box 140165
Dallas, TX 75214
*Aids orphaned or abandoned
children*

Children of the Green Earth
Box 95219
Seattle, WA 98145
Michael Soule, Executive
Director

Children of the Night
14530 Sylvan St.
Van Nuys, CA 91411
Dr. Lois Lee, Executive
Director
Reclaiming the street kids

**Children's Advertising Review
Unit**
c/o Council of Better Business
Bureaus
845 3rd Ave.
New York, NY 10022
Arthur I. Pober, Vice-President
and Director

Children's Aid International
P.O. Box 83220
San Diego, CA 92138
Dr. T. J. Grosser, CEO
*Nutritional, medical, and
educational assistance to
children in Southeast Asia,
Africa and Latin America*

Children's Committee
P.O. Box 16133
Fresno, CA 93755
Vincent J. Lavery, Chairman
*Brings kids from "trouble" spots to
the U.S. for peaceful vacations*

**Children's Creative Response
to Conflict Program**
c/o Fellowship of
Reconciliation
523 N. Broadway
Box 271
Nyack, NY 10960
Priscilla Prutzman,
Coordinator
*Goal is to help children learn to
live peacefully with others*

Children's Defense Fund
25 E St. NW
Washington, DC 20001
Marian Wright Edelman,
President
Long-range advocacy for kids

Children's Foundation
725 15th St. NW, #505
Washington, DC 20005
Kay Hollestelle, Executive
Director
*Deals with social and economic
issues, including child support*

**CHILD
Children's Healthcare Is a
Legal Duty**
P.O. Box 2604
Sioux City, IA 51106
Dr. Rita Swan, President
*Promotes legal rights of children
in obtaining medical care*

Children's Rights Council
220 Eye St. NE
Washington, DC 20002
David L. Levy, President
*Promotes joint custody and
minimalizes hostility between
divorced parents*

Children's Rights of America
655 Ulmerton Rd., #4A
Largo, FL 34641
Kathryn Rosenthal, Director
*Helps find missing children and
assists exploited children*

Children's Wish Foundation International
7840 Roswell Rd., #301
Atlanta, GA 30358
Linda Dozoretz, Executive Director
Wish fulfillment for sick kids

Chiles, Lawton
State Capitol
Tallahassee, FL 32399
Governor of Florida

Chiluba, Frederick T. J.
State House
P.O. Box 135
Lusaka, Zambia
President of Zambia

Chinese Musical and Theatrical Association
24 Pell St.
New York, NY 10013
Stanley S. Chiu, Executive Director

Chissano, Joaquim
Office of the President
Avda Julius Nyerere
Maputo, Mozambique
President of Mozambique

Chocolate Manufacturers Association of the U.S.A.
7900 Westpark Dr., #A-320
McLean, VA 22102
Lawrence T. Graham, President

Choice on Dying—The National Council for the Right to Die
200 Varick St.
New York, NY 10014
Susan Fox Buchanan, Executive Director

Choreographers Guild
256 S. Robertson
Beverly Hills, CA 90211
J. Kutash, President

Chretien, Jean
Office of the Prime Minister
Langevin Block, 80 Wellington St.
Ottawa K1A 042 Canada
Prime Minister of Canada

Christian Children's Fund
2821 Emerywood Pkwy.
Richmond, VA 23294
Dr. Paul McCleary, Executive Director
International, non-sectarian child care organization

Christian Service Brigade
Box 150
Wheaton, IL 60189
Ken Keeler, President

Christopher, Warren M.
Department of State
2201 C Street, NW
Washington, DC 20520
Secretary of State

Chrysalis Records, Inc.
9255 Sunset Blvd., #319
Los Angeles, CA 90069
John Sykes, President
Recording company

Church's Fried Chicken
1333 S. Clearview Pkwy.
Jefferson, LA 70121
Alvin C. Copeland, Chairman
Fast-food chain

Cincinnati Bengals
200 Riverfront Stadium
Cincinnati, OH 45202
Professional football team

Cincinnati Reds
100 Riverfront Stadium
Cincinnati, OH 45202
Professional baseball team

Cinderella Softball Leagues
P.O. Box 1411
Corning, NY 14830
Tony Maio, President

Cinemax
1100 Ave. of the Americas
New York, NY 10036

Cineplex Odeon Corporation
1925 Century Park E., #300
Los Angeles, CA 90067
E. Leo Kolber, Chairman
Movie theater chain

Circus
P.O. Box 265
Mt. Morris, IL 61054
Hard rock magazine

Cisneros, Henry G.
Department of Housing and
   Urban Development
451 7th St., SW
Washington, DC 20410
*Secretary of Housing and Urban
   Development*

**Citizen's Committee to Amend
   Title 18**
P.O. Box 936
Newhall, CA 91321
*(Title 18 exempts non-custodial
   parents from kidnapping
   charges when they take children
   from their custodial parents)*

**Citizens Committee for the
   Right to Keep and Bear
   Arms**
Liberty Park
12500 NE 10th Pl.
Bellevue, WA 98005
John A. Hosford, Executive
   Director

Civil Air Patrol
Bldg. 714
Maxwell AFB, AL 36112-5572
Brig. Gen. Carl Miller,
   Administrator
*Civilian volunteer auxiliary of
   USAF*

Clapton, Eric
9830 Wilshire Blvd.
Beverly Hills, CA 90212
Guitarist, film score composer
birthdate 3/30/45

Clarissa Explains It All
Nickelodeon
1515 Broadway
New York, NY 10036
TV series

Clark, Dick
3003 West Olive Ave.
Burbank, CA 91505
Producer, host
birthdate 11/30/29

Clark, Roy
c/o J. Halsey
3225 S. Norwood Ave.
Tulsa, OK 74135
Singer, musician
birthdate 4/15/33

**Classic Thunderbird Club
   International**
P.O. Box 4148
Santa Fe Springs, CA 90670
Marjorie Price, Executive
   Director
Car club

**Claus, Santa
(also Mrs. Claus, Elves,
   Dancer, Prancer, Donner,
   Vixen, Cupid, Rudolph,
   Dasher, Comet and Blitzen)**
North Pole 30351

Clay, William L.
2306 Rayburn House Office
Bldg.
Washington, DC 20515-2501
Representative from Missouri,
Democrat
First District

Clayton, Eva M.
222 Cannon House Office
Bldg.
Washington, DC 20515-3301
Representative from North
Carolina, Democrat
First District

Clearinghouse on Child Abuse
and Neglect Information
P.O. Box 1182
Washington, DC 20013
Caroline Hughes, Project
Director
Research and information

Clearinghouse on Family
Violence Information
P.O. Box 1182
Washington, DC 20013
Candy Hughes, Director

Cleary, Beverly Atlee
1350 Ave. of the Americas
New York, NY 10020
Author of books for children and
teenagers

Clement, Bob
1230 Longworth House Office
Bldg.
Washington, DC 20515-4205
Representative from Tennessee,
Democrat
Fifth District

Cleveland Browns
Cleveland Stadium
Cleveland, OH 44114
Professional football team

Cleveland Cavaliers
2923 Statesboro Rd.
Richfield, OH 44286
Professional basketball team

Cleveland Indians
Cleveland Stadium
Cleveland, OH 44114
Professional baseball team

Cliff Richard Fan Club of
America
8916 Skokie Blvd., #3
Skokie, IL 60077

Cliff, Jimmy
c/o Victor Chambers
51 Lady Musgrave Rd.
Kingston, Jamaica
Reggae singer

Cline, Patsy, Fan Club
Box 244
Dorchester, MA 02125

Clinger, William F.
2160 Rayburn House Office
Bldg.
Washington, DC 20515-3805
Representative from Pennslyvania,
Republican
Fifth District

Clinton, Bill
The White House
1600 Pennsylvania Ave.
Washington, DC 20500
President of the United States
birthdate 8/19/46

Clinton, Chelsea
The White House
1600 Pennsylvania Ave.
Washington, DC 20500
First daughter

Clinton, Hillary Rodham
The White House
1600 Pennsylvania Ave.
Washington, DC 20500
First Lady and health care czar

Close, Glenn
9830 Wilshire Blvd.
Beverly Hills, CA 90212
Actress
birthdate 3/19/47

Clowns of America,
International
P.O. Box 570
Lake Jackson, TX 77566
Jack Anderson, President

Club Mediterranee
40 W. 57th St.
New York, NY 10019
Jean-Meichel Landau,
President

Clyburn, James E.
319 Cannon House Office
Bldg.
Washington, DC 20515-4006
Representative from South
Carolina, Democrat
Sixth District

CNN
Cable News Network
One CNN Center
P.O. Box 105366
Atlanta, GA 30348

Coach
Universal Television
70 Universal City Plaza
Universal City, CA 91608
TV series

Coalition for America's
Children
1710 Rhode Island Ave., NW,
4th Fl.
Washington, DC 20036
Kay L. Johnson, Contact
Group of child welfare
organizations working together

Coalition to Promote
America's Trade
c/o W. Brendon Harrington
1101 15th St. NW, #1000
Washington, DC 20005

Coalition to Protect Animals in
Entertainment
P.O. Box 2448
Riverside, CA 92516
Nancy Burnett, Executive
Director

Coast Alliance
235 Pennsylvania Ave. SE
Washington, DC 20003
Beth Millemann, Executive
Director

Coastal Conservation
Association
4801 Woodway, #220W
Houston, TX 77056
Walter W. Fondren, III,
Chairman

Coasters, The
141 Dunbar Ave.
Fords, NJ 08863
Pop group

Coats, Dan
404 Senate Russell Office
Bldg.
Washington, DC 20510-1403
Senator from Indiana, Republican

Coble, Howard
403 Cannon House Office
Bldg.
Washington, DC 20515-3306
Representative from North
Carolina, Republican
Sixth District

Cobra
c/o Cannell Productions
7083 Hollywood Blvd.
Hollywood, CA 90028
TV series

Coca Cola Enterprises Inc.
1 Coca-Cola Plaza, NW
Atlanta, GA 30313
Brian G. Dyson, CEO
Soft drink company

**Cocaine Anonymous World
Services**
3740 Overland Ave., #H
Los Angeles, CA 90034-6337

Cochran, Thad
326 Senate Russell Office
Bldg.
Washington, DC 20510-2402
*Senator from Mississippi,
Republican*

Cocker, Joe
c/o A&M
1416 N. LaBrea Ave.
Hollywood, CA 90028
Singer

Code 3
c/o Barbour/Langley
Productions
222 Colorado Ave.
Santa Monica, CA 90404
TV series

Cohen, William S.
322 Senate Hart Office Bldg.
Washington, DC 20510-1901
Senator from Maine, Republican

Cole of California
Subsidiary of Wickes
Companies
1615 Fruitland Ave.
Los Angeles, CA 90058
George Green, President
*Manufactures gymnastic apparel,
water sports apparel, and
swimsuits*

Cole, Natalie
9830 Wilshire Blvd.
Beverly Hills, CA 90212
Singer
birthdate 2/6/50

Coleman, Ronald D.
440 Cannon House Office
Bldg.
Washington, DC 20515-4316
*Representative from Texas,
Democrat
Sixteenth District*

Collins, Barbara-Rose
1108 Longworth House Office
Bldg.
Washington, DC 20515-2215
*Representative from Michigan,
Democrat
Fifteenth District*

Collins, Cardiss
2308 Rayburn House Office
Bldg.
Washington, DC 20515-1307
*Representative from Illinois,
Democrat
Seventh District*

Collins, Gary
151 El Camino
Beverly Hills, CA 90212
Talk show host

Collins, Jackie
13708 Riverside Dr., #608
Sherman Oaks, CA 91423
Author

Collins, Joan
44 Celeborn St.
South Woodham Ferrers
Chelmsford Essex CM3 7AE
England
Actress
birthdate 5/23/33

Collins, Michael A. (Mac)
1118 Longworth House Office
Bldg.
Washington, DC 20515-1003
*Representative from Georgia,
Republican
Third District*

Collins, Phil
822 S. Robertson Blvd., #200
Los Angeles, CA 90035
Singer, songwriter, drummer
birthdate 1/30/51

Color Me Badd
c/o Reprise Records
3300 Warner Blvd.
Burbank, CA 91505
Pop group

Colorado Rockies
1700 Lincoln St.
Denver, CO 80203
Professional baseball team

Columbia Pictures
10202 W. Washington Blvd.
Culver City, CA 90232
Film production company

Columbia Records, Sony Music Entertainment
51 W. 52nd St.
New York, NY 10019
Don Ienner, President
Record company

(Santa Monica Office)
2100 Colorado Blvd.
Santa Monica, CA 90404

Columbo
Universal Television
70 Universal City Plaza
Universal City, CA 91608
TV series

Combest, Larry
1511 Longworth House Office Bldg.
Washington, DC 20515-4319
Representative from Texas, Republican
Nineteenth District

Combs, Holly Marie
15760 Ventura Blvd., #1730
Encino, CA 91436
Actress

Comedy Channel, The
1100 Ave. of the Americas
New York, NY 10036

Comedy Writers Association
c/o Robert Makinson
P.O. Box 023304
Brooklyn, NY 11202-0066

Comic Books
American Business Directories, Inc.
5711 S. 86th Circle, Box 27347
Omaha, NE 68127
List of 1,688 firms dealing in comic books

Comic Buyer's Guide/Price Guide
Krause Publications
700 E. State St.
Iola, WI 54900

Comics Interview
Fictioneer Books
234 Fifth Ave., #301
New York, NY 10001
Magazine about comic artists

Commish, The
2020 Ave. of the Stars, 5th Fl.
Century City, CA 90067
TV series

Commissioner's Office, Baseball
350 Park Ave.
New York, NY 10022

Committee for Children
172 20th Ave.
Seattle, WA 98122
Karen Bachelder, Executive Director
Seeks to prevent physical and sexual abuse through education

Committee for Mother and Child Rights
210 Ole Orchard Dr.
Clear Brook, VA 22624
Elizabeth Owen, National Coordinator
Custody-related problems

Committee for Sustainable Agriculture
P.O. Box 1300
Colfax, CA 95713
Otis Woolen, Executive Director
Organic agriculture

Committee on Public Doublespeak
c/o National Council of Teachers of English
1111 Kenyon Rd.
Urbana, IL 61801
William Lutz, Chairman

Committee to Abolish Sport Hunting
Box 43
White Plains, NY 10605
Luke A. Sommer, Chairman

Committee to Preserve American Color Television
3050 K St. NW, #400
Washington, DC 20007
Paul Cullen, Counsel

Commodores, The
3151 Cahuenga Blvd., W, #235
Los Angeles, CA 90068
Pop group

Compassion International
3955 Cragwood Dr.
P.O. Box 7000
Colorado Springs, CO 80933
Wilt Erickson, President
Help for kids on Indian reservations, inner cities, etc.

Compton, John George Melvin
Office of the Prime Minister
Castries, St. Lucia
Prime Minister of St. Lucia

Computer Music Journal
MIT Press
55 Hayward St.
Cambridge, MA 02142
Stephen Pope, Editor
Magazine

Condit, Gary A.
1123 Longworth House Office Bldg.
Washington, DC 20515-0518
Representative from California, Democrat
Eighteenth District

Confederate Memorial Association
Confederate Memorial Hall
1322 Vermont Ave. NW
Washington, DC 20005
John Edward Hurley, President

Cong, Vo Chi
c/o Council of Ministers
Bac Thao, Hanoi
Vietnam
President of Vietnam

Congress of Racial Equality
1457 Flatbush Ave.
Brooklyn, NY 11210
Roy Innis, Chairman

Congressional Staff Club
805 House Annex I
Washington, DC 20515
Mary T. Geiger, President

Connick, Harry, Jr.
P.O. Box 4450
New York, NY 10101
Jazz musician
born 1967

Conrad, Kent
724 Senate Hart Office Bldg.
Washington, DC 20510-3403
Senator from North Dakota,
Democrat

Conservation Fund
1800 N. Kent St., #1120
Arlington, VA 22209
Patrick F. Noonan, President

Conservation International
1015 18th St. NW, #1000
Washington, DC 20036
Russell A. Mittermeier,
President

Conte, Brig. Gen. Lansana
Office du President
Conakry, Guinea
President of Guinea

Contemporary Christian Music
CCM Publications Inc.
1913 21st Ave. S.
Nashville, TN 37212
John Styll, Editor
Magazine

Converse Inc.
1 Fordham Rd.
N. Reading, MA 01864
Richard B. Loynd, Chairman
Manufactures athletic shoes

Conyers, John, Jr.
2426 Rayburn House Office
Bldg.
Washington, DC 20515-2214
Representative from Michigan,
Democrat
Fourteenth District

Cooder, Ry
c/o Warner Bros.
3300 West Warner Blvd.
Burbank, CA 91505
Recording artist, guitarist

Coolidge, Rita
c/o Jason McCloskey
426 S. Fairview St.
Burbank, CA 91505
Singer
birthdate 5/1/45

Cooper, Alice
4135 E. Keim Dr.
Paradise Valley, AZ 85235
Singer
birthdate 2/4/48

Cooper, Jim
125 Cannon House Office
Bldg.
Washington, DC 20515-4204
Representative from Tennessee,
Democrat
Fourth District

Copperfield, David
9107 Wilshire Blvd., #500
Beverly Hills, CA 90210
Magician

Coppersmith, Sam
1607 Longworth House Office
Bldg.
Washington, DC 20515-0301
Representative from Arizona,
Democrat
First District

Cops
c/o Barbour/Langley
Productions
2225 Colorado Ave.
Santa Monica, CA 90404
TV series

Cornelius, Don
9255 Sunset Blvd., #420
Los Angeles, CA 90039
TV host

Corporation for Public Broadcasting
901 E St. NW
Washington, DC 20004-2037
Richard W. Carlson, CEO and President

Corvette Club of America
P.O. Box 9288
Glenwood, FL 32722
Walt Mentzer, President
Car club

Cosmetic Ingredient Review
1101 17th St. NW, #310
Washington, DC 20036
Dr. Robert L. Elder, Director
Cosmetic industry self-regulatory organization

**Costello, Elvis
(Declan Patrick McManus)**
c/o Warner Bros.
3300 Warner Blvd.
Burbank, CA 91510
Musician, singer
birthdate 8/25/54

Costello, Jerry F.
119 Cannon House Office Bldg.
Washington, DC 20515-1312
*Representative from Illinois, Democrat
Twelfth District*

Costume Collection
c/o Theatre Development Fund
1501 Broadway, #2110
New York, NY 10036
Whitney Blausen, Administrator
Costume assistance for non-profit theaters

Costume Designers Guild
13949 Ventura Blvd., #309
Sherman Oaks, CA 91423
Carole Frazier, Executive Officer
IATSE Local #892 (Union)

Costume Society of America
55 Edgewater Dr.
Earleville, MD 21919-0073
Inez Brooks-Myers, President

Coulier, David
9200 Sunset Blvd., #428
Los Angeles, CA 90069
Actor, comedian, host

Council on Alternate Fuels
1110 N. Glebe Rd., #610
Arlington, VA 22201
Michael S. Koleda, President

Council on Anxiety Disorders
P.O. Box 17011
Winston-Salem, NC 27116
Sarah U. Vaughan, Director

Council on Competitiveness
900 17th St. NW, #1050
Washington, DC 20006
Kent Hughes, President

**Count Dracula Society
Quarterly**
334 W. 54th St.
Los Angeles, CA 90037
Horror magazine

Country Music Association
1 Music Circle S.
Nashville, TN 37203
Edwin Benson, Executive Director

Country Music Television
2806 Opryland Dr.
Nashville, TN 37214
Country music video programming

Coupon Exchange Club
P.O. Box 13708
Wauwatosa, WI 53213
Becky Thompson, Membership
 Director
Cheaper groceries through coupons

Coverdell, Paul D.
204 Senate Russell Office
 Bldg.
Washington, DC 20510-1004
Senator from Georgia, Republican

Cox, Christopher
206 Cannon House Office
 Bldg.
Washington, DC 20515-0547
Representative from California,
 Republican
Forty-seventh District

Coyne, William J.
2455 Rayburn House Office
 Bldg.
Washington, DC 20515-3814
Representative from Pennsylvania,
 Democrat
Fourteenth District

Cracked
Globe Communications
535 5th Ave.
New York, NY 10017
Humor magazine

Crafted With Pride in the
 U.S.A. Council
1045 Ave. of the Americas
New York, NY 10018
Robert E. Swift, Executive
 Director

Craig, Larry E.
313 Senate Hart Office Bldg.
Washington, DC 20510-1203
Senator from Idaho, Republican

Cramer, Robert E. (Bud), Jr.
1318 Longworth House Office
 Bldg.
Washington, DC 20515-0105
Representative from Alabama,
 Democrat
Fifth District

Crane, Phillip M.
233 Cannon House Office
 Bldg.
Washington, DC 20515-1308
Representative from Illinois,
 Republican
Eighth District

Crapo, Michael D.
437 Cannon House Office
 Bldg.
Washington, DC 20515-1202
Representative from Idaho,
 Republican
Second District

Crawford, Cindy
111 E. 22nd, #200
New York, NY 10010
Model, MTV personality

Cray, Robert
Hightone Records
220 Fourth St., #101
Oakland, CA 94607
Guitarist, singer, songwriter

Create-a-Book
The Book Factory
c/o Hotel Del Coronado
1500 Orange Ave.
Coronado, CA 92118
This company will personalize
 books for kids

CREEM
John T. Edwards Publishing
 Ltd.
519 8th Ave., 15th Fl.
New York, NY 10018
Dan Halpern, Publisher
Music magazine

Cremation Association of North America
401 N. Michigan Ave.
Chicago, IL 60611
Jack M. Springer, Executive
  Director

Crime Stoppers International
3736 Eubank NE, #B4
Albuquerque, NM 87111
Tim Kline, Executive Director

Cristiani, Alfredo
Oficina del Presidente
San Salvador, El Salvador
President of El Salvador

Cro
c/o Children's TV Workshop
One Lincoln Plaza
New York, NY 10023
TV series

Crosby, Stills & Nash
1588 Crossroads of the World
Los Angeles, CA 90028
Musicians

Cross, Christopher
P.O. Box 63
Marble Falls, TX 78654
Singer, songwriter

Cruise, Tom
9830 Wilshire Blvd.
Beverly Hills, CA 90212
Actor
birthdate 7/3/62

Cryer, Jon
9560 Wilshire Blvd., 5th Fl.
Beverly Hills, CA 90212
Actor

Culkin, McCauley
8942 Wilshire Blvd.
Beverly Hills, CA 90211
Actor

Cult of the Virgin
65 Hillside Ave., #B-A
New York, NY 10040
Black Virgin fan club

Cunningham, Randy (Duke)
117 Cannon House Office
  Bldg.
Washington, DC 20515-0551
Representative from California,
  Republican
Fifty-first District

Cuomo, Mario M.
State Capitol
Albany, NY 12224
Governor of New York

Curb Records
3907 Alameda Ave., 2nd Fl.
Burbank, CA 91505
Mike Curb, Chairman/
  President
Record company

Current Affair, A
Twentieth Television
P.O. Box 900
Beverly Hills, CA 90213
TV series

Curry, Adam
c/o MTV
1515 Broadway, 23rd Fl.
New York, NY 10036
MTV video countdown veejay

Curry, Tim
c/o Innovative
1999 Ave. of the Stars, #2850
Los Angeles, CA 90069
Actor

Curtis, Jamie Lee
9830 Wilshire Blvd.
Beverly Hills, CA 90212
Actress
birthdate 11/22/58

Cycles Peugeot, USA, Inc.
Subsidiary of Cycles Peugeot
555 Gotham Pkwy.
Carlstadt, NJ 07072
Alexander Sacerdoti, Executive
  Vice-President
Manufacturer, distributor, and
importer of bicycles, equipment
and apparel

Cyrus, Billy Ray
c/o Mercury
825 8th Ave.
New York, NY 10019
Singer

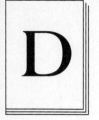

D

A letter is a conversation you can hold.

—NANCY BUNNING

D'Amato, Alfonse M.
520 Senate Hart Office Bldg.
Washington, DC 20510-3202
Senator from New York,
Republican

D'Aviano, Grand Duke Jean
Benoit Guillaume Marie
Robert Louis Antoine
Adolphe Marc
Grand Ducal Place
2013 Luxembourg
Ruler of Luxembourg

D. H. Lawrence Society of
North America
c/o Lydia Blanchard
Southwest Texas State
University
Department of English, GCB
213
San Marcos, TX 78666

D.J. Jazzy Jeff
(Jeff Townes)
1133 Ave. of the Americas
New York, NY 10036
Singer

Dafoe, Willem
9830 Wilshire Blvd.
Beverly Hills, CA 90212
Actor
birthdate 7/22/55

Daily Variety
5700 Wilshire Blvd., #120
Los Angeles, CA 90036
Michael Silverman, Publisher
Entertainment trade paper

Dairy Queen
P.O. Box 35286
Minneapolis, MN 55435
Michael P. Sullivan, CEO
Fast-food chain

Dakin, Inc.
P.O. Box 7746
San Francisco, CA 94120
Harold A. Nizamian, President
Stuffed animal manufacturer

Dallas Cowboys
One Cowboys Pkwy.
Irving, TX 75063
Professional football team

Dallas Mavericks
777 Sports St.
Dallas, TX 75207
Professional basketball team

Dalton, Lacy J.
c/o Capitol Records
1750 Vine St.
Hollywood, CA 90028
Singer

Daltrey, Roger
Left Services
157 W. 57th St.
New York, NY 10019
Musician
birthdate 3/1/44

Daly, Timothy
232 N. Canon Dr.
Beverly Hills, CA 90210
Actor

Danforth, John C.
249 Senate Russell Office
    Bldg.
Washington, DC 20510-2502
Senator from Missouri,
. Republican

Daniels, Charlie
17060 Central Pike
Lebanon, TN 37087
Musician, songwriter
birthdate 10/28/36

Danner, Pat
12178 Longworth House
    Office Bldg.
Washington, DC 20515-2506
Representative from Missouri,
Democrat
Sixth District

Danson, Ted
955 S. Carrillo Dr., 3rd Fl.
Los Angeles, CA 90048
Actor
birthdate 12/29/47

Danza, Tony
8942 Wilshire Blvd.
Beverly Hills, CA 90211
Actor
birthdate 4/21/50

Darden, George W.
2303 Rayburn House Office
    Bldg.
Washington, DC 20515-1007
Representative from Georgia,
Democrat
Seventh District

Dark Tome Magazine
Box 705
Salem, OR 97308
Michelle Marr, Editor
Horror magazine

Daschle, Thomas A.
317 Senate Hart Office Bldg.
Washington, DC 20510-4103
Senator from South Dakota,
Democrat

Dave's World
c/o CBS Entertainment
7800 Beverly Blvd.
Los Angeles, CA 90036
TV series

Davis, Geena
9830 Wilshire Blvd.
Beverly Hills, CA 90212
Actress
birthdate 1/21/57

de Chamorro, Violeta Barrios
Oficina del Presidente
Managua, Nicaragua
President of Nicaragua

De Generes, Ellen
9560 Wilshire Blvd., 5th Fl.
Beverly Hills, CA 90212
Comedienne

de Gortari, Carlos Salinas
Palacio de Gobierno
Mexico City, DF, Mexico
President of Mexico

de la Garza, E. (Kika)
1401 Longworth House Office
Bldg.
Washington, DC 20515-4315
Representative from Texas,
Democrat
Fifteenth District

de Mello, Fernanco Alfonso
Color
Oficina del President
Palacio del Planalto
Praca dos Tres Poderes,
70.150
Brasilia, Brazil
President of Brazil

Dead of Night
916 Shaker Rd., #143
Longmeadow, MA 01106
L. L. Stein, Editor
Horror magazine

Deal, Nathan
1406 Longworth House Office
Bldg.
Washington, DC 20515-1009
Representative from Georgia,
Democrat
Ninth District

Dean, Howard
Pavilion Office Building
Montpelier, VT 05602
Governor of Vermont

Death Row Support Project
P.O. Box 600
Liberty Mills, IN 46946
Rachel Gross, Coordinator
Church of the Brethren members
who write letters to death row
inmates

DeBarge, El
6255 Sunset Blvd., #624
Los Angeles, CA 90028
Singer

Debbie Harry Collector's
Society
124 S. Locust Point Rd.
Mechanicsburg, PA 17055
Fan club

Debby Boone Fan Club
c/o Ms. Chris Bujnovsky
526 Boeing Ave.
Reading, PA 19601

Debtors Anonymous
P.O. Box 400
Grand Central Station
New York, NY 10063
Mary M., Contact

Deby, Colonel Idriss
Office of the President
N'Djamena, Chad
President of Chad

DeConcini, Dennis
328 Senate Hart Office Bldg.
Washington, DC 20510-0302
Senator from Arizona, Democrat

Deep Purple
P.O. Box 254
Sheffield, S6 1DF, England
Rock group

Dees, Rick
KIIS FM
6255 Sunset Blvd.
Los Angeles, CA 90069
Radio personality

Def Leppard
P.O. Box 670
Old Chelsea Station
New York, NY 10113
Rock group

DeFazio, Peter A.
1233 Longworth House Office
Bldg.
Washington, DC 20515-3704
Representative from Oregon,
Democrat
Fourth District

**Defense for Children
International**
United States of America
Division
21 S. 13th St.
Philadelphia, PA 19107
Kenneth Klothen, Executive
Director
*Promotes and protects the rights of
kids*

**DeForest, Calvert
(formerly Larry Bud Melman)**
Worldwide Pants Inc.
1697 Broadway
New York, NY 10019
Comedian

Dehaene, Jean-Luc
16 rue de la Loi
100 Brussels, Belgium
Premier of Belgium

**Del Shannon Appreciation
Society**
6777 Hollywood Blvd., 9th Fl.
Hollywood, CA 90028
Fan club

DeLauro, Rosa L.
327 Cannon House Office
Bldg.
Washington, DC 20515-0703
*Representative from Connecticut,
Democrat
Third District*

DeLay, Tom
407 Cannon House Office
Bldg.
Washington, DC 20515-4322
*Representative from Texas,
Republican
Twenty-second District*

Dellums, Ronald V.
2108 Rayburn House Office
Bldg.
Washington, DC 20515-0509
*Representative from California,
Democrat
Ninth District*

Dempsey, Patrick
9830 Wilshire Blvd.
Beverly Hills, CA 90212
Actor

DeNiro, Robert
9830 Wilshire Blvd.
Beverly Hills, CA 90212
Actor, director
birthdate 8/17/43

Dennehy, Brian
c/o S. Smith
121 N. San Vicente Blvd.
Beverly Hills, CA 90211
Actor
birthdate 7/9/38

Denver Broncos
13655 E. Dove Valley Pkwy.
Englewood, CO 80112
Professional football team

**Denver, John
(Henry John Deutschendorf,
Jr.)**
8942 Wilshire Blvd.
Beverly Hills, CA 90211
Singer, songwriter
birthdate 12/31/43

Denver Nuggets
1635 Clay St.
Denver, CO 80204
Professional basketball team

Depp, Johnny
500 S. Sepulveda Blvd., #500
Los Angeles, CA 90049-3540
Actor
birthdate 6/9/63

Depressives Anonymous:
Recovery from Depression
329 E. 62nd St.
New York, NY 10021
Dr. Helen DeRosis, Founder

Dern, Laura
c/o JPMC
760 N. La Cienega Blvd.
Los Angeles, CA 90069
Actress
born 1966

Derrick, Butler
221 Cannon House Office
Bldg.
Washington, DC 20515-4003
*Representative from South
Carolina, Democrat
Third District*

Dershowitz, Alan
Harvard University School of
Law
Cambridge, MA 02138
Everybody who's anybody's lawyer

DesBarres, Michael
P.O. Box 4160
Hollywood, CA 90078
Singer

Desert Protective Council
P.O. Box 2312
Valley Center, CA 92082-2312

Desert Tortoise Preserve
Committee
P.O. Box 2910
San Bernardino, CA 92406
Tom Dodson, Vice-President

Detroit Lions
1200 Featherstone Rd.
Pontiac, MI 48057
Professional football team

Detroit Pistons
2 Championship Dr.
Auburn Hills, MI 48057
Professional basketball team

Detroit Red Wings
600 Civic Center Dr.
Detroit, MI 48226
Professional hockey team

Detroit Tigers
Tiger Stadium
Detroit, MI 48216
Professional baseball team

Deutsch, Peter
425 Cannon House Office
Bldg.
Washington, DC 20515-0920
*Representative from Florida,
Democrat
Twentieth District*

Deva, King Birendra Bir
Bikram Shah
Narayanhity Royal Palace
Kathmandu, Nepal
Ruler of Nepal

DeVito, Danny
9830 Wilshire Blvd.
Beverly Hills, CA 90212
Actor
birthdate 11/17/44

Dey, Susan
8942 Wilshire Blvd.
Beverly Hills, CA 90211
Actress
birthdate 12/10/52

Diadora America
6529 S. 216th, Bldg. E
Kent, WA 98032
Galliano Mondin, CEO
Manufactures athletic shoes

Diagnosis Murder
c/o Dean Hargrove
Productions
100 Universal City Plaza,
#507-3E
Universal City, CA 91608
TV series

Diamond, Neil
8730 Sunset Blvd., PH-W
Los Angeles, CA 90069
Singer, songwriter
birthdate 1/24/41

**Diaper Service Accreditation
Council**
2017 Walnut St.
Philadelphia, PA 19103
John A. Shiffert, Executive
Director
Licensing for diaper services

Diaz-Balart, Lincoln
509 Cannon House Office
Bldg.
Washington, DC 20515-0921
*Representative from Florida,
Republican
Twenty-first District*

Dickey, Jay
1338 Longworth House Office
Bldg.
Washington, DC 20515-0404
*Representative from Arkansas,
Republican
Fourth District*

Dicks, Norman D.
2467 Rayburn House Office
Bldg.
Washington, DC 20515-4706
*Representative from Washington,
Democrat
Sixth District*

**Dictionary Society of North
America**
c/o Prof. Louis T. Milic
Rhodes Tower 936-7
1983 E. 24th St.
Cleveland, OH 44115-2403

Diddley, Bo
Box 474
Archer, FL 32618
Musician
birthdate 12/20/28

Dillon, Matt
151 El Camino
Beverly Hills, CA 90211
Actor
birthdate 2/18/64

Dimitrov, Filip
Office of the Premier
Sofia, Bulgaria
Premier of Bulgaria

Dingell, John D.
2328 Rayburn House Office
Bldg.
Washington, DC 20515-2216
*Representative from Michigan,
Democrat
Sixteenth District*

Dinosaurs
Walt Disney Television
500 S. Buena Vista St.
Burbank, CA 91521
TV series

Diouf, Abdou
Office of the President
Avenue Roume
BP 168, Dakar
Senegal
President of Senegal

Dire Straits
10 Southwick Mews
London W2 England
Rock group

Direct Currents
DC Comics Inc.
1325 Ave. of the Americas
New York, NY 10019
*Monthly information on what is
coming out from DC Comics*

**Directory of American Youth
Organizations**
Free Spirit Publishing
400 1st Ave. N., #616
Minneapolis, MN 55401

Directory of Humor Magazines & Humor Organizations in America & Canada
Box 1454
Madison Square Station
New York, NY 10159

Directory of Record & CD Retailers
Power Communications
Box 786
Wharton, NJ 07885

Dirt
Corporate Office
230 Park Ave.
New York, NY 10169
Linda Cohen, Publisher
Magazine

Dirt Band, The
Box 1915
Aspen, CO 81611
Rock group

Discovery Channel, The
7700 Wisconsin Ave.
Bethesda, MD 10814

Disney Channel, The
3800 W. Alameda Ave.
Burbank, CA 91505

Disney's The Little Mermaid
Walt Disney Television
Animation
5200 Lankershim Blvd.
N. Hollywood, CA 91601
Animated series

Diving Equipment Manufacturer's Association
15246 Transistor Lane
Huntington Beach, CA 92649-1142
Robert L. Gray, Executive Director

Dixon, Julian C.
2400 Rayburn House Office Bldg.
Washington, DC 20515-0532
Representative from California, Democrat
Thirty-second District

DJ Times
Testa Communications, Inc.
25 Willowdale Ave.
Pt. Washington, NY 11050
Magazine for mobile and club DJs

Djohar, Said Mhammed
Office of the President
Moroni, Comoros
President of Comoros

Dodd, Christopher J.
444 Senate Hart Office Bldg.
Washington, DC 20510-0702
Senator from Connecticut

Dog, Tim
c/o Sony Music
51 W. 52nd St.
New York, NY 10019
Musician

Doherty, Shannen
8380 Melrose Ave., #310
Los Angeles, CA 90069
Actress

Dole, Robert J.
141 Senate Hart Office Bldg.
Washington, DC 20510-1601
Senator from Kansas, Republican

Domenici, Pete V.
434 Senate Dirksen Office Bldg.
Washington, DC 20510-3101
Senator from New Mexico, Republican

Domingo, Placido
c/o Stafford
26 Mayfield Rd.
Weybridge Surrey
KT13 8XB England
Tenor
birthdate 1/21/41

Domino, Fats
(Antoine)
9229 Sunset Blvd., 4th Fl.
Los Angeles, CA 90069
Pianist, singer, songwriter
birthdate 2/26/28

Domino's Pizza, Inc.
P.O. Box 997
Ann Arbor, MI 48106
Tom Monaghan, President
Fast-food chain

Donahue, Phil
30 Rockefeller Plaza
New York, NY 10112
Talk show host
birthdate 12/21/35

Donald Duck
Walt Disney Publications
500 S. Buena Vista
Burbank, CA 91521
Comic

Donaldson, Sam
ABC World News Tonight
47 W. 66th St.
New York, NY 10023
Broadcast journalist

Doobie Brothers
15140 Sonoma Hwy.
Glen Ellen, CA 95442
Rock group

Doohan, James
3349 Cahuenga Blvd., #2
Los Angeles, CA 90068
Actor

Dooley, Calvin M.
1227 Longworth House Office
Bldg.
Washington, DC 20515-0520
Representative from California,
Democrat
Twentieth District

Doolittle, John T.
1524 Longworth House Office
Bldg.
Washington, DC 20515-0504
Representative from California,
Republican
Fourth District

Dorgan, Byron L.
825 Senate Hart Office Bldg.
Washington, DC 20510-3404
Senator from North Dakota,
Democrat

Dorn, Michael
9229 Sunset Blvd., #710
Los Angeles, CA 90069
Actor, Klingon

Dornan, Robert K.
2402 Rayburn House Office
Bldg.
Washington, DC 20515-0546
Representative from California,
Republican
Forty-sixth District

dos Santos, Jose Eduardo
Gabinete de Presidente
Luanda, Angola
President of Angola

Dowiyogo, Bernard
c/o Parliament House
Nauru, Central Pacific
President of Nauru

Down Beat
Maher Publications
180 W. Park Ave.
Elmhurst, IL 60126
John Ephland, Editor
Music magazine

Downey, Robert, Jr.
9830 Wilshire Blvd.
Beverly Hills, CA 90212
Actor
birthdate 4/4/65

Dr. Quinn, Medicine Woman
c/o CBS Entertainment
7800 Beverly Blvd.
Los Angeles, CA 90036
TV series

Dr. Who: Classic Comics
Marvel Entertainment Group
387 Park Ave. S.
New York, NY 10016
Comic

Drake, Larry
232 N. Canon Dr.
Beverly Hills, CA 90210
Actor

Dramatists Guild
234 W. 44th St., 11th Fl.
New York, NY 10036
Andrew W. Farber, Executive
  Director
Playwrights, lyricists, composers

Dread Zeppelin Fan Club
c/o Birdcage Records
Sierra Madre, CA 91024
*Fan club for reggae band that
  does cover versions of Led
  Zeppelin songs*

Dream Factory
315 Guthrie Green
Louisville, KY 40202
Denis P. Heavrin, Executive
  Director
Wishes for terminal kids

Dream Guys
Dream Guys Inc.
Box 7042
New York, NY 10021
Grace Catalano, Editor
Teen magazine

Dreier, David
411 Cannon House Office
  Bldg.
Washington, DC 20515-0528
*Representative from California,
  Republican
Twenty-eighth District*

Drescher, Fran
232 N. Canon Dr.
Beverly Hills, CA 90210
Actress

Dreyer's Grand Ice Cream Inc.
5929 College Ave.
Oakland, CA 94618
T. Gary Rogers, CEO
Ice cream manufacturer

Drifters, The
10 Chelsea Court
Neptune, NJ 07753
Pop group

Drood Review of Mystery
Box 8872
Boston, MA 02114
Jim Huang, Editor
Mystery magazine

Drugs Anonymous
P.O. Box 772
Bronx, NY 10451
James Kaplow, Executive
  Officer

Drum Corps International
P.O. Box 548
Lombard, IL 60148
Don Pesceone, Executive
  Director

Dubuc, Nicole
c/o Gold/Marshak
3500 West Olive Ave.
Burbank, CA 91505
Actress

Duchovny, David
8942 Wilshire Blvd.
Beverly Hills, CA 90211
Actor

Duckburg Times
3010 Wilshire Blvd., #362
Los Angeles, CA 90010
Comic magazine

Duckman
Klasky Csupo Inc.
1258 N. Highland Ave.
Hollywood, CA 90038
Animated series

Dude Rancher's Association
Box 471
Laporte, CO 80535
Amey Grubbs, Executive
  Director

Dudikoff, Michael
8485 Melrose Place, #E
Los Angeles, CA 90069
Actor

Duffy, Patrick
924 Westwood Blvd., #9th Fl.
Los Angeles, CA 90024
Actor
birthdate 3/17/49

Duncan, John J., Jr.
115 Cannon House Office
  Bldg.
Washington, DC 20515-4202
Representative from Tennessee,
  Republican
Second District

Dunlop Manufacturing Inc.
Box 846
Benicia, CA 94510
Manufactures custom logo guitar
  picks

Dunn, Jennifer B.
1641 Longworth House Office
  Bldg.
Washington, DC 20515-4708
Representative from Washington,
  Republican
Eighth District

Duran Duran
Box 600
London NW18 1EN England
Pop group

Durbin, Richard J.
2463 Rayburn House Office
  Bldg.
Washington, DC 20515-1320
Representative from Illinois,
  Democrat
Twentieth District

Durenberger, Davie
154 Senate Russell Office
  Bldg.
Washington, DC 20510-2301
Senator from Minnesota,
  Independent Republican

Durning, Charles
10100 Santa Monica Blvd.,
  25th Fl.
Los Angeles, CA 90067
Actor
birthdate 2/28/23

Dutton, Charles
9830 Wilshire Blvd.
Beverly Hills, CA 90212
Actor

Dylan, Bob
P.O. Box 263, Cooper Station
New York, NY 10003
Singer, composer
birthdate 5/24/41

Dysart, Richard
924 Westwood Blvd., 9th Fl.
Los Angeles, CA 90024
Actor
birthday 3/30

E

A letter is the mind alone without corporeal friend.
—EMILY DICKINSON

E! Entertainment Television
5670 Wilshire Blvd.
Los Angeles, CA 90036
TV channel

E, Sheila
9830 Wilshire Blvd.
Beverly Hills, CA 90212
Musician

Early Six Mustang Registry
428 Madingley Rd.
Linthicum, MD 21090
Rick Mitchell, Contact
Car club

Earth Communications Office
10960 Wilshire Blvd., 16th Fl.
Los Angeles, CA 90024
Bonnie Reiss, Executive
    Director

Earth Day, USA
2 Elm St., Box 470
Peterborough, NH 03458
Gaylord Nelson, Chairman

Earth First!
P.O. Box 5176
Missoula, MT 59806
*Militant environmental
    organization (won't list contact)*

East Coast Rocker
7 Oak Place
P.O. Box 137
Montclair, NJ 07042
James Rensenbrink, Editor
    and Publisher
Music magazine

East End Lights
The Quarterly Magazine for
    Elton John Fans
Voice Communications Corp.
P.O. Box 760
31950 23 Mile Rd.
New Baltimore, MI 48047
Tom Stanton, Editor

Easton, Sheena
151 El Camino
Beverly Hills, CA 90212
Singer
birthdate 4/27/59

Eastwood, Clint
c/o Warner Bros.
4000 Warner Blvd.
Burbank, CA 91523
Actor, director, producer
birthdate 5/31/30

Eckstine, Billy
(William Clarence Eckstine)
c/o Polygram Records
810 7th Ave.
New York, NY 10019
Singer
birthdate 7/8/14

Eddie Rabbitt Fan Club
Box 125
Lewistown, OH 43333

Edelman, Gregg
1501 Broadway, #703
New York, NY 10036
Broadway actor

Edgar, Jim
State Capitol
Springfield, IL 62706
Governor of Illinois

Edmonton Oilers
Northlands Coliseum
Edmonton, Alberta T5B 4M9
  Canada
Professional hockey team

Edwards Theatres Circuit, Inc.
300 Newport Center Dr.
Newport Beach, CA 92660
James Edwards, Sr., Chairman
Movie theater chain

Edwards, Chet
328 Cannon House Office
  Bldg.
Washington, DC 20515-4311
Representative from Texas,
  Democrat
Eleventh District

Edwards, Don
2307 Rayburn House Office
  Bldg.
Washington, DC 20515-0516
Representative from California
Sixteenth District

Edwards, Edwin W.
State Capitol
Baton Rouge, LA 70904
Governor of Louisiana

Eggert, Nicole
120 S. Victory Blvd., #104
Burbank, CA 91501
Actress

Eikenberry, Jill
151 El Camino
Beverly Hills, CA 90212
Actress
birthdate 1/21/47

Electronic Arts
2755 Campus Dr.
San Mateo, CA 94403
Larry Probst, President/CEO
Creates and manufactures the
  software for video games; loves
  to get letters from kids about
  what they think of the games

Electronic Mail Association
1555 Wilson Blvd., #300
Arlington, VA 22209
Michael F. Cavanaugh,
  Executive Director

Electro-voice
600 Cecil St.
Buchanan, MI 49107
Microphone specialists

Elektra Records (also Asylum,
  Nonesuch)
75 Rockefeller Plaza
New York, NY 10019
Bob Krasnow, Chairman
Record label

(Beverly Hills Office)
345 Maple Dr., #123
Beverly Hills, CA 90210

Eleniak, Erika
9200 Sunset Blvd., #625
Los Angeles, CA 90069
Actress

Elfman, Danny
6525 Sunset Blvd., #402
Los Angeles, CA 90028
Composer, singer

Elias, Jorge Serrano
Oficina del Presidente
Guatemala City, Guatemala
President of Guatemala

**Ellery Queen's Mystery
Magazine**
Bantam Doubleday Dell
Publishing Group
666 5th Ave.
New York, NY 10103
Janet Hutchins, Editor

**Elvira
(Cassandra Peterson)**
P.O. Box 38246
Hollywood, CA 90038
"Mistress of the Dark"
birthdate 9/17/51

Elvis Forever TCB Fan Club
P.O. Box 1066
Pinellas Park, FL 34665

**Emerge: A Men's Counseling
Service on Domestic
Violence**
18 Hurley St., #23
Cambridge, MA 02139
David Adams, President

**Emergency Committee for
American Trade**
1211 Connecticut Ave. NW,
#801
Washington, DC 20036
Robert L. McNeill, Executive
Vice-Chairman

Emerson, Bill
2454 Rayburn House Office
Bldg.
Washington, DC 20515-2508
*Representative from Missouri,
Republican
Eighth District*

EMF
**Mark Decloedt, James Atkin,
Zac Foley, Ian Dench, Derry
Brownson**
810 Seventh Ave.
New York, NY 10022
Recording artists

**EMI Records Group (also
SBK, Chrysalis)**
810 7th Ave., 8th Fl.
New York, NY 10019
Charles Koppelman,
Chariman/CEO
Record label

(Los Angeles Office)
8730 Sunset Blvd., 5th Fl.
Los Angeles, CA 90069

Empty Nest
Witt/Thomas/Harris
Productions
1438 N. Gower St.
Hollywood, CA 90028
TV series

En Vogue
75 Rockefeller Plaza, 4th Fl.
New York, NY 10019
Pop group

Engel, Eliot L.
1433 Longworth House Office
Bldg.
Washington, DC 20515-3217
*Representative from New York,
Democrat
Seventeenth District*

Engler, John
State Capitol
Lansing, MI 48909
Governor of Michigan

English, Karan
1024 Longworth House Office
  Bldg.
Washington, DC 20515-0306
Representative from Arizona,
  Democrat
Sixth District

Eno, Brian
(Brian Peter George St. John
  DeLaSalle Eno)
Opal Ltd.
6834 Camrose Dr.
Los Angeles, CA 90068
Composer, musician, producer

Entertainment Tonight
5555 Melrose Ave.
Los Angeles, CA 90038
TV series

Environmental Defense Fund
257 Park Ave. S.
New York, NY 10010
Frederic D. Krupp, Executive
  Director

Epic Records
(Also WTG)
Sony Music Entertainment
2100 Colorado Blvd.
Santa Monica, CA 90404

(New York Office)
Sony Music Entertainment
P.O. Box 4450
New York, NY 10101
Dave Glew, President
Record label

E.S. Originals
20 W. 33rd St.
New York, NY 10001
Ellis Safdeye, President
Manufactures athletic shoes

Esalen Institute
Big Sur, CA 93920
Steve Donovan, President
Non-profit educational center that
  explores trends in behavioral
  sciences, religion and
  philosophy

Eshoo, Anna G.
1505 Longworth House Office
  Bldg.
Washington, DC 20515-0514
Representative from California,
  Democrat
Fourteenth District

ESPN, Inc.
ESPN Plaza
Bristol, CT 06010
Sports channel (cable)

Espy, Mike
Department of Agriculture
The Mall, 12th & 14th Sts.
Washington, DC 20250
Secretary of Agriculture

Estefan, Gloria Maria
6205 Bird Rd.
Miami, FL 33155
Singer, songwriter
birthdate 9/1/57

Etch-A-Sketch Club
c/o The Ohio Art Club
1 Toy St.
Bryan, OH 43506
Lowell T. Wilson, Vice-
  President

Etheridge, Melissa
c/o Island Records
14 E. 4th St.
New York, NY 10012
Singer, songwriter

Eurythmics
(Annie Lennox, Dave Stewart)
P.O. Box 245
London N8 90G England
Rock group

Evans, Janet
c/o U.S. Olympic Committee
1750 E. Boulder St.
Colorado Springs, CO 80909
Gold medalist swimmer

Evans, Lane
2335 Rayburn House Office
Bldg.
Washington, DC 20515-1317
*Representative from Illinois,
Democrat
Seventeenth District*

**Ever Rap/Ever Rat/Ever
Dread**
P.O. Box 99284
Seattle, WA 98199
David Portnow, Publisher
Independent record label

Everett, Terry
208 Cannon House Office
Bldg.
Washington, DC 20515-0102
*Representative from Alabama,
Republican
Second District*

Evergreen International
P.O. Box 3
Salt Lake City, UT 84110
*Homosexuals and friends
dedicated to helping people
change their same sex lifestyle*

**Everlast Sporting Goods
Manufacturing Company**
750 E. 132nd St.
Bronx, NY 10454
Ben Nadorf, President
Sporting goods company

Everything's Archie
Archie Comic Publications
Inc.
325 Fayette Ave.
Mamaroneck, NY 10543
Comic

Evigan, Greg
415 N. Camden Dr., #121
Beverly Hills, CA 90210
Actor
birthdate 10/14/53

Ewing, Thomas W.
1317 Longworth House Office
Bldg.
Washington, DC 20515-1315
*Representative from Illinois,
Republican
Fifteenth District*

Exon, J. James
528 Senate Hart Office Bldg.
Washington, DC 20510-2702
Senator from Nebraska, Democrat

Eyadema, General Gnassingbe
Presidence de la Republique
Lome, Togo
President of Togo

> A letter is a cozy quilt, hand-stitched with the thread of friendship.
>
> —FRAN BULLINGTON

F.A.O. Schwartz
767 Fifth Ave.
New York, NY 10153
John Eyler, President
Great toy store

Fabares, Shelley
151 El Camino
Beverly Hills, CA 90212
Actress
birthdate 1/19/42

Fabulous Thunderbirds Fan Club
P.O. Box 17006
Austin, TX 78760

Faircloth, Lauch
702 Senate Hart Office Bldg.
Washington, DC 20510-3305
Senator from North Carolina, Republican

Fallen Angels International
P.O. Box 13
Southington, CT 06489-0013
David Williams, Director
Persons excommunicated from various religious sects

Family Channel, The
1000 Centerville Turnpike
Virginia Beach, VA 23463

Family Feud
Mark Goodson Productions
5750 Wilshire Blvd., #475W
Los Angeles, CA 90036
Game show

Family Matters
Warner Bros. Television
4000 Warner Blvd.
Burbank, CA 91522
TV series

Famous Fone Friends
9101 Sawyer St.
Los Angeles, CA 90035
Linda Stone-Elster, Executive Officer
Arranges phone calls for sick kids from celebrities

Fan Club Directory
2730 Baltimore Ave.
Pueblo, CO 81003

Fanatic Limited
Robin Hill Corporate Park
Route 22
Patterson, NY 12563
Peter Juen, President
Distributor of Sailboards, accessories, and water sports apparel

Fantastic Four
Marvel Entertainment Group
387 Park Ave. S.
New York, NY 10016
Comic

Farr, Sam
1216 Longworth House Office
  Bldg.
Washington, DC 20515-0517
Representative from California,
  Democrat
Seventeenth District

Fat Boys, The
250 W. 57th St., #1723
New York, NY 10107
Rap group

Faustino, David
10100 Santa Monica Blvd.,
  25th Fl.
Los Angeles, CA 90067
Actor
birthdate 3/3/74

Favorite Country Stars
Media Holdings, Inc.
545 Mainstream Dr., #101
Nashville, TN 37228
Music magazine

Fawell, Harris W.
2342 Rayburn House Office
  Bldg.
Washington, DC 21505-1313
Representative from Illinois,
  Republican
Thirteenth District

Fazio, Vic
2113 Rayburn House Office
  Bldg.
Washington, DC 20515-0503
Representative from California,
  Democrat
Third District

Feingold, Russell D.
502 Senate Hart Office Bldg.
Washington, DC 20510-4904
Senator from Wisconsin, Democrat

Feinstein, Dianne
331 Senate Hart Office Bldg.
Washington, DC 20510-0504
Senator from California

Feinstein, Michael
8942 Wilshire Blvd.
Beverly Hills, CA 90211
Entertainer, musicologist

Felber, Rene
Office of the President
Bundeshaus West
Bundesgasse, 3003 Berne
Switzerland
President of Switzerland

Feldman, Corey
15301 Ventura Blvd., #345
Sherman Oaks, CA 91403
Actor

Feliciano, Jose
c/o Thomas Cassidy
417 Marawood Dr.
Woodstock, IL 60098
Singer
birthdate 9/10/45

Fender, Freddy
(Baldemar Huerta)
3225 S. Norwood Ave.
Tulsa, OK 74135
Singer

Ferguson, Maynard
Box 716
Ojai, CA 93023
Trumpeter

Ferry, Bryan
JEM Records Group
3619 Kennedy Rd. S.
Plainfield, NJ 07080
Singer, songwriter

Field, Sally
9830 Wilshire Blvd.
Beverly Hills, CA 90212
Actress
birthdate 11/6/46

Fields, Cleo
513 Cannon House Office
Bldg.
Washington, DC 20515-1804
Representative from Louisiana,
Democrat
Fourth District

Fields, Jack
2228 Rayburn House Office
Bldg.
Washington, DC 20515-4308
Representative from Texas,
Republican
Eighth District

50,000,000,000,000,000,000,000
Watts
5721 SE Laguna Ave.
Stuart, FL 34997
M. C. Kostek
Independent record label

Filner, Bob
504 Cannon House Office
Bldg.
Washington, DC 20515-0550
Representative from California,
Democrat
Fiftieth District

Find the Children
11811 W. Olympic Blvd.
Los Angeles, CA 90064
Jill Searle, Executive Director
Locates missing children

Finding Our Own Ways
P.O. Box 1545
Lawrence, KS 66044
Support for asexuality

Fine Young Cannibals
1680 N. Vine St., #1101
Hollywood, CA 90028
Rock group

Fingerhut, Eric D.
431 Cannon House Office
Bldg.
Washington, DC 20515-3519
Representative from Ohio,
Democrat
Nineteenth District

Finkle, Fyvush
8730 Sunset Blvd., #480
Los Angeles, CA 90069
Actor

Finnbogadottir, Mrs. Vigdis
Office of the President
Reykjavik, Iceland
President of Iceland

Finney, Joan
State House
Topeka, KS 66612
Governor of Kansas

First Amendment Lawyers
Association
c/o Wayne Gianpietro
125 S. Wacker Dr., #2700
Chicago, IL 60606

First Chair America
c/o Mary Martin
P.O. Box 474
Greenwood, MS 38930
Recognition for 1st chair in
orchestras and bands

Fish Police
Marvel Entertainment Group
387 Park Ave. S.
New York, NY 10016
Comic

Fish, Hamilton
2354 Rayburn House Office Bldg.
Washington, DC 20515-3219
Representative from New York,
  Republican
Nineteenth District

Fishburn, Lawrence
10100 Santa Monica Blvd.,
  25th Fl.
Los Angeles, CA 90067
Actor

Fisher-Price
636 Girard Ave.
East Aurora, NY 14052
Ronald Jackson, CEO
Toy manufacturer

Flake, Floyd H.
1035 Longworth House Office Bldg.
Washington, DC 20515-3206
Representative from New York,
  Democrat
Sixth District

Flash
DC Comics Inc.
1325 Ave. of the Americas
New York, NY 10019
Comic

Fleetwood Mac
29169 W. Heathercliff, #574
Malibu, CA 90265
On-again, off-again rock group

Fleetwood, Mick
c/o Warner Brothers
3300 W. Warner Blvd.
Burbank, CA 91505
Musician

Fleischer, Charles
9300 Wilshire Blvd., #410
Beverly Hills, CA 90212
Actor, Roger Rabbitt voice

Fleiss, Heidi
505 S. Beverly Dr., #508
Beverly Hills, CA 90212-4542
"Hollywood Madam"

Flintstones
Harvey Comics Entertainment, Inc.
100 Wilshire Blvd., #500
Santa Monica, CA 90401
Comic

Fly Without Fear
310 Madison Ave.
New York, NY 10017
Carol Gross, Director
Organization that helps people fly
  without fear

FOCUS
c/o C.A.N.
2421 W. Pratt Blvd., #1173
Chicago, IL 60645
Former members of destructive cult
  groups

Fogelberg, Daniel Grayling
c/o Epic Records
1801 Century Park West
Los Angeles, CA 90067
Composer, recording artist
birthdate 8/13/51

Foglietta, Thomas M.
341 Cannon House Office Bldg.
Washington, DC 20515-3801
Representative from Pennsylvania,
  Democrat
First District

Foley, Thomas S.
1201 Longworth House Office Bldg.
Washington, DC 20515-4705
Representative from Washington,
  Democrat
Fifth District

Follows, Megan
121 N. San Vicente Blvd.
Beverly Hills, CA 90211
Actress

Folsom, Jim, Jr.
State Capitol
Montgomery, AL 36130
Governor of Alabama

Fonda, Bridget
9560 Wilshire Blvd., #500
Beverly Hills, CA 90212
Actress

Fonda, Jane
1050 Techwood Dr. NW
Atlanta, GA 30318
Former actress, entrepreneur
birthdate 12/21/37

Food for the Hungry, Inc.
7729 E. Greenway Rd.
P.O. Box E
Scottsdale, AZ 85260
Ted Yamamori, CEO

Footwear Caucus
235 Cannon House Office
Bldg.
Washington, DC 20515
Rep. John Weinfurter, Contact
*Members of Congress from
footwear-producing states*

**Footwear Industries of
America**
1420 K St. NW, #600
Washington, DC 20005
Fawn Everson, President

Ford, Eileen Otte
344 E. 59th St.
New York, NY 10022-1570
Modeling agent

Ford, Harold E.
2211 Rayburn House Office
Bldg.
Washington, DC 20515-4209
*Representative from Tennessee,
Democrat*
Ninth District

Ford, Harrison
c/o McQueeney
10279 Century Woods Dr.
Los Angeles, CA 90067
Actor
birthdate 7/13/42

Ford, Jack
Court TV
600 3rd Ave.
New York, NY 10016
Host

Ford, Wendell H.
173A Senate Russell Office
Bldg.
Washington, DC 21510-1701
Senator from Kentucky, Democrat

Ford, William D.
2107 Rayburn House Office
Bldg.
Washington, DC 20515-2213
*Representative from Michigan,
Democrat*
Thirteenth District

Fordice, Kirk
P.O. Box 139
Jackson, MS 39205
Governor of Mississippi

Foreigner
1790 Broadway, PH
New York, NY 10019
Rock group

**Formula One Spectators
Association**
8033 Sunset Blvd., #60
Los Angeles, CA 90046
George Goad, President
Racing fans

40 Acres & a Mule
8 St. Felix St., 1st Fl.
Brooklyn, NY 11217
Independent record label

Foster Grandparents Program
1100 Vermont Ave., NW,
  6th Fl.
Washington, DC 20525
Constance M. Burns, Assistant
  Director

Foster Grant Corp.
Foster Grant Plaza
Leominster, MA 01453
Richard Wright, President
Sunglasses manufacturer

Foster, Jodie
8942 Wilshire Blvd.
Beverly Hills, CA 90211
Actress, director
birthdate 11/19/62

**Foundation of Motion Picture
  Pioneers**
244 W. 49th St.
New York, NY 10019
Robert H. Sunshine, Executive
  Director
Helps pioneers in need

**Fournier, Rafael Angel
  Calderon**
Casa Presidencial
Apdo 520 Zapote
San Jose, Costa Rica
President of Costa Rica

Fowler, Tillie K.
413 Cannon House Office
  Bldg.
Washington, DC 20515-0905
*Representative from Florida,
  Republican
Fourth District*

Fox Broadcasting Company
10201 W. Pico Blvd.
Los Angeles, CA 90035
TV network

(New York Office)
40 W. 57th St.
New York, NY 10019

Fox, Michael J.
9830 Wilshire Blvd.
Beverly Hills, CA 90212
Actor
birthdate 6/9/61

Frakes, Jonathan
10100 Santa Monica Blvd.,
  25th Fl.
Los Angeles, CA 90067
Actor

Frampton, Peter
c/o Atlantic Records
75 Rockfeller Plaza
New York, NY 10019
Singer, musician
birthdate 4/22/50

**Franchise of Americans
  Needing Sports**
1808 Sherwood
Sacramento, CA 95822
Michael Ross, Executive
  Director
Sports fans bill of rights

Franco, Tony
Pacific Arts Research and
  Investigation
12301 Wilshire Blvd., #204
Los Angeles, CA 90025
Private investigator

Frank, Barney
2404 Rayburn House Office
  Bldg.
Washington, DC 20515-2104
*Representative from
  Massachusetts, Democrat
Fourth District*

Franklin, Aretha
8450 Linwood St.
Detroit, MI 48206
Singer
birthdate 3/25/42

Franks, Bob
429 Cannon House Office
    Bldg.
Washington, DC 20515-3007
Representative from New Jersey,
    Republican
Seventh District

Franks, Gary A.
435 Cannon House Office
    Bldg.
Washington, DC 20515-0705
Representative from Connecticut,
    Republican
Fifth District

Fraser, Brendan
151 El Camino
Beverly Hills, CA 90212
Actor

Frasier
Paramount
5555 Melrose Ave.
Los Angeles, CA 90038
TV series

Freebies
P.O. Box 20283
Santa Barbara, CA 93120
Abel Magana, Editor
Magazine that lists free things
    that you can order by mail

Fresh!
Ashley Communications, Inc.
19431 Business Ctr. Dr., #27
Northridge, CA 91324
Ralph Benner, Editor
Magazine for black teenagers
    trying to break into
    entertainment

Fresh Prince of Del Air, The
NBC Productions
330 Bob Hope Dr.
Burbank, CA 91523
TV series

Fretted Instrument Guild of
    America
c/o Ann Pertoney
2344 S. Oakley Ave.
Chicago, IL 60608
Banjo, mandolin, guitar guild

Frey, Glenn
151 El Camino
Beverly Hills, CA 90212
Songwriter, vocalist, guitarist

Friars Club
57 E. 55th St.
New York, NY 10022
Jean Pierre Trebot, Executive
    Director
Organization for entertainers

Fricke, Janie
P.O. Box 680785
San Antonio, TX 78268
Singer

Friends Around the World
P.O. Box 10266
Merrillville, IN 46411
Pat Tomlin, President
Pen pal group

Friends of Dennis Wilson
1381 Maria Way
San Jose, CA 95117
Fan club

Friends of Karen
P.O. Box 217
Croton Falls, NY 10519
John G. Murphy, Ph.D.,
    Executive Director
Financial and emotional support
    to kids with life threatening
    diseases

Friends of the Earth
218 D St., SE
Washington, DC 20003
Brent Blackweider, Vice-
President

Friends of the Everglades
101 Westward Dr., #2
Miami Springs, FL 33166
Nancy Carroll Brown,
President

**Friends of the Origami Center
of America**
15 W. 77th St.
New York, NY 10024
Michael Shall, President

Friends of the River
909 12th St., #207
Sacramento, CA 95814
Tom Martens, Executive
Director
Environmental group

Friends of the Tango
99-40 64th Rd.
Rego Park, NY 11374
Julio Prieto, Contact

Friends of the Trees Society
P.O. Box 1064
Tonasket, WA 98855
Michael Pilarski, Contact

Frito-Lay
7701 Legacy Dr.
Plano, TX 75024
Michael H. Jordan, President
Snack food company

Frost, Martin
2459 Rayburn House Office
Bldg.
Washington, DC 20515-4324
*Representative from Texas,
Democrat
Twenty-fourth District*

Fujimori, Alberto Kenyo
Office of the President
Lima, Peru
President of Peru

Full House
Warner Bros. Television
4000 Warner Blvd.
Burbank, CA 91522
TV series

Furse, Elizabeth
316 Cannon House Office
Bldg.
Washington, DC 20515-3701
*Representative from Oregon,
Democrat
First District*

Future Fisherman Foundation
1250 Grove Ave., #300
Barington, IL 60010
Sharon Rushton, Executive
Director

Futures for Children
805 Tijeras NW
Albuquerque, NM 87102
Ruth Frazier, President
*Works to motivate underdeveloped
communities*

A letter sings of love and hope, still warm from the hug of an envelope.

—VICKI RENTZ

G, Kenny
(Gorelick)
648 N. Robertson Blvd.
Los Angeles, CA 90048
Saxophonist

Gabriel, Peter
Probono
132 Liverpool Rd.
London N1 1LA England
Vocalist, composer
birthdate 5/13/50

Galimany, Guillermao Endara
Oficina del Presidente
Valija 50, Panama 1
Panama
President of Panama

Gallegly, Elton
2441 Rayburn House Office
Bldg.
Washington, DC 20515-0523
*Representative from California,
Republican
Twenty-third District*

Gallo, Dean A.
2447 Rayburn House Office
Bldg.
Washington, DC 20515-3011
*Representative from New Jersey,
Republican
Eleventh District*

Galway, James
P.O. Box 1077
Bucks, SL2 4DB England
Flutist
birthdate 12/8/39

Gamblers Anonymous
P.O. Box 17173
Los Angeles, CA 90010
Karen H., Executive Director

**Game Manufacturers
Association**
P.O. Box 570
Grinnell, IA 50112
Winston Hamilton, Executive
Director

Ganilau, Ratu Sir Penaia Kanatabatu
Office of the President
Suva, Fiji
President of Fiji

GAP Inc.
One Harrison
San Francisco, CA 94105
Donald G. Fisher, CEO
Clothing store chain

Gapkids
Gap Stores Inc.
900 Cherry Ave.
San Bruno, CA 94066
Donald G. Fisher, CEO
Kids' division of The Gap

Garcia, Jerry
P.O. Box 12979
San Rafael, CA 94913
Musician

Garfield and Friends
Film Roman Inc.
12020 Chandler Blvd., #200
N. Hollywood, CA 91607
Animated series

Garth, Jennie
c/o Gold/Marshak
3500 West Olive Ave.
Burbank, CA 91505
Actress

Gay and Lesbian Press Association
P.O. Box 8185
Universal City, CA 91608
R. J. Curry, Executive Director

Gayle, Crystal
57 Music Sq. E.
Nashville, TN 37203
Singer
birthdate 1/9/51

Gayoom, Maumoon-Abdul
Office of the President
Male, Maldives
President of Maldives

Geary, Cynthia
151 El Camino
Beverly Hills, CA 90212
Actress

Geffen/DGC Records
9130 Sunset Blvd.
Los Angeles, CA 90069
David Geffen, Chairman
Record label

(New York Office)
1755 Broadway, 6th Fl.
New York, NY 10019

Gejdenson, Sam
2416 Rayburn House Office Bldg.
Washington, DC 20515-0702
Representative from Connecticut, Democrat
Second District

Gekas, George W.
2410 Rayburn House Office Bldg.
Washington, DC 20515-3817
Representative from Pennsylvania, Republican
Seventeenth District

Geldof, Sir Bob
Davington Priory
Faversham, Kent
England
Singer
birthdate 10/5/51

Gemeinhardt
P.O. Box 788
Elkhart, IN 46515
Glenn Edward Holtz, President
Band instrument manufacturing company

General Mills
9200 Wayzatta Blvd.
Minneapolis, MN 55440
H. B. Atwater, Jr., CEO
Food manufacturer

Genesis
81–83 Walton St.
London SW3 England
Pop group

Genesis Information
c/o Brad Lentz
P.O. Box 12250
Overland Park, KS 66212
Fan club

**George Michael International
Fan Club**
P.O. Box 882884
San Francisco, CA 94188

George Sand Society
255 S. SW Harrison St., #14G
Portland, OR 97201
Linda E. Odenborg, Chairman

George Strait Fan Club
P.O. Box 2119
Hendersonville, TN 37077

Gephardt, Richard A.
1432 Longworth House Office
  Bldg.
Washington, DC 20515-2503
*Representative from Missouri,
  Democrat
Third District*

Geren, Pete
1730 Longworth House Office
  Bldg.
Washington, DC 20515-4312
*Representative from Texas,
  Democrat
Twelfth District*

Gerry & The Pacemakers
28A Manor Row
Brodford, BDL 4QU England
*One of original British invasion
  groups*

Geto Boys
c/o Priority
P.O. Box 2186
Hollywood, CA 90078
Rappers

Ghiradelli Chocolate Co.
111 139th St.
San Leandro, CA 94578
Dennis DeDominico,
  Chairman
Candy company

Ghostwriter
c/o Children's TV Workshop
One Lincoln Plaza
New York, NY 10023
TV series

ghs Strings
2813 Wilber Ave.
Battle Creek, MI 49015
Guitar string specialists

Giant Cracked
Globe Communications
535 5th Ave.
New York, NY 10017
Humor magazine

Gibb, Barry
P.O. Box 8179
Miami, FL 33139
Vocalist, songwriter
birthdate 9/1/46

Gibb, Maurice
P.O. Box 8179
Miami, FL 33139
Vocalist, songwriter
birthdate 12/22/49

Gibb, Robin
Borman Sternberg Enterprises
9220 Sunset Blvd., #320
Los Angeles, CA 90069
Vocalist, songwriter
birthdate 12/22/49

Gibbons, Leeza
5555 Melrose Ave.
Los Angeles, CA 90038
Talk show host

Gibbons, Sam M.
2204 Rayburn House Office
  Bldg.
Washington, DC 20515-0911
Representative from Florida,
  Democrat
Eleventh District

Gibson, Debbie
P.O. Box 489
Merrick, NY 11566
Singer, songwriter
birthdate 8/31/70

Gibson, Mel
8942 Wilshire Blvd.
Beverly Hills, CA 90211
Actor
birthdate 1/3/56

**Gifted Children's Pen Pals
International**
c/o Dr. Debby Sue van de
  Vender
166 E. 61st St.
New York, NY 10021

G.I. Joe Special Forces
Box 3989
Schaumburg, IL 60168
A. J. Marsiglia, Executive
  Officer
Doll collectors

Gilardi, Jack
ICM
8942 Wilshire Blvd.
Beverly Hills, CA 90211
Actors' agent (clients include O.J.
  Simpson)

Gilbert and Sullivan Society
c/o Frances Yasprica
1351 65th St.
Brooklyn, NY 11219

Gilbert, Melissa
151 El Camino
Beverly Hills, CA 90212
Actress
birthdate 5/8/64

Gilchrest, Wayne T.
412 Cannon House Office
  Bldg.
Washington, DC 20515-2001
Representative from Maryland,
  Republican
First District

**Guild of Ancient Suppliers of
Gas Appliances Skills, Gins,
Accessories and Substances
(GasGasGas)**
314 S. Bobbin Mill Lane
Broomall, PA 19008
Shirley Innaurato, Assistant
  Clerk-Treasurer
Persons who have served at least
  ten years in the gas industry

Gilder, George
P.O. Box 430
Tyringham, MA 01264
Author

Gillmor, Paul E.
1203 Longworth House Office
  Bldg.
Washington, DC 20515-3505
Representative from Ohio,
  Republican
Fifth District

Gilman, Benjamin A.
2185 Rayburn House Office
  Bldg.
Washington, DC 20515-3220
Representative from New York,
  Republican
Twentieth District

Gilyard, Clarence, Jr.
14724 Ventura Blvd., #401
Sherman Oaks, CA 91403
Actor

Gingrich, Newt
1620 Longworth House Office
 Bldg.
Washington, DC 20515-6538
Representative from Georgia,
 Republican
Sixth District

Ginsburg, Ruth Bader
U.S. Supreme Court Bldg.
One First St. NE
Washington, DC 20543
Supreme Court justice

Girl Groups Fan Club
P.O. Box 69A04
West Hollywood, CA 90069
Honeycone, Orlons, Dee Dee
 Sharp, Martha and the
 Vandellas, Ronnettes,
 Marvelettes, etc.

Girl Scouts of the U.S.A.
420 5th Ave.
New York, NY 10018-2702
Mary Rose Main, Executive
 Director

Give Kids the World
210 S. Bass Rd.
Kissimmee, FL 34746
Julia H. Wylam, Executive
 Vice-President
6-day vacations for terminally ill
 kids; works with Dream Factory,
 Make a Wish, etc.

Glenn, John
503 Senate Hart Office Bldg.
Washington, DC 20510-3501
Senator from Ohio, Democrat

Glenn, Scott
8942 Wilshire Blvd.
Beverly Hills, CA 90211
Actor
birthdate 1/26/42

Glickman, Dan
2371 Rayburn House Office
 Bldg.
Washington, DC 20515-1604
Representative from Kansas,
 Democrat
Fourth District

Gloria Estefan and the Miami
 Sound Machine
8390 S.W. 4th St.
Miami, FL 33144
Latin pop group

Glover, Danny
151 El Camino
Beverly Hills, CA 90212
Actor
born 1947

Go-Go's
345 N. Maple Dr., #325
Beverly Hills, CA 90210
Pop girl group

Gobunovs, Anatolijs
Presidium of Lativian
Riga, Latvijas Republika
President of Latvia

Goldberg, Whoopi
9830 Wilshire Blvd.
Beverly Hills, CA 90212
Actor, comedian

Golden Gloves Association of
 America
3535 Kenilworth Lane
Knoxville, TN 37914
Jerry Miller, Secretary-
 Treasurer

Golden State Warriors
Oakland Coliseum
Oakland, CA 94621
Professional basketball team

Goldman, Bo
9830 Wilshire Blvd.
Beverly Hills, CA 90212
Screenwriter

Goldman, William
9830 Wilshire Blvd.
Beverly Hills, CA 90212
Screenwriter, novelist

Goldthwait, Bobcat
232 N. Canon Dr.
Beverly Hills, CA 90210
Comedian, actor
born 1962

Goncz, Arpad
Office of the President
1055 Budapest
Kossuth Lajos ter 1
Hungary
President of Hungary

Gonzalez, Henry B.
2413 Rayburn House Office
Bldg.
Washington, DC 20515-4320
*Representative from Texas,
Democrat
Twentieth District*

Good Clean Fun
1190 Maria Privada
Mountain View, CA 94040
Magazine

Gooding, Cuba, Jr.
151 El Camino
Beverly Hills, CA 90212
Actor

Goodlatte, Bob
214 Cannon House Office
Bldg.
Washington, DC 20515-4606
*Representative from Virginia,
Republican
Sixth District*

Goodling, William F.
2263 Rayburn House Office
Bldg.
Washington, DC 20515-3819
*Representative from Pennsylvania,
Republican
Nineteenth District*

Goodman, John
P.O. Box 5617
Beverly Hills, CA 90210
Actor
birthdate 6/23/50

**Goodwill Industries of
America**
9200 Wisconsin Ave.
Bethesda, MD 20814
David M. Cooney, President
and CEO

Goof Troop
Walt Disney Television
Animation
5200 Lankershim Blvd.
N. Hollywood, CA 91601
Animated series

Gordon, Bart
103 Cannon House Office
Bldg.
Washington, DC 20515-4206
*Representative from Tennessee,
Democrat
Sixth District*

Gore, Al
Admiral House
34th and Massachusetts
Washington, DC 20005
Vice-President of the United States
born 1948

Gorton, Slade
730 Senate Hart Office Bldg.
Washington, DC 20510-4701
*Senator from Washington,
Republican*

Gospel Music Association
P.O. Box 23201
Nashville, TN 37202
Bruce Koblish, Executive
Director

Gosselaar, Mark-Paul
c/o Cunningham
261 S. Robertson Blvd.
Beverly Hills, CA 90210
Actor

Gossett, Louis, Jr.
9830 Wilshire Blvd.
Beverly Hills, CA 90212
Actor
birthdate 5/27/36

Gottfried, Gilbert
1350 Ave. of the Americas
New York, NY 10019
Comedian

Grace Under Fire
c/o Carsey-Werner Co.
4024 Radford Ave., #3
Studio City, CA 91604
TV series

Graham, Bob
524 Senate Hart Office Bldg.
Washington, DC 20510-0903
Senator from Florida, Democrat

Graham, Fred
Court TV
600 3rd Ave.
New York, NY 10016
Reporter

Gramm, Phil
370 Senate Russell Office
Bldg.
Washington, DC 20510-4302
Senator from Texas, Republican

Grammer, Kelsey
10000 Santa Monica Blvd.,
#305
Los Angeles, CA 90067
Actor
birthday 2/20

Grams, Rod
1713 Longworth House Office
Bldg.
Washington, DC 20515-2306
*Representative from Minnesota,
Republican
Sixth District*

Grand Ole Opry
2804 Opryland Dr.
Nashville, TN 37214

Grandparents Anonymous
1924 Beverly
Sylvan Lake, MI 48320
Luella M. Davison, Founder
*Grandparents rights (visitation
after divorce, etc.) and
grandchildren's rights*

Grandy, Fred
418 Cannon House Office
Bldg.
Washington, DC 20515-1505
*Representative from Iowa,
Republican
Fifth District; former actor*

Grant, Amy
P.O. Box 50701
Nashville, TN 37205
Singer
birthdate 12/25/60

Grant, Jennifer
329 N. Wetherly Dr., #101
Beverly Hills, CA 90211
Actress

Grassley, Charles E.
135 Senate Hart Office Bldg.
Washington, DC 20510-1501
Senator from Iowa, Republican

Grateful Dead, The
P.O. Box 1566, Main Office St.
Montclair, NJ 07043
Cult rock group

Gray Panthers
1424 16th NW, #602
Washington, DC 20036
Jule Sugarman, Executive
 Director
Senior citizen activists

Great American Truck Racing
P.O. Box 162
Cato, NY 13033
Michael Bohannon, President

Great Lakes United
State University College at
 Buffalo
Cassety Hall
1300 Elmwood Ave.
Buffalo, NY 14222
Terry Yonker, Executive
 Director

Great White
P.O. Box 67487
Los Angeles, CA 90067
Rock band

Greater Yellowstone Coalition
13 S. Wilson
P.O. Box 1874
Bozeman, MT 59715
Ed Lewis, Executive Director

Green Arrow
DC Comics Inc.
1325 Ave. of the Americas
New York, NY 10019
Comic

Green Bay Packers
1265 Lombardi Ave.
Green Bay, WI 54304
Professional football team

Green Lantern
DC Comics Inc.
1325 Ave. of the Americas
New York, NY 10019
Comic

Green, Brian Austin
9320 Wilshire Blvd., 3rd Fl.
Beverly Hills, CA 90212
Actor

Green, Gene
1004 Longworth House Office
 Bldg.
Washington, DC 20515-4329
*Representative from Texas,
 Democrat
 Twenty-ninth District*

Greene, Graham
121 N. San Vicente Blvd.
Beverly Hills, CA 90211
Actor

Greenpeace U.S.A.
1436 U St. NW
Washington, DC 20009
Barbara Dudley, Executive
 Director
Environmental action group

Greenward Foundation
104 Prospect Park W.
Brooklyn, NY 11215
Robert Makla, Director
*Works for the improvement of
 natural landscapes in urban
 parks*

Greenwood, James C.
515 Cannon House Office
 Bldg.
Washington, DC 20515-3808
*Representative from Pennsylvania,
 Republican
 Eighth District*

Gregg, Judd
393 Senate Russell Office
 Bldg.
Washington, DC 20510-2904
*Senator from New Hampshire,
 Republican*

Grey, Jennifer
9830 Wilshire Blvd.
Beverly Hills, CA 90212
Actress

Gross, Porter J.
330 Cannon House Office
Bldg.
Washington, DC 20515-0914
*Representative from Florida,
Democrat*
Fourteenth District

Grue Magazine
Hell's Kitchen Productions
Box 370,
Times Square Station
New York, NY 10108
Horror magazine

Guardian Angels
982 E. 89th St.
Brooklyn, NY 11236
Curtis Sliwa, Founder
Civilian protection organization

Guess Inc.
1444 S. Alameda St.
Los Angeles, CA 90021
Maurice Marziano, President
Clothing manufacturer

Gunderson, Steve
2235 Rayburn House Office
Bldg.
Washington, DC 20515-4903
*Representative from Wisconsin,
Republican*
Third District

Guns N' Roses
9130 Sunset Blvd.
Los Angeles, CA 90069
Rock group

Gutierrez, Luis V.
1208 Longworth House Office
Bldg.
Washington, DC 20515-1304
*Representative from Illinois,
Democrat*
Fourth District

Guttenberg, Steve
151 El Camino
Beverly Hills, CA 90212
Actor
birthdate 8/24/58

Guy, Jasmine
8942 Wilshire Blvd.
Beverly Hills, CA 90212
Actress, dancer
birthdate 3/10/64

Gypsy Lore Society
5607 Greenleaf Rd.
Cheverly, MD 20785
Sheila Salo, Treasurer

H

News from home is best carried in a letter, and so much can be written on a little piece of paper. Inside the envelope can be sunshine or dark dismal days.

—HANS CHRISTIAN ANDERSEN

Haagen-Dazs Co. Inc.
Glen Pointe
Teaneck, NJ 07666
Michael Bailey, President
Ice cream manufacturer

Haas, Lukas
9830 Wilshire Blvd.
Beverly Hills, CA 90212
Actor

Habyariman, Major General Juvenal
Presidence de la Republique
Kigali, Rwanda
President of Rwanda

Haggard, Merle
P.O. Box 536
Palo Cedro, CA 96073
Singer

Haim, Corey
15301 Ventura Blvd., #345
Sherman Oaks, CA 91403
Actor

Hall, Arsenio
5555 Melrose Ave.
Los Angeles, CA 90038
Actor, former talk show host
birthdate 2/12/58

Hall, Daryl
Champion Entertainment
130 W. 57th St., #12B
New York, NY 10019
Musician
birthdate 10/11/49

Hall, Ralph M.
2236 Russell House Office
Bldg.
Washington, DC 20515-4304
*Representative from Texas,
Democrat
Fourth District*

Hall, Tom T.
P.O. Box 1246
Franklin, TN 37065
Songwriter, performer
birthdate 5/25/36

Hall, Tony P.
2264 Rayburn House Office
Bldg.
Washington, DC 20515-3503
*Representative from Ohio,
Democrat
Third District*

Hallmark Cards
2501 McGee Trafficway,
#419580
Kansas City, MO 64141
Irvine O. Hockaday, Jr., CEO
Greeting card company

Hamburg, Dan
114 Cannon House Office
Bldg.
Washington, DC 20515-0501
Representative from California,
Democrat
First District

Hamilton, Lee H.
2187 Rayburn House Office
Bldg.
Washington, DC 20515-1409
Representative from Indiana,
Democrat
Ninth District

Hamilton, Linda
8942 Wilshire Blvd.
Beverly Hills, CA 90212
Actress

Hammer
(formerly M.C.)
(Stanley Kirk Burrell)
1750 N. Vine St.
Hollywood, CA 90028
Rapper

Hancock, Herbie
9830 Wilshire Blvd.
Beverly Hills, CA 90212
Composer, pianist
birthdate 4/12/40

Hancock, Mel
129 Cannon House Office
Bldg.
Washington, DC 20515-2507
Representative from Missouri,
Republican
Seventh District

Handgun Control Inc.
1225 Eye St. NW, #1100
Washington, DC 20005
Richard M. Abourne,
President

Handicapped Scuba
Association
7172 W. Stanford Ave.
Littleton, CO 80123
Jim Gataare, Program Director

Hanks, Tom
P.O. Box 1276
Los Angeles, CA 90049
Actor
birthdate 7/9/56

Hansen, James V.
2466 Rayburn House Office
Bldg.
Washington, DC 20515-4401
Representative from Utah,
Republican
First District

Harald V, King
Royal Palace
Oslo, Norway
King of Norway

Hard Copy
Paramount Domestic TV
5555 Melrose Ave.
Los Angeles, CA 90038
TV series

Harding, Tonya
4632 SE Oxbow Pkwy.
Gresham, OR 97080
Former figure skater

Hardison, Kadeem
1999 Ave. of the Stars, #2850
Los Angeles, CA 90067
Actor
birthday 7/24

Harkin, Tom
531 Senate Hart Office Bldg.
Washington, DC 20510-1502
Senator from Iowa, Democrat

**Harley Davidson Motor
   Company**
3700 W. Juneau Ave.
Milwaukee, WI 53208
Vaughn Le Roy Beals, Jr.,
   President
*Last American motorcycle
   company*

Harlin, Renny
1033 Gayley Ave., #208
Los Angeles, CA 90024
Film director

Harman, Jane
325 Cannon House Office
   Bldg.
Washington, DC 20515-0536
*Representative from California,
   Democrat
Thirty-sixth District*

Harmon, Mark
9830 Wilshire Blvd.
Beverly Hills, CA 90212
Actor
birthdate 9/2/51

**Harness Horse Youth
   Foundation**
14950 Greyhound Ct., #210
Carmel, IN 46032
Ellen Taylor, Executive
   Director

Harrelson, Woody
9830 Wilshire Blvd.
Beverly Hills, CA 90212
Actor
birthdate 7/23/61

Harris, Emmylou
c/o Monty Hitchcock
Box 159007
Nashville, TN 37215
Singer
birthdate 4/2/47

Harris, Neal Patrick
8942 Wilshire Blvd.
Beverly Hills, CA 90212
Actor
birthdate 6/15/73

Harrison, George
Handmade Films Ltd.
26 Cadogan Sq.
London SW1 England
Singer, producer
birthdate 2/25/43

Harry Connick, Jr., Fan Club
260 Brookline St., #200
Cambridge, MA 02139

**Harry, Debbie
(Deborah Ann Harry)**
c/o Overland
1775 Broadway
New York, NY 10019
Singer
birthdate 7/1/45

Hartford Whalers
One Civic Center Plaza
Hartford, CT 06103
Professional hockey team

Harts of the West
Kushner-Locke Co.
11601 Wilshire Blvd., 21st Fl.
Los Angeles, CA 90025
TV series

Hasbro Inc.
1027 Newport Ave.
Pawtucket, RI 02862
Alan G. Hassenfeld, CEO
Toy and game manufacturer

Haskins, Dennis
c/o Stone
8091 Selma Ave.
Los Angeles, CA 90046
Actor

Hassan II, King
Royal Palace
Rabat, Morocco
Ruler of Morocco

Hassanali, Noor Mohammed
President's House
St. Ann's, Trinidad and
 Tobago
President of Trinidad and Tobago

Hasselhoff, David
151 El Camino
Beverly Hills, CA 90212
Actor, producer, singer
birthdate 7/17/52

Hastert, J. Dennis
2453 Rayburn House Office
 Bldg.
Washington, DC 20515-1314
Representative from Illinois,
 Republican
Fourteenth District

Hastings, Alcee L.
1039 Longworth House Office
 Bldg.
Washington, DC 20515-0923
Representative from Florida,
 Democrat
Twenty-third District

Hatch, Orrin G.
135 Senate Russell Office
 Bldg.
Washington, DC 20510-4402
Senator from Utah, Republican

Hatcher, Teri
151 El Camino
Beverly Hills, CA 90212
Actress

Hatfield, Mark O.
711 Senate Hart Office Bldg.
Washington, DC 20510-3701
Senator from Oregon, Republican

Hawke, Ethan
9830 Wilshire Blvd.
Beverly Hills, CA 90212
Actor

Hawkins, Sophie B.
c/o Columbia Records
51 W. 52nd St.
New York, NY 10019
Singer

Hayes, Isaac
c/o Columbia Records
51 W. 52nd St.
New York, NY 10019
Composer, singer
birthdate 8/20/42

Hayes, James A.
2432 Rayburn House Office
 Bldg.
Washington, DC 20515-1807
Representative from Louisiana,
 Democrat
Seventh District

HBO
Home Box Office
1100 Ave. of the Americas
New York, NY 10036

Healing the Children
North 1603 Belt
Spokane, WA 99205
Terry Rutherford, Executive
 Secretary
Medical attention for
 underprivileged kids

Heart Fan Club
219 1st Ave., #333
Seattle, WA 98109

Heavy Metal
Metal Mammoth Inc.
155 Ave. of the Americas
New York, NY 10013
Comic

Hefley, Joel
2442 Rayburn House Office
Bldg.
Washington, DC 20515-0605
Representative from Colorado,
Republican
Fifth District

Heflin, Howell
728 Senate Hart Office Bldg.
Washington, DC 20510-0101
Senator from Alabama, Democrat

Hefner, W. G. (Bill)
2470 Rayburn House Office
Bldg.
Washington, DC 20515-3308
Representative from North
Carolina, Democrat
Eighth District

Helms, Jesse A.
403 Senate Dirksen Office
Bldg.
Washington, DC 20510-3301
Senator from North Carolina,
Republican

Henderson, Florence
9000 Sunset Blvd., #1200
Los Angeles, CA 90069
Brady Bunch *mom*
birthdate 2/14/34

Henley, Don
9130 Sunset Blvd.
Los Angeles, CA 90069
Singer, songwriter

Henry, Paul B.
1526 Longworth House Office
Bldg.
Washington, DC 20515
Representative from Michigan,
Republican
Third District

Herger, Wally
2433 Rayburn House Office
Bldg.
Washington, DC 20515-0502
Representative from California,
Republican
Second District

Herman's Head
Witt/Thomas Productions
1438 N. Gower St.
Hollywood, CA 90028
TV series

Hershey Foods
100 Mansion Rd.
Hershey, PA 17033
R. A. Zimmerman, CEO
Chocolate manufacturer

Hershey, Barbara
9830 Wilshire Blvd.
Beverly Hills, CA 90212
Actress
birthdate 2/5/48

Hershiser, Orel
L.A. Dodgers
1000 Elysian Park Ave.
Los Angeles, CA 90012
Baseball player

Hewitt, Love
c/o London & Lichtenberg
11601 Wilshire Blvd., #400
Los Angeles, CA 90025
Singer

Hickel, Walter J.
P.O. Box A
Juneau, AK 99811
Governor of Alaska

Highlander
Gaumont Television
24 rue Jacques Dulud
92002 Neuilly,
Paris, France
TV series

Hilliard, Earl F.
1007 Longworth House Office
Bldg.
Washington, DC 20515-0107
Representative from Alabama,
Democrat
Seventh District

Hinchey, Maurice D.
1313 Longworth House Office
Bldg.
Washington, DC 20515-3226
Representative from New York,
Democrat
Twenty-sixth District

Hines, Gregory
9830 Wilshire Blvd.
Beverly Hills, CA 90212
Dancer, actor, singer
birthdate 2/14/46

Hip Magazine
Square Foot Publications
Box 1212
Orange, CT 06477
Allison Zito, Editor
Music magazine

Hit Parader
Hit Parade Publications, Inc.
40 Violet Ave.
Poughkeepsie, NY 12601
Andy Secher, Editor
Heavy metal magazine

Hoagland, Peter
1113 Longworth House Office
Bldg.
Washington, DC 20515-2702
Representative from Nebraska,
Democrat
Second District

Hobby Industry Association of
America
319 E. 54th St.
Elmwood Park, NJ 07407
Particia Koziol, Executive
Director

Hobson, David L.
1507 Longworth House Office
Bldg.
Washington, DC 20515-3507
Representative from Ohio,
Republican
Seventh District

Hochbrueckner, George J.
229 Cannon House Office
Bldg.
Washington, DC 20515-3201
Representative from New York,
Democrat
First District

Hocker International
Federation
78 Unquowa Pl.
Fairfield, CT 06430
Sheila Dearie, Executive
Officer
Hybrid of soccer, basketball,
volleyball, hockey and football

Hoekstra, Peter
1319 Longworth House Office
Bldg.
Washington, DC 20515-2202
Representative from Michigan,
Republican
Second District

Hogestyn, Drake
9255 Sunset Blvd., #515
Los Angeles, CA 90069
Actor

Hoke, Martin R.
212 Cannon House Office
  Bldg.
Washington, DC 20515-3510
Representative from Ohio,
  Republican
Ninth District

Holbrook, Hal
9000 Sunset Blvd., #1200
Los Angeles, CA 90069
Actor
birthdate 2/17/25

Holden, Tim
1421 Longworth House Office
  Bldg.
Washington, DC 20515-3806
Representative from Pennsylvania,
  Democrat
Sixth District

Hollings, Ernest F.
125 Senate Russell Office
  Bldg.
Washington, DC 20510-4002
Senator from South Carolina,
  Democrat

Hollywood Foreign Press
  Association
292 S. La Cienega Blvd.
Beverly Hills, CA 90211
Mirjana Van Blaricom,
  President
Governing body for the Golden
  Globes

Hollywood Pictures
500 S. Buena Vista St.
Burbank, CA 91521
Film production company

Hollywood Reporter, The
5055 Wilshire Blvd.,
Los Angeles, CA 90036
Robert J. Dowling, Publisher
  and Editor in Chief
Daily "trade" publication

Holt International Children's
  Services
P.O. Box 2880
Eugene, OR 97402
Donald D. Ware, Executive
  Director
Works to deinstitutionalize kids

Home Improvement
Touchstone Television
500 S. Buena Vista St.
Burbank, CA 91521
TV series

Hooker, John Lee
P.O. Box 210103
San Francisco, CA 94121
Singer, guitarist

Hooks, Jan
151 El Camino
Beverly Hills, CA 90212
Actress
birthdate 4/23/57

Horatio Alger Society
4907 Allison Dr.
Lansing, MI 48910
Carl T. Hartmann, Secretary

Horn, Stephen
1023 Longworth House Office
  Bldg.
Washington, DC 20515-0538
Representative from California,
  Republican
Thirty-eighth District

Horne, Lena
c/o White
5950 Canoga Ave.
Woodland Hills, CA 91367
Singer
birthdate 6/30/17

Horne, Marilyn
Metropolitan Opera
  Association
147 W. 39th St.
New York, NY 10019
Mezzo-soprano
birthdate 1/16/34

Hornsby, Bruce
c/o BMG
6363 Sunset Blvd.
Hollywood, CA 90028
Musician

Houdini Historical Center
330 E. College Ave.
Appleton, WI 54911
Moira Thomas, Curator

Houghton, Amo
1110 Longworth House Office
  Bldg.
Washington, DC 20515-3231
Representative from New York,
  Republican
Thirty-first District

Houphouet-Boigny, Felix
Presidence de la Republique
Abidjan, Cote d'Ivoire
President of Cote d'Ivoire

House of Ruth
501 H St. NE
Washington, DC 20002
Ellen M. Rocks, Executive
  Director
Shelter for battered, pregnant or
  homeless women and their
  children

Houston Astros
P.O. Box 288
Houston, TX 77001
Professional baseball team

Houston Oilers
6910 Fannin St.
Houston, TX 77030
Professional football team

Houston Rockets
The Summit
Houston, TX 77277
Professional basketball team

Houston, Whitney
6 W. 57th St.
New York, NY 10019
Singer, actress
birthdate 8/9/63

Howling Wind
Strangelove Press
6202 N. 16th St.
Phoenix, AZ 85016
Phil Mershon, Editor
Music magazine

Hoyer, Steny H.
1705 Longworth House Office
  Bldg.
Washington, DC 20515-2005
Representative from Maryland,
  Democrat
Fifth District

Hoyte, Hugh Desmond
Office of the President
New Garden St.
Georgetown, Guyana
President of Guyana

Hrawi, Elias
Office of the President
Beirut, Lebanon
President of Lebanon

Hudson Soft
400 Oyster Point Blvd., #515
S. San Francisco, CA 94080
Electronic games software
  manufacturer

Huffington, Michael
113 Cannon House Office
  Bldg.
Washington, DC 20515-0522
Representative from California,
  Republican
Twenty-second District

Huffy Corporation
P.O. Box 1204
Mimisburg, OH 45401
Harry A. Shaw III, President
Bicycle, bicycle accessory, and
basketball manufacturer

Hug-A-Tree and Survive
c/o Jacqueline Hunt
6465 Lance Way
San Diego, CA 92120
What to do when you're lost

Hughes, William J.
241 Cannon House Office
Bldg.
Washington, DC 20515-3002
Representative from New Jersey,
Democrat
Second District

Humane Society of the United
States
2100 L St. NW
Washington, DC 20037
John A. Hoyt, Chief Executive

Hunt, Bonnie
9830 Wilshire Blvd.
Beverly Hills, CA 90212
Actress

Hunt, Helen
9830 Wilshire Blvd.
Beverly Hills, CA 90212
Actress

Hunt, Jim
State Capitol
Raleigh, NC 27603
Governor of North Carolina

Hunter, Duncan
133 Cannon House Office
Bldg.
Washington, DC 20515-0552
Representative from California,
Republican
Fifty-second District

Hussein I, King
Royal Palace
Amman, Jordan
Ruler of Jordan

Hussein, Saddam
Revolutionary Command
Council
Baghdad, Iraq
President of Iraq

Huston, Anjelica
8942 Wilshire Blvd.
Beverly Hills, CA 90211
Actress
birthdate 7/8/51

Hutchinson, Y. Tim
1541 Longworth House Office
Bldg.
Washington, DC 20515-0403
Representative from Arkansas,
Republican
Third District

Hutchison, Kay Bailey
703 Senate Hart Office Bldg.
Washington, DC 20510-4304
Senator from Texas, Republican

Hutto, Earl
2435 Rayburn House Office
Bldg.
Washington, DC 20515-0901
Representative from Florida,
Democrat
First District

Hyde, Henry J.
2110 Rayburn House Office
Bldg.
Washington, DC 20515-1306
Representative from Illinois,
Republican
Sixth District

I

Persons do not become a society by living in physical proximity, any more than a man ceases to be socially influenced by being so many feet or miles removed from others. A letter may institute a more intimate association between human beings separated thousands of miles from each other than exists between dwellers under the same roof.

—JOHN DEWEY

IBM
(International Business Machines)
Old Orchard Rd.
Anorak, NY 10504
John Fellow Akers, President
Personal computer manufacturer

I.R.S. Records
3939 Lankershim Blvd.
Universal City, CA 91604
Miles Copeland, President
Record label

(New York Office)
594 Broadway, #901
New York, NY 10012

Ibsen Society of America
DeKalb Hall, 3
Pratt Institute
Brooklyn, NY 11205
Rolf Fjelde, President

Ice Cube
c/o Priority
P.O. Box 2186
Hollywood, CA 90078
Rapper

Ice Screamers
Box 5387
2733 Lititz Pike
Lancaster, PA 17601
Ed Marks, President
Club for ice cream fanatics

Ice-T
c/o Sire Records
75 Rockefeller Plaza
New York, NY 10019
Rapper

Idol, Billy
c/o EMI/Chrysalis
810 7th Ave., 8th Fl.
New York, NY 10019
Singer
birthdate 11/30/55

Iliescu, Ion
Office of the President
Bucharest, Romania
President of Romania

Illusion Theater
528 Hennepin Ave., #704
Minneapolis, MN 55403
Michael H. Robins, Executive Producer-Director
"Relevant" theater, specializes in child sexual abuse prevention education

Iman
924 Westwood Blvd., 9th Fl.
Los Angeles, CA 90024
Model

In Living Color
Twentieth Television
P.O. Box 900
Beverly Hills, CA 90213
TV series

In the Heat of the Night
The Fred Silverman Co.
12400 Wilshire Blvd.
Los Angeles, CA 90025
TV series

Incest Survivors Anonymous
P.O. Box 5613
Long Beach, CA 90805-0613

**Incorporated Society of Irish/
American Lawyers**
15140 Farmington Rd.
Livonia, MI 48154
Hon. James R. McCann,
Secretary-Treasurer
*Universal liberty, equal rights and
justice for all*

**Incredible Hulk
(Tales to Astonish)**
Marvel Entertainment Group
387 Park Ave. S.
New York, NY 10016
Comic

Indiana Pacers
300 E. Market St.
Indianapolis, IN 46204
Professional basketball team

Indianapolis Colts
P.O. Box 53500
Indianapolis, IN 46253
Professional football team

Industrial Light and Magic
P.O. Box 2459
San Rafael, CA 94912-2459
George Lucas, Founder
Special-effects wizards

Infant Formula Council
5775 Peachtree-Dunwoody Rd.,
#500G
Atlanta, GA 30342
Robert C. Geraldi, Executive
Director
Rates formulas

Ingenue
Bantam Doubleday Dell
Publishing Group
666 5th Ave.
New York, NY 10103
Barney O'Hara, Advertising
Director
Magazine

Inglis, Bob
1237 Longworth House Office
Bldg.
Washington, DC 20515-4004
*Representative from South
Carolina, Republican
Fourth District*

Ingraham, Hubert
P.O. Box N10846
Nassau, Bahamas
Prime Minister of the Bahamas

Ingram, James
c/o Warner Brothers Records
3300 Warner Blvd.
Burbank, CA 91505
*Rhythm and blues songwriter,
performer*

Inhofe, James M.
442 Cannon House Office
Bldg.
Washington, DC 20515-3601
*Representative from Oklahoma,
Republican
First District*

Ink Spots, The
1385 York Ave., #15H
New York, NY 10021
Pop group

Inouye, Daniel K.
722 Senate Hart Office Bldg.
Washington, DC 20510-1102
Senator from Hawaii, Democrat

Inside Edition
King World Productions Inc.
1700 Broadway, 35th Fl.
New York, NY 10019
TV series

Inside Hollywood
World Publishing
990 Grove St.
Evanston, IL 60201
Jim Turano, Editor
Fan magazine

Inslee, Jay
1431 Longworth House Office
Bldg.
Washington, DC 20515-4704
*Representative from Washington,
Democrat
Fourth District*

Institute for American Values
1841 Broadway, #211
New York, NY 10023
David Blankenhorn, President

Institute for Palestine Studies
Washington Office
3501 M St. NW
Washington, DC 20007
Dr. Philip Mattar, Executive
Director

**Institute for the Achievement
of Human Potential**
8801 Stenton Ave.
Philadelphia, PA 19118
Glenn J. Doman, Chairman
*Works with brain-damaged and
disabled children*

**Institute for the Advanced
Study of Black Family Life
and Culture**
175 Filbert St., #202
Oakland, CA 94607
Wade Nobles, Ph.D., Executive
Director

**Institute for the Development
of the Harmonius Human
Being**
P.O. Box 370
Nevada City, CA 95959
Lee Perry, President

**Institute of Clean Air
Companies**
1707 L St. NW, #570
Washington, DC 20036
Jeffrey C. Smith, Executive
Director

Interflora, Inc.
29200 Northwestern Hwy.
Southfield, MI 48037
John A. Borden, Secretary-
Treasurer
Flowers, flowers everywhere

**International Animated Film
Society**
P.O. Box 787
Burbank, CA 91503
Girard Miller, Executive
Secretary

**International Anti-Euthanasia
Task Force**
P.O. Box 760
Steubenville, OH 43952
Rita Marker, Director

**International Association for
Computer Security**
6 Swarthmore Lane
Dix Hills, NY 11746
Robert J. Wilk, Founder and
President

International Association for the Child's Right to Play
c/o Mr. Robin Moore
Box 7701, NCSU
Raleigh, NC 27695
Believes in kids' right to have fun

International Association of Amusement Parks and Attractions
1448 Duke St.
Alexandria, VA 22314
John R. Graff, Executive Director

International Association of Arson Investigators
5616 Bardstown Rd.
P.O. Box 91119
Louisville, KY 40291
Benny King, Executive Secretary

International Association of Buddhist Studies
c/o Institute of Buddhist Studies
1900 Addison St.
Berkeley, CA 94704
Lou Lancaster, Treasurer

International Association of Sand Castle Builders
172 N. Pershing Ave.
Akron, OH 44313
Thomas A. Morrison, President

International Barbie Doll Collector's Club
P.O. Box 79
Bronx, NY 10464
Ruth Cronk, President

International Bluegrass Music Association
326 St. Elizabeth St.
Owensboro, KY 42301
Dan Hayes, Executive Director

International Bocce Association
187 Proctor Blvd.
Utica, NY 13501
Paul F. Vitagliano, President
Italian lawn bowling

International Boxing Federation
134 Evergreen Pl., 9th Fl.
East Orange, NJ 07018
Marian Muhammad, Executive Secretary

International Boxing Hall of Fame Museum
Hall of Fame Dr.
P.O. Box 425
Canastota, NY 13032
Edward P. Brophy, Executive Director

International Chain Saw Wood Sculptors Association
c/o Tome Rine
14041 Carmody Dr.
Eden Prairie, MN 55347

International Cheerleading Foundation
10660 Barkely
Overland Park, KS 66212
Randy Neil, President

International Child Care (U.S.A.)
Box 2645
Toledo, OH 43606
Rev. Allan F. Waterson, Contact
Better life for Haitian kids

International Child Resource Institute
1810 Hopkins
Berkeley, CA 94707
Ken Jaffe, Executive Director
Deals with issues of day care, abuse, neglect, and has lawyers for kids

International Christian Youth
756 Haddon Ave.
Collingswood, NJ 08108
R. Norris Clark, Chairman

**International Erosion Control
Association**
Box 4904
Steamboat Springs, CO 80477
Ben Northcutt, Executive
Director

**International Fan Club
Organization**
P.O. Box 177
Wild Horse, CO 80862

**International Fan Club
Organization Journal/
Directory**
Tri-Son Inc.
Box 40328
Nashville, TN 37204

**International Federation of
Children's Choirs**
120 S. 3rd St.
Shallway Bldg.
Connellsville, PA 15425
L. Fry, President

**International Foundation for
Airline Passengers**
985 Birch Ct.
P.O. Box 159
Marchel Island, FL 33969
Monte Lazarus, Director

**International Foundation of
Employee Benefit Plans**
18700 W. Bluemound Rd.
P.O. Box 69
Brookfield, WI 53008
John A. Altobelli, CEO

**International Gay and Lesbian
Human Rights Commission**
520 Castro St.
San Francisco, CA 94114
Julie Dorf, Executive Director

International Gay Travel
Association
P.O. Box 4974
Key West, FL 33041
Walt Marlowe, Administrator

**International Handicapper's
Net**
P.O. Box 1185
Ashland, OR 97520
Calvin J. Burt, President
*Radio amateurs who are physically
challenged*

International Hockey League
3850 Priority Way S. Dr., #104
Indianapolis, IN 46240
N. T. Berry, Jr., Commissioner

**International Jet Ski Boating
Association**
1239 E. Warner Ave.
Santa Ana, CA 92705
Bruce Stjernstrom, Vice-
President

**International Jugglers
Association**
P.O. Box 218
Montague, MA 01351
Richard Dingman, Secretary-
Treasurer

International Kart Federation
4650 Arrow Hwy., #B4
Montclair, CA 91763
Jan Gaspar, Office Manager
Go-kart racing

**International Laser Display
Association**
1126 Ashland Ave.
Santa Monica, CA 90405
Barbara Inatsugu, Executive
Director

International Magic Dealers Association
Hank Lee's Magic
102 North St.
Medford, MA 02155
Hank Lee, Secretary

International Mountain Bicycling Association
P.O. Box 412043
Los Angeles, CA 90041
Jim Hasenauer, President

International Nanny Association
P.O. Box 26522
Austin, TX 78755-0522
Kelly Campbell, President

International Pen Friends
P.O. Box 290065
Brooklyn, NY 11229
Leslie Fox, Regional
Representative

International Planned Parenthood Federation
Western Hemisphere Region
902 Broadway, 10th Fl.
New York, NY 10010
Hernan Sanhueza, Regional
Director

International Plastic Modelers Society
P.O. Box 6138
Warner Robins, GA 31095
Frederick P. Horky, President

International Rock 'N' Roll Music Association
P.O. Box 158946
Nashville, TN 37215
Bernard G. Walters, President

International Save the Pun Foundation
P.O. Box 5040, Station A
Toronto, ON, Canada
  M5W IN4
John S. Crosbie, Chairman of
the Bored

International Security and Detective Alliance
P.O. Box 6303
Corpus Christi, TX 78466-6303
H. Roehm, Ph.D., Executive
Director

International Sinatra Society
P.O. Box 5195
Anderson, SC 29623
Fan club

International Sled Dog Racing Association
P.O. Box 446
Nordman, ID 83848
Donna Hawley, Executive
Director

International Soap Box Derby
P.O. Box 7233
Akron, OH 44306
Jeff Jula, General Manager

International Society for General Semantics
P.O. Box 728
Concord, CA 94522
Paul Dennithorne-Johnston,
Executive Director

International Society for Prevention of Child Abuse and Neglect
1205 Oneida St.
Denver, CO 80220
Helen Agathonos, President

International Society for the History of Rhetoric
c/o Michael Leff
Northwestern University
1815 Chicago Ave.
Evanston, IL 60208

International Society for the Study of Time
P.O. Box 815
Westport, CT 06881-0815
Dr. J. T. Fraser, Founder

International Swimming Hall of Fame
1 Hall of Fame Dr.
Ft. Lauderdale, FL 33316
Dr. Samuel James Freas,
Executive Director

International Tap Association
3220 Connecticut Ave. NW,
#112
Washington, DC 20008
Linda Christensen, Executive
Director

International Tennis Hall of Fame
100 Park Ave., 10th Fl.
New York, NY 10017
Jane G. Brown, President

International Unicycling Federation
1560 Baylor Ct.
Eagan, MN 55122
Kenneth G. Fuchs, Secretary-
Treasurer

International Wheelchair Road Racers Club
c/o Joseph M. Dowling
30 Myano Lane, Box 3
Stamford, CT 06902

International Wildlife Society
c/o New York Zoological
Society
Bronx, NY 10460
John G. Robinson, Director

International Willie Nelson Fan Club
P.O. Box 7104
Lancaster, PA 17604

International Windsurfer Class Association
2030 E. Gladwick St.
Compton, CA 90220
Diane Schweitzer, Executive
Secretary

International Wizard of Oz Club
Box 95
Kinderhook, IL 62345
Fred M. Meyer, Secretary
*L. Frank Baum appreciation
society*

Iron Butterfly Information Network
c/o Easy Action
P.O. Box 1658
Fontana, CA 92334
Fan club

Iron Maiden
P.O. Box 391
London, W41LZ England
Rock group

Isaak, Chris
c/o Warner Bros./Reprise
3300 Warner Blvd.
Burbank, CA 91510
Singer

Island Records
400 Lafayette St.
New York, NY 10003
Chris Blackwell, Chairman
Record label

(Los Angeles Office)
8920 Sunset Blvd., 2nd Fl.
Los Angeles, CA 90069

Istook, Ernest J.
1116 Longworth House Office
  Bldg.
Washington, DC 20515-3605
Representative from Oklahoma,
  Republican
Fifth District

It's Showtime at the Apollo
801 Second Ave.
New York, NY 10017
TV series

Itsy Bitsy Spider, The
Hyperion Animation
111 N. Maryland Ave., #200
Glendale, CA 91206
Animated series

Ivanesivich, Goren
U.S. Tennis Association
1212 Ave. of the Americas
New York, NY 10036
Tennis player

Izaak Walton League of
  America
1401 Wilson Blvd., Level B
Arlington, VA 22209
Maitland Sharpe, Executive
  Director

J

Whatever happens to us in our lives, we find questions recurring that we would gladly discuss with some friend. Yet it is hard to find just the friend we should talk to. Often it is easier to *write* to someone whom we do not expect to ever see.

—ELEANOR ROOSEVELT

Jack and Jill of America
346 Commerce St.
Alexandria, VA 22314
Barbara B. Hofman, Executive
  Secretary
*Promotes awareness of community
  needs*

Jack-in-the-Box Restaurants
9330 Balboa Ave.
San Diego, CA 92112
Jack W. Goodall, Jr., Chairman
Fast-food chain

Jackson, Janet (Damita)
338 N. Foothill Rd.
Beverly Hills, CA 90210
Singer
birthdate 5/16/66

Jackson, Joe
c/o Direct Mgmt. Group
947 N. La Cienega Blvd.
West Hollywood, CA 90069
Musician, singer, songwriter

Jackson, Michael
c/o Gallin/Morey Association
8730 Sunset Blvd., PH W
Los Angeles, CA 90069
Singer
birthdate 8/29/58

Jacobs, Andrew, Jr.
2313 Rayburn House Office
  Bldg.
Washington, DC 20515-1410
*Representative from Indiana,
  Democrat
Tenth District*

Jacobs, Sir Wilfrid E.
Office of the Governor
  General
St. John's, Antigua, West
  Indies
*Governor General of Antigua/
  Barbuda*

Jagger, Mick
c/o RZO
110 W. 57th St.
New York, NY 10019
Rock performer
birthdate 7/26/43

Janie's Friends
P.O. Box 680785
San Antonio, TX 78268
Janie Fricke fan club

Janis Ian Fan Club
P.O. Box 475
New York, NY 10023

Jansen, Dan
U.S. Olympic Committee
1750 E. Boulder St.
Colorado Springs, CO 80909
Speed skater

Jarreau, Al
c/o Patrick Rains
9034 Sunset Blvd., #250
West Hollywood, CA 90069
Musician
birthdate 3/12/40

Jawara, Sir Dawda K.
Office of the President
Banjul, the Gambia
President of the Gambia

Jefferson, William J.
428 Cannon House Office
    Bldg.
Washington, DC 20515-1802
Representative from Louisiana,
    Democrat
Second District

Jeffords, James M.
513 Senate Hart Office Bldg.
Washington, DC 20510-4503
Senator from Vermont, Republican

Jenkins, Jerrold
Publishers Distribution
6893 Sullivan Rd.
Grawn, MI 49637
Book distributor

Jeopardy!
Merv Griffin Enterprises
9860 Wilshire Blvd.
Beverly Hills, CA 90210
Game show

Jerry Jeff Walker Fan Club
c/o Tried and True Music
P.O. Box 39
Austin, TX 78767

Jet Lag Magazine
8419 Hals Ferry
Mailman Bldg.
St. Louis, MO 63147
Steve Pick, Editor
Alternative music magazine

Jeter, Michael
924 Westwood Blvd., 9th Fl.
Los Angeles, CA 90024
Actor

Jethro Tull
12 Stratford Place
London, W1N 9AF England
Rock group

Jetsons
Harvey Comics Entertainment,
    Inc.
100 Wilshire Blvd., #500
Santa Monica, CA 90401
Comic

**JFK Assassination Information
    Center**
603 Munger Ave., #3110, Box
    40
Dallas, TX 75202
Larry N. Howard, President

**Jimi Hendrix Information
    Management Institute**
Box 374
Des Plaines, IL 60016
Fan club

**Jimmy Page/Robert Plant
International Newsletter**
1660 Broadmoor Dr. E.
Seattle, WA 98112
Led Zeppelin fan club

Jockey Club, The
40 E. 52nd St.
New York, NY 10022
Hans G. Stahl, Executive
    Director
Rules for breeding horses, etc.

Joe Public
51 W. 52nd St.
New York, NY 10019
Recording artists

Joel, Billy
(William Martin)
Maritime Music Inc.
200 W. 57th St.
New York, NY 10019
Singer, songwriter
birthdate 5/9/49

John Larroquette Show, The
Witt/Thomas Productions
1438 N. Gower St.
Hollywood, CA 90028
TV series

John Paul II, His Holiness
(Karol Wojtyla)
Apostolic Palace
Vatican City
The Pope of the Roman Catholic
Church

John, Elton
(Reginald Kenneth Dwight)
c/o John Reid
32 Galena Rd.
London W6 OLT England
Singer, songwriter
birthdate 3/25/47

Johns and Call Girls United
Against Repression
P.O. Box 021011
Brooklyn, NY 11202-0022
Hugh Montgomery, President
Goal is to make prostitution legal
in the U.S.

Johnson, Don
226 Cannon House Office
Bldg.
Washington, DC 20515-1010
Representative from Georgia,
Democrat
Tenth District

Johnson, Earvin "Magic"
c/o First Team Marketing
1801 Ave. of the Stars
Los Angeles, CA 90067
AIDS activist, former basketball
player

Johnson, Eddie Bernice
1721 Longworth House Office
Bldg.
Washington, DC 20515-4330
Representative from Texas,
Democrat
Thirtieth District

Johnson, Nancy L.
343 Cannon House Office
Bldg.
Washington, DC 20515-0706
Representative from Connecticut,
Republican
Sixth District

Johnson, Sam
1030 Longworth House Office
Bldg.
Washington, DC 20515-4303
Representative from Texas,
Republican
Third District

Johnson, Tim
2438 Rayburn House Office
Bldg.
Washington, DC 20515-4101
Representative from South Dakota,
Democrat At Large

Johnston, Harry
204 Cannon House Office
Bldg.
Washington, DC 20515-0919
Representative from Florida,
Democrat
Nineteenth District

Johnston, J. Bennett
136 Senate Hart Office Bldg.
Washington, DC 20510-1802
Senator from Louisiana, Democrat

Jones, Brereton C.
State Capitol
Frankfort, KY 40601
Governor of Kentucky

Jones, Etta
Houston Person
160 Goldsmith Ave.
Newark, NY 07112
Singer

Jones, George
c/o Buddy Lee Attractions
38 Music Alley
Nashville, TN 37212
Country music singer, songwriter
birthdate 9/12/31

Jones, James Earl
5750 Wilshire Blvd., #512
Los Angeles, CA 90036
Actor
birthdate 1/17/31

Jones, Jenny
9169 Sunset Blvd.
Los Angeles, CA 90069
Talk show host

Jones, Quincy
P.O. Box 48249
Los Angeles, CA 90048
Composer, producer

Jones, Tom
10100 Santa Monica Blvd.,
  #205
Los Angeles, CA 90067
Singer
birthdate 6/7/40

Jones, Tommy Lee
8942 Wilshire Blvd.
Beverly Hills, CA 90211
Actor
birthdate 9/15/46

Jordan, Michael
c/o Falk and Association
5335 Wisconsin Ave.
Washington, DC 20015
Former basketball player

Joseph R. McCarthy
  Foundation
P.O. Box 8040
Appleton, WI 54913
G. Vance Smith, CEO
Honors the late "red scare"
  senator

Journey
P.O. Box 404
San Francisco, CA 94101
Rock group

Juan Carlos I
Palacio de la Zarzuela
Madrid, Spain
King of Spain

Judd, Naomi
P.O. Box 17087
Nashville, TN 37217
Singer

Judy Garland Memorial Club
153 5th St.
Lock Haven, PA 17745

Jugnauth, Aneerood
Government House
Port Louis, Mauritius
Prime Minister of Mauritius

Juice Newton Fan Club
P.O. Box 293323
Lewisville, TX 75029

Junior Bowhunter Program
c/o National Field Archery
  Association
31407 Outer Interstate 10
Redlands, CA 92373
Pam Shilling, Executive
  Secretary

Just for Laughs
JFL Communications
22 Miller Ave.
Mill Valley, CA 94941
Hut Landon, Editor
Stand-up comedy magazine

Just Say No International
2101 Webster St., #1300
Oakland Creek, CA 94612
Ivy Cohen, President
Anti-drug youth group

Justice League of America
DC Comics Inc.
1325 Ave. of the Americas
New York, NY 10019
Comic

As long as there are postmen, life will have zest.

—WILLIAM JAMES

K-Mart Corp.
3100 W. Big Beaver
Troy, MI 48084
Joseph E. Antonini, COO
Department store chain

Kafi, Ali
Presidence de la Republique
El Moradia, Algiers, Algeria
President of Algeria

Kalember, Patricia
232 N. Canon Dr.
Beverly Hills, CA 90210
Actress

Kanjorski, Paul E.
2429 Rayburn House Office
Bldg.
Washington, DC 20515-3811
*Representative from Pennsylvania,
Democrat
Eleventh District*

Kansas City Chiefs
1 Arrowhead Dr.
Kansas City, MO 64129
Professional football team

Kansas City Royals
P.O. Box 419969
Kansas City, MO 64141
Professional baseball team

Kaplan, Stuart
435 Roxbury Dr., #210
Beverly Hills, CA 90210
Dermatologist

Kaptur, Marcy
2104 Rayburn House Office
Bldg.
Washington, DC 20515-3509
*Representative from Ohio,
Democrat
Ninth District*

Karamanlis, Konstantinos G.
Office of the President
Odos Zalokosta 10
Athens, Greece
President of Greece

**Karaoke International Sing-
Along Association**
2321-B Tapo Street, #114
Simi Valley, CA 93063
Neal L. Friedman, Executive
Director

**Karen A. Carpenter Memorial
Foundation**
P.O. Box 1368
Downey, CA 90240
*Scholarship fund for young
musicians and funding for
anorexia nervosa research*

Kasem, Casey
11755 Wilshire Blvd., #2320
Los Angeles, CA 90025
DJ
born 1933

Kasich, John R.
1131 Longworth House Office
Bldg.
Washington, DC 20515-3512
Representative from Ohio,
Republican
Twelfth District

Kassebaum, Nancy L.
302 Senate Russell Office
Bldg.
Washington, DC 21510-1602
Senator from Kansas, Republican

Katz, Ilana
19430 Business Center Dr.
Northridge, CA 91324
Children's book author

Kaufman, Philip
9830 Wilshire Blvd.
Beverly Hills, CA 90212
Screenwriter

Kaufman, Wendy
Snapple, Inc.
175 N. Central Ave.
Valley Stream, NY 11580-3842
Spokesperson

Kaufmann, Mark D.
The Dramatic Publishing
Company
311 Washington St.
Woodstock, IL 60098
Playwright

Keanan, Staci
8730 Sunset Blvd., #202
Los Angeles, CA 90069
Actress

Keating, Charles
#H32037 California Men's
Colony
P.O. Box 8101
San Luis Obispo, CA 93409
Convicted of state securities fraud
over savings and loan crisis

Keating, Paul
Parliament House
Canberra, A.C.T., Australia
Prime Minister of Australia

Keebler Company
1 Hollow Tree Lane
Elmhurst, IL 60126
Thomas M. Garvin, CEO
Cookies and crackers baked by
elves

Keep America Beautiful
Mill River Plaza
9 W. Broad St.
Stamford, CT 06902
Roger W. Powers, President

Kelley, DeForest
415 N. Camden Dr., #121
Beverly Hills, CA 90210
Actor
birthdate 1/20/20

Kelly, Moira
1999 Ave. of the Stars, #2850
Los Angeles, CA 90067
Actress

Kempthorne, Dirk
B40, Suite 3, Senate Dirksen
Office Bldg.
Washington, DC 20510-1204
Senator from Idaho, Republican

Kennedy, Anthony M.
U.S. Supreme Court Bldg.
One First Street NE
Washington, DC 20543
Supreme Court justice

Kennedy, Edward M.
315 Senate Russell Office
Bldg.
Washington, DC 20510-2101
Senator from Massachusetts,
Democrat

Kennedy, Joseph P. II
1210 Longworth House Office
Bldg.
Washington, DC 20515-2108
Representative from
Massachusetts, Democrat
Eighth District

Kennelly, Barbara B.
201 Cannon House Office
Bldg.
Washington, DC 20515-0701
Representative from Connecticut,
Democrat
First District

Kenner Products
1014 Vine St.
Cincinnati, OH 45202
David Mauer, President
Toy and game manufacturer

KFC
Kentucky Fried Chicken
P.O. Box 32070
Louisville, KY 40232
Richard P. Mayer, Chairman
Fast-food chain

Kerrey, Bob
303 Senate House Office Bldg.
Washington, DC 20510-2704
Senator from Nebraska, Democrat

Kerrigan, Nancy
7 Cedar Ave.
Stoneham, MA 02180
Figure skater, Olympic medalist

Kerry, John F.
421 Senate Russell Office
Bldg.
Washington, DC 20510-2102
Senator from Massachusetts,
Democrat

Kevin Collins Foundation for
Missing Children
P.O. Box 59073
San Francisco, CA 94159
David Collins, President
Encourages hope of recovery for
abducted children; maintains
child abduction response
team

Kevorkian, Dr. Jack
223 S. Main St.
Royal Oaks, MI 58067
"Dr. Death"

al-Khalifa, Sheikh Isa bin-
Sulman
Rifa's Palace
Manama, Bahrain
Emir of Bahrain

Khan, Chaka
c/o Geffen Records
9130 Sunset Blvd.
West Hollywood, CA 90069
Singer
birthdate 3/23/53

Khan, Ghulam Ishaq
Office of the President
Constitution Ave.
Islamabad, Pakistan
President of Pakistan

Kidbits
North American Youth Sport
Institute
4985 Oak Garden Dr.
Kernersville, NC 27284
Jack Hutslar, Editor
Magazine

Kidman, Nicole
9830 Wilshire Blvd.
Beverly Hills, CA 90212
Actress

Kids for a Clean Environment
P.O. Box 158254
Nashville, TN 37215
Trish Poe, Contact

Kids Fund
Box 35A
217 W. 80th St.
New York, NY 10024
Nancy Lewis, Associate
    Director
Works to develop self-respect

Kildee, Dale E.
2239 Rayburn House Office
    Bldg.
Washington, DC 20515-2209
Representative from Michigan,
    Democrat
Ninth District

Kilmer, Val
9830 Wilshire Blvd.
Beverly Hills, CA 90212
Actor

Kim, Jay C.
502 Cannon House Office
    Bldg.
Washington, DC 20515-0541
Representative from California,
    Republican
Forty-first District

Kimbrough, Charles
9200 Sunset Blvd., #710
Los Angeles, CA 90069
Actor

King, B.B.
(Riley B. King)
c/o Sidney A. Seidenberg
1414 Ave. of the Americas
New York, NY 10019
Singer, guitarist
birthdate 9/10/25

King, Bruce
State Capitol
Santa Fe, NM 87503
Governor of New Mexico

King, Carole
Free Flow Productions
1209 Baylor St.
Austin, TX 78703
Composer, singer

King, Peter T.
118 Cannon House Office
    Bldg.
Washington, DC 20515-3203
Representative from New York,
    Republican
Third District

King, Stephen
9830 Wilshire Blvd.
Beverly Hills, CA 90212
Author, screenwriter, producer

Kingston, Jack
1229 Longworth House Office
    Bldg.
Washington, DC 20515-1001
Representative from Georgia,
    Republican
First District

Kinnear, Greg
5670 Wilshire Blvd.
Los Angeles, CA 90036
Talk show host

Kirby, Bruno
9320 Wilshire Blvd., 3rd Fl.
Beverly Hills, CA 90212
Actor
born 1949

KISS
P.O. Box 840
Westbury, NY 11590
Rock group

Kiss Konnection Fan Club
P.O. Box 5626
San Angelo, TX 76902

Kitaen, Tawny
9169 Sunset Blvd.
Los Angeles, CA 90069
Actress, host

Kiwanis International
3636 Woodview Terrace
Indianapolis, IN 46268-3196
Kevin Kepinevich, Secretary

Klanwatch
P.O. Box 548
Montgomery, AL 36104
Danny Welch, Contact
Keeping track of the Ku Klux
Klan

Kleczka, Gerald D.
2301 Rayburn House Office
Bldg.
Washington, DC 20515-4904
Representative from Wisconsin,
Democrat
Fourth District

Klein, Herbert C.
1728 Longworth House Office
Bldg.
Washington, DC 20515-3008
Representative from New Jersey,
Democrat
Eighth District

Klestil, Thomas
Prasidentschaftskanzlei
Hofburg, 1014 Vienna, Austria
President of Austria

Klink, Ron
1130 Longworth House Office
Bldg.
Washington, DC 20515-3804
Representative from Pennsylvania,
Democrat
Fourth District

Klug, Scott L.
1224 Longworth House Office
Bldg.
Washington, DC 20515-4902
Representative from Wisconsin,
Republican
Second District

Knight, Gladys (Maria)
c/o Shakeji Inc.
1589 Golden Arrow Dr.
Las Vegas, NV 89109
Singer
birthdate 5/28/44

Knollenberg, Joe
1218 Longworth House Office
Bldg.
Washington, DC 20515-2211
Representative from Michigan,
Republican
Eleventh District

Koala Club News
Zoological Society of San
Diego
Box 551
San Diego, CA 92112
Georgeanne Irvine, Editor
Animal and conservation
magazine

Koenig, Walter
c/o Gold/Marshak
3500 West Olive Ave.
Burbank, CA 91505
Actor

Kohl, Helmut
Marbacher Strasse 11
6700 Ludwigshafen/Rhein
Federal Republic of Germany
Chancellor of Germany

Kohl, Herb
330 Senate Hart Office Bldg.
Washington, DC 20510-4903
Senator from Wisconsin, Democrat

Koivisto, Mauno Henrik
Presidential Palace
Helsinki, Finland
President of Finland

Kol Ha T'Nuah
National Young Judaea
50 W. 58th St.
New York, NY 10019
Daniel Miller, Editor
Magazine

Kolbe, Jim
405 Cannon House Office
Bldg.
Washington, DC 20515-0305
Representative from Arizona,
Republican
Fifth District

Kolingba, General Andre
Presidence de la Republique
Bangui, Central African
Republic
President of the Central African
Republic

Koontz, Dean
P.O. Box 235
Bedford Hills, NY 10607
Author

Kopetski, Michael J.
218 Cannon House Office
Bldg.
Washington, DC 20515-3705
Representative from Oregon,
Democrat
Fifth District

Kosher Wine Institute
175 5th Ave.
New York, NY 10010
David Herzog, President

Kozak, Harley Jane
9560 Wilshire Blvd., 5th Fl.
Beverly Hills, CA 90212
Actress

Kravchuk, Leonid M.
Office of the President
Kyiv, Ukraine
President of the Ukraine

Kreidler, Mike
1535 Longworth House Office
Bldg.
Washington, DC 20515-4709
Representative from Washington,
Democrat
Ninth District

Kriss Cross
51 W. 52nd St.
New York, NY 10019
Hip hop group

Kris Kristofferson
International Fan Club
313 Lakeshore Dr.
Marietta, GA 30067

Kristofferson, Kris
c/o CBS Special Records
51 W. 52nd St.
New York, NY 10019
Composer, singer, actor

Kucan, Milan
Office of the President
Ljubljana, Slovenija
President of Slovenia

Kung Fu: The Legend
Continues
Warner Bros. Television
4000 Warner Blvd.
Burbank, CA 91522
TV series

Kurtz, Swoosie
151 El Camino
Beverly Hills, CA 90212
Actress
birthdate 9/6/44

Kyl, Jon
2440 Rayburn House Office
Bldg.
Washington, DC 20515-0304
Representative from Arizona,
Republican
Fourth District

People in the flesh are a lot more complicated than they appear on paper, which is both one of the attractions and one of the shortcomings of carrying on a prolonged correspondence.

—SHANA ALEXANDER

La Leche League International
9616 Minneapolis Ave.
P.O. Box 1209
Franklin Park, IL 60131
Betty Wagner, Executive
    Director
Pro–breast feeding

La's
(Lee Mavers, Neil Mavers,
    Cammy Power, John Power)
825 Eighth Avenue
New York, NY 10022
Recording artists

LaBelle, Patti
c/o MCA Records
100 Universal City Plaza
Universal City, CA 91608
Singer
birthdate 10/4/44

Lacalle, Luis Alberto
Oficina del Presidente
Montevideo, Uruguay
President of Uruguay

Lacrosse Foundation
113 W. University Pkwy.
Baltimore, MD 21210
Steve Senersen, Executive
    Director

Lacy J. Dalton Fan Club
P.O. Box 1109
Mount Juliet, TN 37122

LADIES (Life After Divorce Is
    Eventually Sane)
P.O. Box 2974
Beverly Hills, CA 90213
Ex-wives of famous men

Ladies Professional Bowlers
    Tour
7171 Cherryvale Blvd.
Rockford, IL 61112
John F. Falzone, President

Ladies Professional Golf
    Association
LPGA
2570 Volusia Ave., #B
Daytona, FL 32114
Charles S. Mechem,
    Commissioner

LaFalce, John J.
2310 Rayburn House Office
    Bldg.
Washington, DC 20515-3229
Representative from New York,
    Democrat
Twenty-ninth District

Lake Upsata Guest Ranch
Box 6
Ovanda, MT 59854
Richard Howe, Owner
Unique wildlife vacations

Lake, Ricki
151 El Camino
Beverly Hills, CA 90212
Talk show host

Lamas, Lorenzo
15301 Ventura Blvd., #345
Sherman Oaks, CA 91403
Actor
birthdate 1/20/58

Lambert, Blanche M.
1204 Longworth House Office
  Bldg.
Washington, DC 20515-0401
Representative from Arkansas,
  Democrat
First District

Lambs, The
3 W. 51st St.
New York, NY 10019
Richard L. Charles, Shepherd
Social organization for the
  entertainment industry

Lancaster, H. Martin
2436 Rayburn House Office
  Bldg.
Washington, DC 20515-3303
Representative from North
  Carolina, Democrat
Third District

Lando, Joe
5750 Wilshire Blvd., #512
Los Angeles, CA 90036
Actor

Landsbergis, Vytautas
Office of the President
Vilnius, Lietuvos Respublika
President of Lithuania

lang, k.d.
c/o Sire Records
75 Rockefeller Plaza
New York, NY 10019
Country music singer, composer
birthdate 11/2/61

Lange, Jessica
588 Broadway, #1212
New York, NY 10022
Actress
birthdate 4/20/49

Lantos, Tom
2182 Rayburn House Office
  Bldg.
Washington, DC 20515-0512
Representative from California,
  Democrat
Twelfth District

LaRocco, Larry
1117 Longworth House Office
  Bldg.
Washington, DC 20515-1201
Representative from Idaho,
  Democrat
First District

Larroquette, John
P.O. Box 6910
Malibu, CA 90265
Actor
birthdate 11/25/47

Larry Gatlin and Gatlin
  Brothers International Fan
  Club
P.O. Box 153452
Irving, TX 75015

LaSorda, Tommy
L.A. Dodgers
1000 Elysian Park Ave.
Los Angeles, CA 90012
Baseball manager

Lassie
16133 Soledad Canyon Rd.
Canyon Country, CA 91351
Famous dog

Latest Jokes
Box 023304
Brooklyn, NY 11202
Joke magazine

Laugh
Archie Comic Publications
Inc.
325 Fayette Ave.
Mamaroneck, NY 10543
Comic

Laughlin, Greg
236 Cannon House Office
Bldg.
Washington, DC 20515-4314
Representative from Texas,
Democrat
Fourteenth District

Lauper, Cyndi
c/o Dave Wolff
853 7th Ave.
New York, NY 10019
Singer
birthdate 6/20/53

Lauren, Ralph
1107 Fifth Ave.
New York, NY 10128
Fashion designer

Lautenberg, Frank R.
506 Senate Hart Office Bldg.
Washington, DC 20510-3002
Senator from New Jersey, Democrat

Law & Order
Universal Television
70 Universal City Plaza
Universal City, CA 91608
TV series

Lawrence, Joey
9200 Sunset Blvd., #710
Los Angeles, CA 90069
Actor, singer

Lawrence, Vicki
151 El Camino
Beverly Hills, CA 90212
Talk show host
birthdate 3/26/49

Lazio, Rick A.
314 Cannon House Office
Bldg.
Washington, DC 20515-3202
Representative from New York,
Republican
Second District

Leach, Jim
2186 Rayburn House Office
Bldg.
Washington, DC 21505-1501
Representative from Iowa,
Republican
First District

Leach, Robin
1 Dag Hammarskjold Plaza
885 Second Ave.
New York, NY 10017
TV host
birthdate 8/29/41

League of American Theatres
and Producers
226 W. 47th St.
New York, NY 10036
Harvey Sabinson, Executive
Director
Parents of the Tony Awards

League of American
Wheelmen
190 W. Ostend St., #120
Baltimore, MD 21230
Gil Clark, Executive Director
Bicyclists

League of Historic American
Theatres
1511 K St. NW, #923
Washington, DC 20005
Mary Margaret Shoenfeld,
Executive Director

**League of Off-Broadway
Theatres and Producers**
c/o George Elmer
Productions Ltd.
130 W. 42nd St., #1300
New York, NY 10036

League of Resident Theatres
c/o Harry Weintraub
Garry & Weintraub, RC
1501 Broadway, #2401
New York, NY 10036

Leahy, Patrick J.
433 Senate Russell Office
Bldg.
Washington, DC 20510-4502
Senator from Vermont, Democrat

**Learning Disabilities
Association of America**
4156 Library Rd.
Pittsburgh, PA 15234
Jean Petersen, Executive
Director

Leavitt, Mike
210 State Capitol
Salt Lake City, UT 84114
Governor of Utah

L.E.G.I.O.N.
DC Comics Inc.
1325 Ave. of the Americas
New York, NY 10019
Comic

Legion of Superheroes
DC Comics Inc.
1325 Ave. of the Americas
New York, NY 10019
Comic

Lehman, Richard
1226 Longworth House Office
Bldg.
Washington, DC 20515-0519
*Representative from California,
Democrat
Nineteenth District*

Leibovitz, Annie
55 Vandam St.
New York, NY 10013
Photographer

Leigh, Jennifer Jason
8942 Wilshire Blvd.
Beverly Hills, CA 90211
Actress

Leighton, Laura
924 Westwood Blvd., 9th Fl.
Los Angeles, CA 90024
Actress

Lennox, Annie
Box 245
London N89 QG England
Singer

**Lesbian Herstory Educational
Foundation, Inc.**
P.O. Box 1258
New York, NY 10116
Joan Nestle, Sec.
Lesbian herstory archives

Letterman, David
Worldwide Pants Inc.
1697 Broadway
New York, NY 10019
Talk show host
birthdate 4/12/47

Levi Strauss
1155 Battery St.
San Francisco, CA 94111
Robert D. Hass, President
Jeans manufacturer

Levin, Carl
459 Senate Russell Office
Bldg.
Washington, DC 20510-2202
Senator from Michigan, Democrat

Levin, Sander M.
106 Cannon House Office
 Bldg.
Washington, DC 20515-2212
Representative from Michigan,
 Democrat
Twelfth District

Levine, Arthur
Newsmaker Interviews
8217 Beverly Blvd.
Los Angeles, CA 90048
Editor of newsletter for TV &
 radio stations noting who is
 currently available for
 interviews

Levine, Michael
8730 Sunset Boulevard,
 6th Floor
Los Angeles, CA 90069
Author of The Address Book

Levinson, Barry
9830 Wilshire Blvd.
Beverly Hills, CA 90212
Director, writer, producer

Levy, David A.
116 Cannon House Office
 Bldg.
Washington, DC 20515-3204
Representative from New York,
 Republican
Fourth District

**Lewis Carroll Society of North
 America**
617 Rockford Rd.
Silver Spring, MD 20902
Charles Lovett, President

Lewis, Huey
P.O. Box 819
Mill Valley, CA 94942
Singer
birthdate 7/5/51

Lewis, Jerry
151 El Camino
Beverly Hills, CA 90211
French cultural icon, fund-raiser

Lewis, Jerry
2312 Rayburn House Office
 Bldg.
Washington, DC 20515-0540
Representative from California,
 Republican
Fortieth District

Lewis, Jerry Lee
P.O. Box 3864
Memphis, TN 37173
Country-rock singer, musician
birthdate 9/29/35

Lewis, John
329 Cannon House Office
 Bldg.
Washington, DC 20515-1005
Representative from Georgia,
 Democrat
Fifth District

Lewis, Tom
2351 Rayburn House Office
 Bldg.
Washington, DC 20515-0916
Representative from Florida,
 Republican
Sixteenth District

Lieberman, Joseph I.
316 Senate Hart Office Bldg.
Washington, DC 20510-0703
Senator from Connecticut,
 Democrat

Lifetime Television
10880 Wilshire Blvd., #2010
Los Angeles, CA 90024

Light, Christopher Upjohn
Old Kent Bank Bldg.
136 E. Michigan Ave.
Kalamazoo, MI 49007
Computer musician

Light, Judith
8942 Wilshire Blvd.
Beverly Hills, CA 90211
Actress
birthdate 2/9/50

Lightfoot, Gordon (Meredith)
40 W. 57th St.
New York, NY 10019
Singer, songwriter
birthdate 11/17/38

Lightfoot, Jim Ross
2444 Rayburn House Office
Bldg.
Washington, DC 21505-1503
Representative from Iowa,
Republican
Third District

Lighthawk
P.O. Box 8163
Santa Fe, NM 87504
Michael M. Stewatt, Executive
Director
Air support for conservationists

Limbaugh, Rush
Multimedia Entertainment
45 Rockefeller Plaza, 35th Fl.
New York, NY 10111
Talk show host

Lincoln Center for the
Performing Arts
70 Lincoln Center Plaza
New York, NY 10023-6583
Nathan Leventhal, President

Linder, John
1605 Longworth House Office
Bldg.
Washington, DC 20515-1004
Representative from Georgia,
Republican
Fourth District

Linn-Baker, Mark
8942 Wilshire Blvd.
Beverly Hills, CA 90211
Actor
birthdate 6/17/53

Lions Clubs International
300 22nd St.
Oak Brook, IL 60521
Mark C. Lukas, Executive
Administrator

Liotta, Ray
9830 Wilshire Blvd.
Beverly Hills, CA 90212
Actor
birthday 12/18

Lipinski, William O.
1501 Longworth House Office
Bldg.
Washington, DC 20515-1303
Representative from Illinois,
Democrat
Third District

Lithgow, John
9830 Wilshire Blvd.
Beverly Hills, CA 90212
Actor
birthdate 10/19/45

Little League Baseball
P.O. Box 3485
Williamsport, PA 17701
Dr. Creighton J. Hale,
President & CEO

Little People of America
7238 Piedmont Dr.
Dallas, TX 75227-9324
Mary Carten, President
Association of little people

Little Richard
(Richard Wayne Penniman)
c/o BMI
8730 Sunset Blvd., 3rd Fl.
Los Angeles, CA 90069
Pianist, songwriter
birthdate 12/5/32

Little River Band
87-91 Palmerstin Cres.
Albert Park
Melbourne Victoria 3206
   Australia
Rock group

Livingston, Bob
2368 Rayburn House Office
   Bldg.
Washington, DC 20515-1801
Representative from Louisiana,
   Republican
First District

LL Cool J
(Ladies Love Cool James)
298 Elizabeth St.
New York, NY 10012
Rapper

Lloyd Webber, Andrew
19/22 Tower St.
London WC2H 9NS England
Composer

Lloyd, Marilyn
2406 Rayburn House Office
   Bldg.
Washington, DC 20515-4203
Representative from Tennessee,
   Democrat
Third District

Locklear, Heather
151 El Camino
Beverly Hills, CA 90211
Actress
birthdate 9/25/61

Loggins, Kenny
(Kenneth Clarke Loggins)
151 El Camino
Beverly Hills, CA 90212
Singer, songwriter
birthdate 1/17/47

Lois & Clark: The New
   Adventures of Superman
Warner Bros. Television
4000 Warner Blvd.
Burbank, CA 91522
TV series

Long, Jill
1513 Longworth House Office
   Bldg.
Washington, DC 20515-1404
Representative from Indiana,
   Democrat
Fourth District

Looking Up
P.O. Box K
Augusta, ME 04332
Kathy Lamb, Executive
   Director
Organization for survivors of
   incest and sexual abuse

Loose Teeth
Fantagraphics Books Inc.
7563 Lake City Way N.E.
Seattle, WA 98115
Comic

Lopez, Mario
c/o NBC Productions
300 Bob Hope Dr.
Burbank, CA 91523
Actor

Loretta Lynn Fan Club
P.O. Box 177
Wild Horse, CO 80862

Los Angeles Clippers
3939 S. Figueroa
Los Angeles, CA 90037
Professional basketball team

Los Angeles Dodgers
Dodger Stadium
Los Angeles, CA 90012
Professional baseball team

Los Angeles Kings
3900 W. Manchester Blvd.
Inglewood, CA 90306
Professional hockey team

Los Angeles Lakers
Great Western Forum
Inglewood, CA 90306
Professional basketball team

Los Angeles Raiders
332 Center St.
El Segundo, CA 90245
Professional football team

Los Angeles Rams
2327 W. Lincoln Ave.
Anaheim, CA 92801
Professional football team

Los Lobos
P.O. Box 1304
Burbank, CA 91507
Recording artists

Lott, Trent
487 Senate Russell Office
    Bldg.
Washington, DC 20510-2403
*Senator from Mississippi,
    Republican*

**Lou Christie International Fan
    Club**
c/o Harry Young
P.O. Box 748
Chicago, IL 60690

Loughlin, Lori
151 El Camino
Beverly Hills, CA 90212
Actress

Louis-Dreyfus, Julia
9560 Wilshire Blvd., 5th Fl.
Beverly Hills, CA 90212
Actress

Love Connection
c/o Eric Lieber Production
    Inc.
9220 Sunset Blvd., #200
Los Angeles, CA 90069
Game show

Lovitz, Jon
9830 Wilshire Blvd.
Beverly Hills, CA 90212
Comedian
birthdate 7/21/57

Lowey, Nita M.
1424 Longworth House Office
    Bldg.
Washington, DC 20515-3218
*Representative from New York,
    Democrat
Eighteenth District*

Lowry, Mike
State Capitol
Olympia, WA 98504
Governor of Washington

Lubbers, Ruud
Office of the Prime Minister
The Hague, Netherlands
President of the Netherlands

Lucci, Susan
40 W. 57th St.
New York, NY 10019
Actress
birthdate 12/23/49

Lugar, Richard G.
306 Senate Hart Office Bldg.
Washington, DC 20510-1401
Senator from Indiana, Republican

LuPone, Patti
232 N. Canon Dr.
Beverly Hills, CA 90212
Singer, actress
birthdate 4/21/49

Lynn, Loretta
c/o MCA Records Inc.
70 Universal City Plaza
Universal City, CA 91608
Singer
birthday 4/14

Excuse me for not answering your letter sooner, but I've been so busy not answering letters that I couldn't get around to yours in time.

—GROUCHO MARX

M&M/Mars
High Street
Hackettstown, NJ 07840
Howard Walker, President
Candy company

Ma, Yo Yo
40 W. 57th St.
New York, NY 10019
Cellist

Machtley, Ronald K.
326 Cannon House Office
  Bldg.
Washington, DC 20515-3901
*Representative from Rhode Island,
  Republican
First District*

Mack, Connie
517 Senate Hart Office Bldg.
Washington, DC 20510-0904
Senator from Florida, Republican

Mad
E.C. Publications, Inc.
485 Madison Ave.
New York, NY 10022
John Ficarra, Editor
Humor magazine

Mad About You
TriStar Television
9336 W. Washington Blvd.
Culver City, CA 90232
TV series

**Madonna
(Madonna Louise Veronica
  Ciccone)**
75 Rockefeller Plaza
New York, NY 10019
Singer
birthdate 8/16/58

Magical Youths International
61551 Bremen Hwy.
Mishawaka, IN 46544
Steve Kelley, Publisher
Kid magicians

Magope, Kgosi Lucas
Department of the Presidency
Private Bag X2005
Mafikeng, Bophuthatswana
South Africa
President of Bophuthatswana

**Mahal, Taj
(Henry St. Clair Fredericks)**
Folklore Productions
1671 Appian Way
Santa Monica, CA 90401
Composer, musician

Mail for Tots
25 New Chardon St.
P.O. Box 8699
Boston, MA 02114
Edmund G. Burns, President
Letters of cheer to seriously ill or
physically challenged kids

Major, John
10 Downing St.
London S.W. 1, England
United Kingdom
Prime Minister of the United
Kingdom

Make-A-Wish Foundation of
America
2600 N. Central Ave., #936
Phoenix, AZ 85004
Janet Hayes, Executive
Director
Wishes for ill children

Malkovich, John
1322 Genessee St.
Los Angeles, CA 90019
Actor
birthdate 12/9/53

Maloney, Carolyn B.
1504 Longworth House Office
Bldg.
Washington, DC 20515-3214
Representative from New York,
Democrat
Fourteenth District

Mamaloni, Solomon
Office of the Prime Minister
P.O. Box GO1
Honiara, Guadalcanal
Solomon Islands
Prime Minister of the Solomon
Islands

Mamet, David
P.O. Box 381589
Cambridge, MA 02238
Playwright, screenwriter

Mandela, Nelson
Tuynhuys
Cape Town 8000, South Africa
President of South Africa

Mandrell, Barbara Ann
World Class Talent
1522 Demonbreun St.
Nashville, TN 37203
Singer
birthdate 12/25/48

Mandylor, Costas
151 El Camino
Beverly Hills, CA 90212
Actor

Mangione, Chuck
(Charles Frank Mangione)
1850 Winton Road S.
Rochester, NY 14618
Jazz musician, composer
birthdate 11/29/40

Manhattan Transfer, The
3575 Cahuenga Blvd., W.,
#450
Los Angeles, CA 90068
Pop group

Manilow, Barry
Stiletto Ltd.
6640 Sunset Blvd., #110
Los Angeles, CA 90028
Singer, songwriter, arranger
birthdate 6/17/46

Mann, David S.
503 Cannon House Office
Bldg.
Washington, DC 20515-3501
Representative from Ohio,
Democrat
First District

Manton, Thomas J.
203 Cannon House Office
  Bldg.
Washington, DC 20515-3207
Representative from New York,
  Democrat
Seventh District

Manzullo, Donald A.
506 Cannon House Office
  Bldg.
Washington, DC 20515-1316
Representative from Illinois,
  Republican
Sixteenth District

Margolies-Mezvinsky, Marjorie
1516 Longworth House Office
  Bldg.
Washington, DC 20515-3813
Representative from Pennsylvania,
  Democrat
Thirteenth District

Marie, Teena
c/o Sony Music
51 W. 52nd St.
New York, NY 10019
Singer

Marinaro, Ed
1999 Ave. of the Stars, #2850
Los Angeles, CA 90067
Actor

Marine Corps Toys for Tots
  Foundation
4053 Maple Rd., #101
Amherst, NY 14226
Bill Grein, Contact

Markey, Edward J.
2133 Rayburn House Office
  Bldg.
Washington, DC 20515-2107
Representative from
  Massachusetts, Democrat
Seventh District

Marky Mark
(Mark Wahlberg)
10900 Wilshire Blvd.
Los Angeles, CA 90024
Rapper

Marsalis, Branford
c/o The Tonight Show
3000 W. Alameda
Burbank, CA 91523
Musician

Marsalis, Wynton
9000 Sunset Blvd., #1200
Los Angeles, CA 90069
Musician

Marshall, Penny
9830 Wilshire Blvd.
Beverly Hills, CA 90212
Director, actress
birthdate 10/15/43

Martin
c/o HBO Independent
  Production Inc.
2049 Century Park East,
  41st Fl.
Los Angeles, CA 90067
TV series

Martin, Kellie
151 El Camino
Beverly Hills, CA 90212
Actress

Martinez, A
151 El Camino
Beverly Hills, CA 90212
Actor

Martinez, Matthew G.
2231 Rayburn House Office
  Bldg.
Washington, DC 20515-0531
Representative from California,
  Democrat
Thirty-first District

Marvel Age
Marvel Entertainment Group
387 Park Ave. S.
New York, NY 10016
Comic

Marx Brothers Study Unit
Darien 28
New Hope, PA 18938
Paul G. Wesolowski, Director

Marx, Richard
1750 N. Vine St.
Hollywood, CA 90028
Singer

Masire, Quett Ketumile Joni
State House
Private Bag 001, Gabornoe
Botswana
President of Bostwana

Mastrantonio, Mary Elizabeth
8942 Wilshire Blvd.
Beverly Hills, CA 90212
Actress
birthdate 11/17/58

Mathews, Harlan
506 Senate Dirksen Office
   Bldg.
Washington, DC 20510-4203
Senator from Tennessee, Democrat

Matlock
c/o Dean Hargrove
   Production
100 Universal City Plaza,
   #507-3E
Universal City, CA 91608
TV series

Matsui, Robert T.
2311 Rayburn House Office
   Bldg.
Washington, DC 20515-0505
Representative from California,
   Democrat
Fifth District

Mattea, Kathy
c/o Robert T. Titley
706 18th Ave. S.
Nashville, TN 37212
Vocalist, songwriter

Mattel
5150 Rosecrans Ave.
Hawthorne, CA 90250
Thomas J. Kalinske, President
Toy company

Mayfield, Curtis
P.O. Box 724677
Atlanta, GA 30339
Musician
birthdate 6/3/42

Mazar, Debi
9057 Nemo St., #A
West Hollywood, CA 90069
Actress

Mazzoli, Romano L.
2246 Rayburn House Office
   Bldg.
Washington, DC 20515-1703
Representative from Kentucky,
   Democrat
Third District

Mbasogo, Colonel Teodoro
   Obiang Nguema
Oficina del Presidente
Malabo, Equatorial Guinea
President of Equatorial Guinea

MCA Records
70 Universal Plaza
Universal City, CA 91608
Al Teller, Chairman
Record label

(Nashville Office)
1514 South St.
Nashville, TN 37212

(New York Office)
1755 Broadway
New York, NY 10019

McCain, John
111 Senate Russell Office
Bldg.
Washington, DC 20510-0303
Senator from Arizona, Republican

McCandless, Alfred A.
2422 Rayburn House Office
Bldg.
Washington, DC 20515-0544
Representative from California,
Republican
Forty-fourth District

McCartney, Paul
MPL Communications Ltd.
1 Soho Sq.
London W1V 6BQ England
Singer, composer
birthdate 6/18/42

McCloskey, Frank
306 Cannon House Office
Bldg.
Washington, DC 20515-1408
Representative from Indiana,
Democrat
Eighth District

McCollum, Bill
2266 Rayburn House Office
Bldg.
Washington, DC 20515-0908
Representative from Florida,
Republican
Eighth District

McConnell, Mitch
120 Senate Russell Office
Bldg.
Washington, DC 20510-1702
Senator from Kentucky,
Republican

McCormick, Maureen
9744 Wilshire Blvd., #308
Beverly Hills, CA 90212
Actress, "Marcia Brady"

McCrory, Jim
225 Cannon House Office
Bldg.
Washington, DC 20515-1805
Representative from Louisiana,
Republican
Fifth District

McCurdy, Dave
2344 Rayburn House Office
Bldg.
Washington, DC 20515-3604
Representative from Oklahoma,
Democrat
Fourth District

McDade, Joseph M.
2370 Rayburn House Office
Bldg.
Washington, DC 20515-3810
Representative from Pennsylvania,
Republican
Tenth District

McDermott, Jim
1707 Longworth House Office
Bldg.
Washington, DC 20515-4707
Representative from Washington,
Democrat
Seventh District

McDonald's Corporation
One McDonald Plaza
Oak Brook, IL 60521
Fred L. Turner, CEO
Fast-food chain

McDonnell, Mary
15760 Ventura Blvd., #1730
Encino, CA 91436
Actress

McEntire, Reba
1514 South Street
Nashville, TN 37212
Singer
birthdate 3/28/54

McFerrin, Bobby
ProbNoblem Music
Original Artists
128 W. 69th St.
New York, NY 10023
Singer, musician
birthdate 3/11/50

McGinley, Ted
151 El Camino
Beverly Hills, CA 90212
Actor

McHale, Paul
511 Cannon House Office
Bldg.
Washington, DC 20515-3815
Representative from Pennsylvania,
Democrat
Fifteenth District

McHugh, John M.
416 Cannon House Office
Bldg.
Washington, DC 20515-3224
Representative from New York,
Republican
Twenty-fourth District

McInnis, Scott
512 Cannon House Office
Bldg.
Washington, DC 20515-0603
Representative from Colorado,
Republican
Third District

McKeon, Howard P. (Buck)
307 Cannon House Office
Bldg.
Washington, DC 20515-0525
Representative from California,
Republican
Twenty-fifth District

McKernan, John R., Jr.
State House
Augusta, ME 04333
Governor of Maine

McKinney, Cynthia A.
124 Cannon House Office
Bldg.
Washington, DC 21505-1011
Representative from Georgia,
Democrat
Eleventh District

McLaughlin, John
Olive Productions
1211 Connecticut Ave. NW,
#810
Washington, DC 20007

McMillan, Alex
401 Cannon House Office
Bldg.
Washington, DC 20515-3309
Representative from North
Carolina, Republican
Ninth District

McNulty, Michael R.
217 Cannon House Office
Bldg.
Washington, DC 20515-3221
Representative from New York,
Democrat
Twenty-first District

McRaney, Gerald
329 N. Wetherly Dr., #101
Beverly Hills, CA 90211
Actor
birthdate 8/19/47

McVie, Christine Perfect
c/o Warner Bros. Records
3300 W. Warner Blvd.
Burbank, CA 91505
Musician

McWherter, Ned
State Capitol
Nashville, TN 37219
Governor of Tennessee

Medical Network for Missing Children
67 Pleasant Ridge Rd.
Harrison, NY 10528
Peter S. Liebert, M.D.,
Director
Maintains archive of medical and dental records of missing children

Meehan, Martin T.
1223 Longworth House Office Bldg.
Washington, DC 21505-2105
Representative from Massachusetts, Democrat Fifth District

Meek, Carrie P.
404 Cannon House Office Bldg.
Washington, DC 20515-0917
Representative from Florida, Democrat Seventeenth District

Mellencamp, John Cougar
Champion Entertainment
130 W. 57th St., #12B
New York, NY 10019
Singer, songwriter

Melrose Place
Spelling Television
5700 Wilshire Blvd.
Los Angeles, CA 90036
TV series

Men at Work
Box 289
Abbotsford, Victoria 3067
Australia
Pop group

Menem, Carlos Saul
Casa de Gobierno
Balcarce 50, 1064 Buenos Aires
Argentina
President of Argentina

Menendez, Eric
Menendez, Lyle
Los Angeles County Jail
441 Bouchet St.
Los Angeles, CA 90012
Famous patricide defendants

Menendez, Robert
1531 Longworth House Office Bldg.
Wasbington, DC 20515-3013
Representative from New Jersey, Democrat Thirteenth District

Menken, Alan
500 S. Buena Vista St.
Burbank, CA 91521
Disney animated musical composer (Aladdin, Little Mermaid, etc.)

Mercury Records
PolyGram Label Group
Worldwide Plaza, 825 8th Ave.
New York, NY 10019
Ed Eckstine, President
Record label

(Los Angeles Office)
11150 Santa Monica Blvd., 10th Fl.
Los Angeles, CA 90025

Merrie Melodies Starring Bugs Bunny and Friends
Warner Bros. Animation Inc.
15303 Ventura Blvd., #1100
Sherman Oaks, CA 91403
Animated series

Merrill, Steve
State House, Room 208
Concord, NH 03301
Governor of New Hampshire

Messies Anonymous
c/o Sandra Felton
5025 SW 114th Ave.
Miami, FL 33165

Metal Mania
Tempo Publishing
475 Park Ave. S.
New York, NY 10016
Fan magazine

Metal Muscle
Faces Magazine, Inc.
63 Grand Ave., #230
River Edge, NJ 07661
Music magazine

Metallica
75 Rockefeller Plaza
New York, NY 10019
Heavy metal group

Metheny, Patrick Bruce
c/o T. Kurland
173 Brighton Ave.
Boston, MA 02134
Musician

Mettalix
Pilot Communications
25 W. 39th St.
New York, NY 10018
Heavy metal magazine

Metzenbaum, Howard M.
140 Senate Russell Office
    Bldg.
Washington, DC 20510-3502
Senator from Ohio, Democrat

Meyers, Jan
2338 Rayburn House Office
    Bldg.
Washington, DC 20515-1603
Representative from Kansas,
    Republican
Third District

Mfume, Kweisi
2419 Rayburn House Office
    Bldg.
Washington, DC 20515-2007
Representative from Maryland,
    Democrat
Seventh District

Miami Dolphins
2269 NW 199 St.
Miami, FL 33056
Professional football team

Miami Heat
Miami Arena
Miami, FL 33136
Professional basketball team

Mica, John L.
427 Cannon House Office
    Bldg.
Washington, DC 20515-0907
Representative from Florida,
    Republican
Seventh District

Michael, George
Ixworth Place, 1st Fl.
London, SW1, England
Singer
birthdate 6/26/63

Michel, Robert H.
2112 Rayburn House Office
    Bldg.
Washington, DC 20515-1318
Representative from Illinois,
    Republican
Eighteenth District

Midkiff, Dale
232 N. Canon Dr.
Beverly Hills, CA 90210
Actor

Midler, Bette
500 S. Buena Vista, #1G2
Burbank, CA 91521
Singer, actress
birthdate 12/1/45

Midnight Graffiti
13101 Sudan Rd.
Poway, CA 92064
Fantasy and horror magazine

Midnight Oil
c/o Sony
51 W. 52nd St.
New York, NY 10019
Rock Group

Midwest Stock Exchange
1 Financial Place
440 S. LaSalle St.
Chicago, IL 60605
John L. Fletcher, Chairman

Mighty Ducks, The
P.O. Box 61077
Anaheim, CA 92803
Professional hockey team

**Mighty Morphin Power
   Rangers**
Fox Broadcasting Company
10201 W. Pico Blvd.
Los Angeles, CA 90035

Mikulski, Barbara A.
709 Senate Hart Office Bldg.
Washington, DC 20510-2003
Senator from Maryland, Democrat

**Milking Machine
   Manufacturers Council**
10 South Riverside Plaza,
   #1220
Chicago, IL 60606
J. B. Ebbinghaus, Vice-
   President

Miller, Bob
State Capitol
Carson City, NV 89710
Governor of Nevada

Miller, Dan
510 Cannon House Office
   Bldg.
Washington, DC 20515-0913
*Representative from Florida,
   Republican
Thirteenth District*

Miller, George
2205 Rayburn House Office
   Bldg.
Washington, DC 20515-0507
*Representative from California,
   Democrat
Seventh District*

Miller, Steve
P.O. Box 4127
Mercer Island, WA 98040
Musician

Miller, Walter Dale
State Capitol
Pierre, SD 57501
Governor of South Dakota

Miller, Zell
State Capitol
Atlanta, GA 30334
Governor of Georgia

Milsap, Ronnie
12 Music Circle Sq.
Nashville, TN 37203
Singer
birthdate 1/16/44

Milton Bradley Co.
443 Shaker Rd.
East Longmeadow, MA 01028
George R. Ditamassi, President
Game manufacturer

Milwaukee Brewers
Milwaukee County Stadium
Milwaukee, WI 53215
Professional baseball team

Milwaukee Bucks
1001 N. 4th St.
Milwaukee, WI 53203
Professional basketball team

Mindell, Dr. Earl
10739 W. Pico Blvd.
Los Angeles, CA 90046
Vitamin expert

Mineta, Norman Y.
2221 Rayburn House Office
  Bldg.
Washington, DC 20515-0515
Representative from California,
  Democrat
Fifteenth District

Minge, Dave
1508 Longworth House Office
  Bldg.
Washington, DC 20515-2302
Representative from Minnesota,
  Democrat
Second District

Miniature Arms Collectors/
  Makers Society
c/o Donald Beck
3329 Palm St.
Granite City, IL 62040
Mini–war model enthusiasts

Miniature Book Society
P.O. Box 127
Sudbury, MA 01776-0001
Rev. Joseph L. Curran,
  Treasurer
Books less than 3" in height

Miniature Golf Association of
  America
P.O. Box 32353
Jacksonville, FL 32237
Skip Laun, Executive Director

Miniatures Industry
  Association of America
1100-H Brandywine Blvd.
P.O. Box 2188
Zanesville, OH 43702
Patty Parrish, Manager

Mink, Patsy T.
2135 Rayburn House Office
  Bldg.
Washington, DC 20515-1102
Representative from Hawaii,
  Democrat
Second District

Minnelli, Liza
1776 Broadway
New York, NY 10019
Performer
birthdate 3/12/46

Minnesota North Stars
7901 Cedar Ave. S.
Bloomington, MN 55425
Professional hockey team

Minnesota Timberwolves
600 First Ave. N.
Minneapolis, MN 55403
Professional basketball team

Minnesota Twins
501 Chicago Ave., S.
Minneapolis, MN 55415
Professional baseball team

Minnesota Vikings
9520 Viking Dr.
Eden Prairie, MN 55344
Professional football team

Missing Children . . . Help
  Center
410 Ware Blvd., #400
Tampa, FL 33619
Ivana DiNora, Executive
  Director
Acts as the Missing Children
  Division of the National
  Child Safety Council

Missing Children of America
P.O. Box 670-949
Chugiak, AK 99567
Dolly Whaley, Executive
  Director

Missing Persons
c/o Cannell Productions
7083 Hollywood Blvd.
Hollywood, CA 90028
TV series

Mister Roger's Neighborhood
WQED/Pittsburgh
4802 Fifth Ave.
Pittsburgh, PA 15213
TV series

Mitchell, George J.
176 Senate Russell Office
   Bldg.
Washington, DC 20510-1902
Senator from Maine, Democrat

Mitchell, James
Prime Minister's Office
Kingstown, St. Vincent
*Prime Minister of St. Vincent and
   the Grenadines*

**Mitterand, Francois Maurice
   Marie**
Palais de l'Elysee
55-57 rue du Faubourg Saint-
   Honore
75008 Paris, France
President of France

Miyazawa, Kiichi
House of Representatives
Tokyo, Japan
Prime Minister of Japan

Moakley, John Joseph
235 Cannon House Office
   Bldg.
Washington, DC 20515-2109
*Representative from
   Massachusetts, Democrat
Ninth District*

Model Industry Association
P.O. Box 28129
Denver, CO 80228
Steve Shue, Executive Director

Moe, Tommy
U.S. Olympic Committee
1750 E. Boulder St.
Colorado Springs, CO 80909
Skier

Mohammed, All Mahdi
Office of the President
Mogadishu, Somalia
President of Somalia

Moi, Daniel Arap
Office of the President
P.O. Box 30510
Nairobi, Kenya
President of Kenya

Molinari, Susan
123 Cannon House Office
   Bldg.
Washington, DC 20515-3213
*Representative from New York,
   Republican
Thirteenth District*

Moll, Richard
270 N. Canon Dr., PH
Beverly Hills, CA 90210
Actor
birthdate 1/13/43

Mollohan, Alan B.
2242 Rayburn House Office
   Bldg.
Washington, DC 20515-4801
*Representative from West Virginia,
   Democrat
First District*

Mommies, The
Paramount
5555 Melrose Ave.
Los Angeles, CA 90038
TV series

**Momoh, Major General
   Joseph Saidu**
Office of the President
Freetown, Sierra Leone
President of Sierra Leone

Mona Lisas and Mad Hatters
Rte. 1, Box 200
Todd, NC 28684
Elton John fan club

Monday Night Football
c/o ABC Sports
47 W. 66th St.
New York, NY 10023

**Monkees, Boyce and Hart
Photo Fan Club, The**
P.O. Box 411
Watertown, SD 57201

**Monteiro, Antonia
Mascarenhas**
Office of the President
Cidade de Praia
Sao Tiago, Cape Verde
President of Cape Verde

Montgomery, G. V.
2184 Rayburn House Office
Bldg.
Washington, DC 20515-2403
*Representative from Mississippi,
Democrat
Third District*

Montoya, Carlos Garcia
c/o Kolmar/Luth
Entertainment Inc.
165 W. 46th St., #1202
New York, NY 10036
Classical guitarist

Montreal Canadiens
2313 St. Catherine St., West
Montreal, Quebec H3H 1N2
Canada
Professional hockey team

Montreal Expos
P.O. Box 500, Station M
Montreal, QUE H1V 3P2
Canada
Professional baseball team

**Monty Python Special Interest
Group**
c/o H. E. Roll
2419 Greensburg Pike
Pittsburgh, PA 15221

Moody Blues
151 El Camino
Beverly Hills, CA 90212
Rock group

Moore, Demi
9830 Wilshire Blvd.
Beverly Hills, CA 90212
Actress

Moore, Dudley
8942 Wilshire Blvd.
Beverly Hills, CA 90212
Actor, musician
birthdate 4/19/35

Moorhead, Carlos J.
2346 Rayburn House Office
Bldg.
Washington, DC 20515-0517
*Representative from California,
Republican
Twenty-seventh District*

Moran, James P.
430 Cannon House Office
Bldg.
Washington, DC 20515-4608
*Representative from Virginia,
Democrat
Eighth District*

Moran, Terry
Court TV
600 3rd Ave.
New York, NY 10016
TV journalist

Morella, Constance A.
223 Cannon House Office
Bldg.
Washington, DC 20515-2008
*Representative from Maryland,
Republican
Eighth District*

Morgan Creek Music Group
1875 Century Park E., #600
Los Angeles, CA 90067
James G. Robinson,
  Chairman/CEO
Record label

Morgan, Shelley Taylor
12456 Ventura Blvd., #1
Studio City, CA 91604
Talk show host

Mormorstein, Wayne
The Pine Mine
7974 Melrose Ave.
Los Angeles, CA 90046
Furniture store owner

Morrison, Van
c/o Sony
51 W. 52nd St.
New York, NY 10019
Musician

Morrow, Rob
151 El Camino
Beverly Hills, CA 90212
Actor

Morse Telegraph Club
1101 Maplewood Dr.
Normal, IL 61761

Moseley-Braun, Carol
320 Senate Hart Office Bldg.
Washington, DC 20510-1303
Senator from Illinois, Democrat

Moss, Kate
c/o R. Lauren
1107 Fifth Ave.
New York, NY 10128
Waif model

M.A.D.D.
**(Mothers Against Drunk
  Driving)**
511 E. John Carpenter Fwy.,
  #700
Irving, TX 75062
Robert J. King, Executive
  Director

**Motion Picture and Television
  Fund**
23388 Mulholland Dr.
Woodland Hills, CA 91364
William Hang, Executive
  Director
Welfare agency

**Motion Picture Association of
  America**
1600 Eye St. NW
Washington, DC 20006
Jack J. Valenti, President

Mötley Crüe
345 North Maple Dr., #123
Beverly Hills, CA 90210
Rock group

Motorcycle Safety Foundation
2 Jenner St., #150
Irvine, CA 92718-3800
Alan R. Isley, Executive
  Officer

Motown Records
6255 Sunset Blvd., 17th Fl.
Los Angeles, CA 90028
Jheryl Busby, President/CEO
Record label

(New York Office)
1350 Ave. of the Americas,
  20th Fl.
New York, NY 10019

Mouse Club, The
2056 Cirone Way
San Jose, CA 95124
Kim McEuen, Executive
  Officer
Disney "stuff" collectors

Movie Channel, The
1633 Broadway
New York, NY 10019

Moynihan, Daniel Patrick
464 Senate Russell Office
Bldg.
Washington, DC 20510-3201
Senator from New York, Democrat

Mrs. Field's Cookies
P.O. Box 680370
Park City, UT 84068
Debbie Fields, Founder
Cookie company

Mswati III
Royal Palace
Mbabane, Swaziland
Ruler of Swaziland

MTV Networks
1515 Broadway
New York, NY 10019

Mubarak, Hosni
Presidential Palace
Abdeen, Cairo
Egypt
President of Egypt

Mugabe, Robert
Office of the President
Harare, Zimbabwe
Executive President of Zimbabwe

Muldaur, Maria
P.O. Box 5535
Mill Valley, CA 94942
Singer

Mulligan, Gerry
1416 N. LaBrea Ave.
Hollywood, CA 90028
*Jazz composer, arranger, musician,
    songwriter*

Mulroney, Dermot
9830 Wilshire Blvd.
Beverly Hills, CA 90212
Actor

**Munsters & the Addams
    Family Reunion**
Fan Club Publishing Company
Box 69A04
West Hollywood, CA 90069
Fan magazine

Muppet Babies
Harvey Comics Entertainment
    Inc.
100 Wilshire Blvd., #500
Santa Monica, CA 90401
Comic

Murder, She Wrote
Universal Television
70 Universal City Plaza
Universal City, CA 91608
TV series

Murkowski, Frank H.
706 Senate Hart Office Bldg.
Washington, DC 20510-0202
Senator from Alaska, Republican

Murphy Brown
Warner Bros. Television
4000 Warner Blvd.
Burbank, CA 91522
TV series

Murphy, Austin J.
2210 Rayburn House Office
    Bldg.
Washington, DC 20515-3820
*Representative from Pennsylvania,
    Democrat
Twentieth District*

Murray, Bill
9830 Wilshire Blvd.
Beverly Hills, CA 90212
Actor
birthdate 9/21/50

Murray, Patty
302 Senate Hart Office Bldg.
Washington, DC 20510-4704
Senator from Washington,
Democrat

Murtha, John P.
2423 Rayburn House Office
Bldg.
Washington, DC 20515-3812
Representative from Pennsylvania,
Democrat
Twelfth District

Museum of Broadcasting, The
25 W. 52nd St.
New York, NY 10019
Dr. Robert M. Batscha,
President

Museveni, Yoweri Kaguta
Office of the President
Kampala, Uganda
President of Uganda

Mushroom Caucus
2267 Rayburn House Office
Bldg.
Washington, DC 20515
Rep. Richard Schulze,
Chairman
Members of Congress from
mushroom producing states

Music City News
50 Music Sq. W., #601
Nashville, TN 37203
Country music magazine

Musician
33 Commercial St., #2
Gloucester, MA 01930
Bill Flanagan, Editor
Magazine for the serious pop
musician

Mwinyi, Ali Hassan
c/o Office of the President
Dar-es-Salaam, United
Republic of Tanzania
President of Tanzania

Myers, John T.
2372 Rayburn House Office
Bldg.
Washington, DC 20515-1407
Representative from Indiana,
Republican
Seventh District

Myers, Mike
30 Rockefeller Center
New York, NY 10112
Actor, comedian, Wayne

Mystery Science Theatre 3000
Best Brains Inc.
7615 Golden Triangle Dr.
Eden Prairie, MN 55344
Joel Hodgson, Creator
Jim Mallon, Producer
Trace Beaulieu, Actor/Writer
Mike Nelson, Headwriter/
Actor
TV series (cable)

Mystery Writers of America
17 E. 47th St., 6th Fl.
New York, NY 10017
Priscilla Ridgway, Executive
Director

N

A writer lives in awe of words for they can be cruel or kind, and they can change their meanings right in front of you. They pick up flavors and odors like butter in a refrigerator.

Nader, Ralph
P.O. Box 19367
Washington, DC 20036
Consumer advocate

Nadler, Jerrold
424 Cannon House Office
   Bldg.
Washington, DC 20515-3208
Representative from New York,
   Democrat
Eighth District

al-Nahayan, Sheikh Zayed bin
   Sultan
Amiti Palace
Abu Dhabi, United Arab
   Emirates
President of the United Arab
   Emirates

'Nam, The
Marvel Entertainment Group
387 Park Ave. S.
New York, NY 10016
Comic

Namaliu, Rabbie
The Prime Minister's Office
Government Buildings
Port Moresby
Papua, New Guinea
Prime Minister of New Guinea

Nanny, The
TriStar Television
9336 W. Washington Blvd.
Culver City, CA 90232
TV series

Narcotics Anonymous
P.O. Box 9999
Van Nuys, CA 91409
Joe Gossett, Director

Nash, Graham
c/o Atlantic Records
75 Rockefeller Pl.
New York, NY 10019
Singer, composer
birthdate 2/2/42

Nashville Network, The
2806 Opryland Dr.
Nashville, TN 37214
Music television

Natcher, William H.
2333 Rayburn House Office
   Bldg.
Washington, DC 20515-1702
Representative from Kentucky,
   Democrat
Second District

National Abortion Federation
1436 U St. NW, #103
Washington, DC 20009
Barbara Radford, Executive
Director

National Academy of Popular Music
875 3rd Ave., 8th Fl.
New York, NY 10022
Christian Malone, Managing
Director

National Academy of Recording Arts and Sciences
303 N. Glenoaks Blvd., #140
Burbank, CA 91502-1178
Christine N. Farnon, Executive
Vice-President

National Adoptee Information Clearinghouse
11426 Rockville Pike, #410
Rockville, MD 20852
Debra G. Smith, Director

National Alcoholic Beverage Control Association
4216 King St. W.
Alexandria, VA 22302
Paul C. Dufek, Executive
Director

National Amputee Golf Association
P.O. Box 1228
Amherst, NH 03031
Bob Wilson, Executive
Director

National Amusement Park Historical Association
P.O. Box 83
Mt. Prospect, IL 60056
James E. Abbate, President

National Anti Hunger Coalition
c/o FRAC
1875 Connecticut Ave. NW,
#540
Washington, DC 20009-5728
Michele Tingling-Clemmons,
Contact

National Arson and Action Coalition
c/o James Lescault
P.O. Box 5059
Holyoke, MA 01041

National Assault Prevention Center
P.O. Box 02005
Columbus, OH 43202
Cheryl Howard, Executive
Director

National Association for Family Day Care
725 15th St. NW, #505
Washington, DC 20005
Linda Geigle, President

National Association for Native American Children of Alcoholics
P.O. Box 18736
Seattle, WA 98118
Anna Whiting-Sorrell,
President

National Association for Outlaw and Lawman History
c/o Richard J. Miller
615-C N. 8th St.
Killeen, TX 76541

National Association for Search and Rescue
P.O. Box 3709
Fairfax, VA 22038
Peggy McDonald, Executive
Director

**NASCAR
National Association for Stock
  Car Auto Racing**
P.O. Box 2875
1801 Volusia Ave.
Daytona Beach, FL 32120
William C. France, President

**NAACP
National Association for the
  Advancement of Colored
  People**
4805 Mt. Hope Dr.
Baltimore, MD 21215
Benjamin L. Hooks, Executive
  Director

**National Association for the
  Preservation and
  Perpetuation of Storytelling**
P.O. Box 309
Jonesborough, TN 37659
Jimmy Neil Smith, Executive
  Director

**National Association for the
  Self-Employed**
P.O. Box 612067
DFW Airport, TX 75261-2067
Robert Hughes, President

**National Association of Auto
  Racing Memorabilia**
P.O. Box 12226
St. Petersburg, FL 33733
Ken S. Breslauer, President

**National Association of
  Chewing Gum
  Manufacturers**
2 Greentree Centre, #225
P.O. Box 955
Marlton, NJ 08053
William L. MacMillan, III,
  Secretary-Treasurer

**National Association of
  Counsel for Children**
1205 Oneida St.
Denver, CO 80220
Laura Freeman Michaels,
  Executive Director
Legal representatives for kids

**National Association of Doll
  and Stuffed Toy
  Manufacturers**
200 E. Post Rd.
White Plains, NY 10601
Ralph P. Katz, Administrator

**National Association of Fan
  Clubs**
2730 Baltimore Ave.
Pueblo, CO 81003

**National Association of Home
  Based Businesses**
P.O. Box 30220
Baltimore, MD 21270
Rudolph Lewis, President

**National Association of
  Neighborhoods**
1651 Fuller NW
Washington, DC 20009
Marla Anderson, Executive
  Director

**National Association of Pet
  Sitters**
418 E. King St.
P.O. Box 1030
King, NC 27021
Patti J. Moran, Executive
  Director

**National Association of Resale
  and Thrift Shops**
153 Halsted
Chicago Heights, IL 60411
Trudy Miller, President

National Association of Rocketry
P.O. Box 177
Altoona, WI 54720
J. Patrick Miller, President

National Association of Theatre Owners
4605 Lankershim Blvd., #340
N. Hollywood, CA 91602
Mary Ann Grasso, Executive Director
Movie theater owners

National Association to Advance Fat Acceptance
P.O. Box 188620
Sacramento, CA 95818
Sally E. Smith, Executive Director

National Audubon Society
950 3rd Ave.
New York, NY 10022
Peter A. A. Berle, President

National Band Association
P.O. Box 121292
Nashville, TN 37212
L. Howard Nicar, Jr., Secretary/Treasurer

National Basketball Association
645 5th Ave., 10th Fl.
New York, NY 10022
David J. Stern, Commissioner

National Beauty Culturists' League
25 Logan Circle NW
Washington, DC 20005
Mrs. Cleolif Richardson, President

National Beep Baseball Association
9623 Spencer Hwy.
La Porte, TX 77571
Dr. Ed Bradley, President
Baseball for the blind

National Black Child Development Institute
1023 15th St., NW, #600
Washington, DC 20005
Evelyn K. Moore, Executive Director

National Board of Fur Farm Organizations
c/o Robert Buckler
405 Sibley St., #120
St. Paul, MN 55101

National Board of Review of Motion Pictures
P.O. Box 589
New York, NY 10021
Inez Salinger Glucksman, President

National Boating Safety Advisory Council
c/o Mr. A. J. Marmo
U.S. Coast Guard, G-NAB
Washington, DC 20593-0001

National Business League
1629 K St. NW, #605
Washington, DC 20006
Sherman Copilia, President
Organizational vehicle for minority business people

National Campers and Hikers Association
4804 Transit Rd., Bldg. 2
Depew, NY 14043
Fran Opela, Office Manager

National Captioning Institute
1443 Beachwood Dr.
Hollywood, CA 90026
Closed captioning for music videos

National Center for Computer Crime Data
1222 17th Ave., #3
Santa Cruz, CA 95062
Jay J. BloomBecker, Director

National Center for Employee Ownership
2201 Broadway, #807
Oakland, CA 94612
Corey Rosen, Executive Director

National Center for Film and Video Preservation
c/o American Film Institute
2021 N. Western Ave.
Los Angeles, CA 90027
Gregory Lukow, Deputy Director

National Center for Missing & Exploited Children
2101 Wilson Blvd., #550
Arlington, VA 22201
800-843-5678 HOT LINE
Ernest E. Allen, President

National Chastity Association
P.O. Box 402
Oak Forest, IL 60452
Mary Meyer, President and Founder

National Child Support Enforcement Association
Hall of States
400 N. Capitol NW, #372
Washington, DC 20001
Kathleen Duggan, Executive Director

National Chimney Sweep Guild
18115 Georgia Ave.
P.O. Box 429
Olney, MD 20830
John E. Bittner, Executive Director

National Circus Preservation Society
P.O. Box 59710
Potomac, MD 20859
Irvin G. Hohler, Secretary-Treasurer

National Clearinghouse on Marital and Date Rape
2325 Oak St.
Berkeley, CA 94708
Laura X, Contact

National Clogging and Hoedown Council
P.O. Box 71015
Durham, NC 27722
Garland Steele, President

National Coal Association
1130 17th St. NW
Washington, DC 20036
Richard L. Lawson, President

National Coalition Against Censorship
275 7th Ave., 20th Fl.
New York, NY 10001
Leanne Katz, Executive Director

National Coalition Against Domestic Violence
P.O. Box 34103
Washington, DC 20043-4103
Deborah White, Coordinator

National Coalition Against Sexual Assault
P.O. Box 21378
Washington, DC 20009
Marybeth Carter, President

National Coalition Against Surrogacy
1130 17th St. NW, #630
Washington, DC 20036
Jeremy Rifkin, Co-Chair

National Coalition Against the Misuse of Pesticides
701 E St. SE, #200
Washington, DC 20003
Jay Feldman, Coordinator

National Coalition for the Homeless
1621 Connecticut Ave. NW, #400
Washington, DC 20009
Fred Kanas, Jr., Executive Director

National Coalition on Television Violence
P.O. Box 2157
Champaign, IL 61825
Carole Lieberman, M.D., Contact

National Coalition to Abolish the Death Penalty
1325 G St. NW, Lower Level B
Washington, DC 20005
Leigh Dingerson, Director

National Committee for Fair Divorce and Alimony Laws
11 Park Place, #1116
New York, NY 10007
Sidney Siller, General Counsel

National Committee for Prevention of Child Abuse
332 S. Michigan Ave., #1600
Chicago, IL 60604
Anne Harris Cohn, Executive Director

National Committee for Responsible Philanthropy
2001 S St. NW, #620
Washington, DC 20009
Robert O. Bothwell, Executive Director

National Committee for Sexual Civil Liberties
98 Olden Lane
Princeton, NJ 08540
Dr. Arthur C. Warner, Chairman

National Conference of Personal Managers
210 E. 51st St.
New York, NY 10022
Gerard W. Purcell, President

National Conference of State Historic Preservation Officers
Hall of States
444 N. Capitol St. NW, #372
Washington, DC 20001
Eric Hertfelder, Executive Director

National Consumer Law Center
11 Beacon St.
Boston, MA 02108
Willard Ogburn, Executive Director

National Council of Young Men's Christian Associations of the United States of America (YMCA)
101 N. Wacker Dr.
Chicago, IL 60606
Leslie Cohn, Contact

National Council on Child Abuse and Family Violence
1155 Connecticut Ave. NW, #300
Washington, DC 20036
Alan Davis, President

National Court Appointed Special Advocates Association
2722 Eastlake Ave. E., #220
Seattle, WA 98102
Beth Waid, Executive Director
Advocates for children

National Cowboy Hall of Fame and Western Heritage Center
1700 NE 63rd St.
Oklahoma City, OK 73111
Byron Price, Director

National Deaf Bowling Association
9244 E. Mansfield Ave.
Denver, CO 80237
Don Gene Warnick, Secretary-Treasurer

National Easter Seal Society
70 E. Lake St.
Chicago, IL 60601
James E. Williams, Jr., President

National Exchange Club Foundation for the Prevention of Child Abuse
3050 Central Ave.
Toledo, OH 43606
George Mezinko, Director
Volunteer parent aids to help prevent child abuse

National Family Farm Coalition
110 Maryland Ave., Box 9
Washington, DC 20002
Katherine Ozer, Executive Officer

National Federation of Music Clubs
1336 N. Delaware St.
Indianapolis, IN 46202
Patricia M. Midgley, Executive Secretary

National Fishing Lure Collectors Club
P.O. Box 0184
Chicago, IL 60609
Steve Lumpkin, Secretary-Treasurer

National Football Foundation and Hall of Fame
Bell Tower Bldg.
1865 Palmer Ave.
Larchmont, NY 10538
Robert Casciola, Jr., Director

National Football League
410 Park Ave.
New York, NY 10022
Paul Tagliabue, Commissioner

National Foundation for Unemployment Compensation and Workers Compensation
600 Maryland Ave. SW, #603
Washington, DC 20024
J. Eldred Hill, Jr., President
Researches issues, works to improve compensation

National Foundation of Wheelchair Tennis
940 Calle Amancer, #B
San Clemente, CA 92672
Bradley Parks, President

National Frozen Pizza Institute
1764 Old Meadow Lane, #350
McLean, VA 22102
Francis G. Williams, Executive Director

National Glass Association
8200 Greensboro Dr., #302
McLean, VA 22102
Philip J. James, CAE, CEO

National Handicapped Sports
451 Hungerford Dr., #100
Rockville, MD 20850
Kirk M. Bauer, Executive Director

National High School Rodeo Association
11178 N. Huron, #7
Denver, CO 80234
Kent Sturman, General Manager

National Hockey League
League Headquarters
Sun Life Bldg.
Montreal, Quebec H3B 2W2
Gil Stein, President

National Horseshoe Pitchers Association of America
c/o Donnie Roberts
Box 7927
Columbus, OH 43207

National Ice Carving Association
P.O. Box 3593
Oak Brook, IL 60522-3593
Chuck Wagner, Executive Director

National Institute for Child Support Enforcement
7200 Wisconsin Ave., #500
Bethesda, MD 20814
Athena M. Kaye, Director

National Jousting Association
c/o Sandy Izer
P.O. Box 14
Mt. Solon, VA 22843

National Lampoon
10850 Wilshire Blvd.
Los Angeles, CA 10013
Chris Macil, Editor
Humor magazine

National League of Professional Baseball Clubs
350 Park Ave.
New York, NY 10022
William D. White, President

National Leather Association
P.O. Box 17463
Seattle, WA 98107
George Nelson, Secretary
Sadomasochism, fetishism

National Little Britches Rodeo Association
1045 W. Rio Grande
Colorado Springs, CO 80906
Jim Chamley, General Manager

National Muscle Car Association
3404 Democrat Rd.
Memphis, TN 38118
Russ Smitnieks, Director
Car club

National Museum of Racing and Hall of Fame
Union Ave.
Saratoga Springs, NY 12866
Peter H. Hammell, Director

National Network of Runaway and Youth Services
1319 F St. NW, #401
Washington, DC 20004
Della M. Hughes, Executive Director

National Ocean Access Project
Annapolis City Marina
P.O. Box 3377
Annapolis, MD 21403
Water sports for the physically challenged

National Organization for Victim Assistance
1757 Park Rd. NW
Washington, DC 20010
Marlene A. Young, Ph.D., Executive Director

National Organization for Women
1000 16th St. NW, #700
Washington, DC 20036
Patricia Ireland, President

National Organization of Adolescent Pregnancy and Planning
4421 A East-West Hwy.
Bethesda, MD 20814
Kathleen Sheeran, Executive Director

National Organization of Circumcision Information Resource Centers
P.O. Box 2512
San Anselmo, CA 94979
Marilyn Fayre Milos, R.N., Executive Director
Hopes to end routine infant circumcision

National Ornamental Goldfish Growers Association
6916 Black's Mill Rd.
Thurmont, MD 21788
Raymond W. Klinger, Executive Secretary

National Paddleball Association
6529 S. Westridge
Portage, MI 49002
Lorri Bingham, Secretary-Treasurer

National Pawnbrokers Association
600 S. Federal St., #400
Chicago, IL 60605
James G. Callas, Executive Director

National Pest Control Association
8100 Oak St.
Dunn Loring, VA 22027
Harvey S. Gold, Executive Vice-President

National Pocket Billiard Association
P.O. Box 34025
Milwaukee, WI 53234
Arthur J. Manske, President

National Police Bloodhound Association
509 Hemlock Lane
Lebanon, PA 17042
James Shaffer, Chairman

National Pop Can Collectors
P.O. Box 7862
Rockford, IL 61126
Tom Kirschbaum, Director

National Press Club
National Press Bldg.
529 14th St. NW
Washington, DC 20045
Greg Spears, President

National Professional Soccer League
229 Third St., NW
Canton, OH 44702
Paul Luchowski, Director

National Public Radio
2025 M St. NW
Washington, DC 20036
Douglas Bennet, President

National Pygmy Goat Association
10000 Greenacres Dr.
Bakersfield, CA 93312
Pam Ames, Business Manager

National Restaurant Association
1200 17th St. NW
Washington, DC 20036
William P. Fisher, Executive Vice-President

National Safe Kids Campaign
111 Michigan Ave. NW
Washington, DC 20010
Herta B. Feely, Executive
   Director
*Works to create safe homes and
   communities for kids*

National Safety Council
1121 Spring Lake Dr.
Itasca, IL 60143-3201
T. C. Gilchrest, President

National Scrabble Association
c/o Williams & Co.
P.O. Box 700
Greenport, NY 11944

**National Semi-Professional
   Baseball Association**
P.O. Box 29965
Atlanta, GA 30359
Lt. Co. McDonald Valentine,
   Jr., Executive Director
*Conducts the "Fastest Kid on the
   Bases" contest*

**National Shuffleboard
   Association**
c/o Harold Edmondson
704 52nd Ave. Dr. W.
Bradenton, FL 38207
Howard Raiylend, President

**National Society of Stress
   Analysts**
1442 Wood Lake Circle
St. Cloud, FL 34772
C. R. McQuiston, Executive
   Director
Stress analysis for truth detection

**National Society of Student
   Keyboardists**
361 Pin Oak Lane
Westbury, NY 11590
Dr. Albert DeVito, President

**National Soft Drink
   Association**
1101 16th St. NW
Washington, DC 20036
William L. Ball, III, President

**National Sporting Goods
   Association**
Lake Center Plaza Bldg.
1699 Wall St.
Mount Prospect, IL 60056-
   5780
Thomas B. Doyle, Director

**National Street Rod
   Association**
4030 Park Ave.
Memphis, TN 38111
Gilbert L. Bugg, Jr., Office
   Manager
Car club

National Teen Challenge
P.O. Box 1015
Springfield, MO 65801
Charles E. Hackett, President

**National Touch Football
   League**
1039 Coffey Ct.
Crestwood, MO 63126
Charles G. Middleton,
   Executive Director

**National Tractor Pullers
   Association**
6969 Worthington-Galena Rd.,
   #L
Worthington, OH 43085
David P. Schreier, President

**National Transsexual-
   Transvestite Feminization
   Union**
P.O. Box 297
Peru, IL 61354
Jean Stevens, Director

National Trust for Historic Preservation
1785 Massachusetts Ave. NW
Washington, DC 20036
Richard Moe, President

National United Law Enforcement Officers Association
256 E. McLemore Ave.
Memphis, TN 38106
Clyde R. Venson, Executive Director

National Urban League
500 E. 62nd St.
New York, NY 10021
John E. Jacob, CEO and President

National Wheelchair Athletic Association
3595 E. Fountain Blvd., #E-1
Colorado Springs, CO 80910
Patricia Long, Operations Manager

National Wheelchair Basketball Association
University of Kentucky
110 Seaton Bldg.
Lexington, KY 40506
Stan Labanowich, Executive Director

National Wheelchair Softball Association
1616 Todd Ct.
Hastings, MN 55033
Jon Speake, Commissioner

National Wildlife Federation
1400 16th St. NW
Washington, DC 20036
Lynn Bowersox, President

National Woman Abuse Prevention Project
1112 16th St. NW, #920
Washington, DC 20336
Mary Pat Brygger, Director

National Woman's Christian Temperance Union
1730 Chicago Ave.
Evanston, IL 60201
Rachel B. Kelly, President
Anti-alcohol group

National Women's History Project
7738 Bell Rd.
Windsor, CA 95492
Molly MacGregor, Director

National Woodcarvers Association
7424 Miami Ave.
Cincinnati, OH 45243
Edward F. Gallenstein, President

National Youth Sports Coaches Association
2611 Old Okeechobee Rd.
West Palm Beach, FL 33409
Fred C. Engh, President

Nationwide Patrol
P.O. Box 2629
Wilkes Barre, PA 18703
George Dewey III, President
Assists in locating missing children

Natural Resources Defense Council
40 W. 20th St.
New York, NY 10011
John H. Adams, Executive Director

Nature Conservancy, The
1815 N. Lynn St.
Arlington, VA 22209
John C. Sawhill, Contact

Naturists and Nudists
Opposing Pornographic
Exploitation
P.O. Box 2085
Rancho Cordova, CA 95741-
2085
Nikki Craft, Director

Naughty by Nature
c/o Tommy Boy Records
1747 First Ave.
New York, NY 10128
Recording artists

Nazarbeyev, Nursultan A.
Office of the President
Alma-Ata, Kazak Respublikasy
President of the Kazak Republic

NBC
National Broadcasting Co., Los
Angeles
3000 W. Alameda Ave.
Burbank, CA 91523
TV network

(New York Office)
30 Rockefeller Plaza
New York, NY 10112

Ndamase, Chief Tutor
Nyangilizwe
Office of the President
Transkei, South Africa
President of Transkei

Neal, Richard E.
131 Cannon House Office
Bldg.
Washington, DC 20515-2102
Representative from
Massachusetts, Democrat
Second District

Neal, Stephen L.
2469 Rayburn House Office
Bldg.
Washington, DC 20515-3305
Representative from North
Carolina, Democrat
Fifth District

Neeson, Liam
9830 Wilshire Blvd.
Beverly Hills, CA 90212
Actor

Nelson
(Matt and Gunnar)
9130 Sunset Blvd.
Los Angeles, CA 90069
Singing duo, third generation of
musical Nelsons

Nelson, Ben
State Capitol
Lincoln, NE 69509
Governor of Nebraska

Nelson, Craig T.
8942 Wilshire Blvd.
Beverly Hills, CA 90211
Actor
birthdate 4/4/46

Nelson, Willie
P.O. Box 2689
Danbury, CT 06813
Singer, songwriter
birthdate 4/30/33

Nestle Food Corp.
100 Manhattanville Rd.
Purchase, NY 10577
C. A. MacDonald, President
Candy company

Neurotics Anonymous
International Liaison
11140 Bainbridge Dr.
Little Rock, AR 72212
Grover Boydston, Chairman

Neville Brothers
(Aaron, Art, Charles, Cyril)
A & M Records
1416 N. LaBrea Ave.
Los Angeles, CA 90028
Singing group and solo artists

**New Adventures of Captain
Planet and the Planeteers**
Hanna-Barbera Cartoons, Inc.
3400 Cahuenga Blvd.
Hollywood, CA 90068
Animated series

**New Adventures of Speed
Racer, The**
Fred Wolf Films Inc.
4222 W. Burbank Blvd.
Burbank, CA 91505
Animated series

New England Patriots
Foxboro Stadium
Foxboro, MA 02035
Professional football team

New Expressions
Youth Communication
207 S. Wabash Ave.
Chicago, IL 60604
Roberta English, Editor
Teen magazine for and by teens

New Jersey Devils
Meadowlands Arena
E. Rutherford, NJ 07073
Professional hockey team

New Jersey Nets
Meadowlands Arena
E. Rutherford, NJ 07073
Professional basketball team

New Orleans Saints
1500 Poydras St.
New Orleans, LA 70003
Professional football team

New York Board of Trade
P.O. Box 3020
Rockefeller Center Station
New York, NY 10185
William J. Sloboda, President

New York Giants
Giants Stadium
E. Rutherford, NJ 07073
Professional football team

New York Islanders
Nassau Coliseum
Uniondale, NY 11553
Professional hockey team

New York Jets
1000 Fulton Ave.
Hempstead, NY 11550
Professional football team

New York Knickerbockers
4 Pennsylvania Plaza
New York, NY 10001
Professional basketball team

New York Mets
Shea Stadium
Flushing, NY 11368
Professional baseball team

New York Rangers
4 Pennsylvania Plaza
New York, NY 10001
Professional hockey team

New York Stock Exchange
11 Wall St.
New York, NY 10005
Judith Poole, Executive Officer

New York Yankees
Yankee Stadium
Bronx, NY 10451
Professional baseball team

Newborn Rights Society
P.O. Box 48
St. Peters, PA 19470
Leroy O'Byle, Contact

Newman, Paul
1120 Fifth Ave., #1C
New York, NY 10128-0144
Actor
birthdate 1/26/25

Newman, Randy
Renaissance Management
  Corporation
21241 Ventura Blvd., #251
Woodland Hills, CA 91364
Singer, songwriter, musician
birthdate 11/28/43

Newsline Fan Club
P.O. Box 1926
Sandy, UT 84091
*Huey Lewis and the News fan
  club*

Newton-John, Olivia
P.O. Box 690
Beverly Hills, CA 90213
Singer
birthdate 9/26/47

NFL Films
330 Fellowship Rd.
Mount Laurel, NJ 08054
Video production

Nicholson, Jack
15760 Ventura Blvd., #1730
Encino, CA 91436
Actor
birthdate 4/28/37

Nickles, Don
133 Senate House Office Bldg.
Washington, DC 20510-3602
*Senator from Oklahoma,
  Republican*

**Nicks, Stevie
(Stephanie)**
P.O. Box 6907
Alhambra, CA 91802
Singer
birthdate 5/26/48

Nielsen, Leslie
15760 Ventura Blvd., #1730
Encino, CA 91436
Actor
birthdate 2/11/26

Nike
3900 SW Murray Blvd.
Beaverton, OR 97005
Philip H. Knight, Chairman
Athletic shoe manufacturer

Nilsson, Harry
CL Sims Corp.
11330 Ventura Blvd.
Studio City, CA 91604
Singer, songwriter

Nine Lives of Felix the Cat
Harvey Comics Entertainment
  Inc.
100 Wilshire Blvd., #500
Santa Monica, CA 90401
Comic

19th-Century Music
University of California Press
2120 Berkeley Way
Berkeley, CA 94704
Magazine

Nintendo
4820 150th Ave., NE
Redmond, WA 98052
Hiroshi Yamauchi, President
Video game manufacturer

Nirvana
9130 Sunset Blvd.
Los Angeles, CA 90069
Alternative rock group

**NKOTB
(formerly New Kids on the
  Block)**
P.O. Box 7001
Quincy, MA 02269
Pop group
Jonathan Knight 11/29/68,
  Jordan Knight 5/17/70,
  Joe McIntyre 12/31/72,
  Donnie Wahlberg 8/17/69,
  Danny Wood 5/14/69

Nocturnal News
Baker Street Publicatons
Box 994
Metairie, LA 70004
Sharida Rizzuto, Editor
Horror magazine

Nolte, Nick
6174 Bonsall Dr.
Malibu, CA 90265
Actor
birthdate 2/8/40

Noone, Peter
VH-1
1515 Broadway
New York, NY 10036
"My Generation" host, Herman of Herman's Hermits

Norris, Chuck
P.O. Box 872
Navasota, TX 77868
Actor
birthdate 3/10/40

North American Association of Ventriloquists
800 W. Littleton Blvd.
P.O. Box 420
Littleton, CO 80160
Clinton Detweiler, President

North American Bungee Association
1500 E. Kearns Blvd., #E300
Park City, UT 84060
Thomas Woodard, Executive Officer

North American Falconers Association
820 Jay Pl.
Berthoud, CO 80513
John Hegan, Corresponding Secretary

North American Gaming Regulators Association
P.O. Box 21886
Lincoln, NE 68543-1886
John Willems, President

North American Man/Boy Love Association
P.O. Box 174, Midtown Station
New York, NY 10018
Renato Corazza, Contact
Advocates legalization of sexual relationships between men and underage boys

North American Swing Club Association
P.O. Box 7128
Buena Park, CA 90622
Robert L. McGinley, Ph.D., President
Swingers

Nujoma, Sam Shafilshuna
c/o Office of the President
Windhoek, Namibia
President of Namibia

Nunn, Sam
303 Senate Dirksen Office Bldg.
Washington, DC 20510-3521
Senator from Georgia, Democrat

Nussle, Jim
308 Cannon House Office Bldg.
Washington, DC 21505-1502
Representative from Iowa, Republican
Second District

O

The world did not impact upon me until I got to the post office.

—Christopher Morley

100 Flowers
c/o Happy Squid Records
P.O. Box 94565
Pasadena, CA 91109
Rock group

1000 Home DJ's
c/o Megaforce Entertainment
210 Bridge Plaza Dr.
Manalapan, NJ 07726
Rock group

101 Records
159 S. Highway 101
Solana Beach, CA 92075
Marc Wintriss, Contact
Independent record label

111 East Records
161 Hudson St., 5th Fl.
New York, NY 10013
James Bratton, Contact
Independent record label

**1334 North Beechwood Drive
  Irregulars**
c/o Sue Roach
1719 Gardenia, #2
Royal Oak, MI 48067
Monkees fan club

148th St Block
Work It!
P.O. Box 180, Cooper Station
New York, NY 10276
Recording artists

O'Connor, Sandra Day
U.S. Supreme Court Bldg.
One First Street NE
Washington, DC 20543
Supreme Court justice

O'Connor, Sinead
13 Red Lion Square, 10 Halsey
  House
London WC1 England
Singer
birthdate 12/8/67

O'Donnell, Chris
9560 Wilshire Blvd., 5th Fl.
Beverly Hills, CA 90212
Actor

O'Donnell, Rosie
8942 Wilshire Blvd.
Beverly Hills, CA 90211
Actress, comedienne, host

O'Leary, Hazel R.
Department of Energy
1000 Independence Ave., SW
Washington, DC 20585
Secretary of Energy

O'Neal, Shaquille
1 Magic Place
Orlando, FL 32801
Professional basketball player,
actor

Oak Ridge Boys
329 Rockland Rd.
Hendersonville, TN 37075-
3423
Country and western group

Oakland A's
Oakland Coliseum
Oakland, CA 94621
Professional baseball team

Oberstar, James L.
2366 Rayburn House Office
Bldg.
Washington, DC 20515-2308
Representative from Minnesota,
Democrat
Eighth District

Obey, David R.
2462 Rayburn House Office
Bldg.
Washington, DC 20515-4907
Representative from Wisconsin,
Democrat
Seventh District

Obsessive–Compulsive
Anonymous
P.O. Box 215
New Hyde Park, NY 11040
Roy C., Contact

Ocasek, Rick
9830 Wilshire Blvd.
Beverly Hills, CA 90212
Rock vocalist, songwriter,
producer, guitarist

Ochirbat, Punsalmaagiyn
Presidential Palace
Ulan Bator
Mongolian People's Republic
President of the Mongolian
People's Republic

Odyssey Institute Corporation
5 Hedley Farms Rd.
Westport, CT 06880
Judianne Densen-Gerber,
M.D., Chairperson
Research, education, child
advocacy

Official Country Music
Directory
Entertainment Media Corp.
Box 2772
Palm Springs, CA 92263

Official Electronic Keyboard
Blue Book
Sights and Sound, Inc.
1220 Mound Ave.
Racine, WI 53404
Valuation of used keyboards

Official Overstreet Comic
Book Price Guide
House of Collectibles
201 E. 50th St.
New York, NY 10022

Ohio Penal Racing Association
c/o L. F. Campbell
Ohio State Reformatory
Box 1368
Mansfield, OH 44901
Services, maintains, and helps set
up a late-model stock car for
racing

Olmos, Edward James
10000 Santa Monica Blvd.,
#305
Los Angeles, CA 90067
Actor, activist
birthdate 2/24/47

Olsen, Mary Kate and Ashley
c/o Full House
4000 Warner Blvd.
Burbank, CA 91522
Actresses

Oltcr, Bailey
Government
Pohnpei, Micronesia
Head of State

Olver, John W.
1323 Longworth House Office
Bldg.
Washington, DC 20515-2101
Representative from
Massachusetts, Democrat
First District

One-Arm Dove Hunt
Association
Box 582
Olney, TX 76374
Jack R. Northrup, Co-Founder
Physically challenged hunters

Ono, Yoko
One W. 72nd St.
New York, NY 10023
Singer, artist, famous widow

Opening Door
Rte. 2, Box 1805
Woodford, VA 22580
William A. Duke, Jr., President
Travel and lodging for the
physically challenged

Orbach, Jerry
1930 Century Park West, #403
Los Angeles, CA 90067
Actor
birthdate 10/20/35

Organization for the Lifelong
Establishment of Paternity
P.O. Box 1725
Eugene, OR 97401
Madeline Smith, President
Promotes responsible fatherhood

Organization of American
States
17th St. and Constitution Ave.
NW
Washington, DC 20006
Joao Baena Soares, Secretary
General

Orlando Magic
1 Magic Place
Orlando, FL 32801
Professional basketball team

Orphan Foundation of
America
1500 Massachusetts Ave. NW,
#448
P.O. Box 14261
Washington, DC 20005
Eileen McCaffrey, President

Ortiz, Solomon P.
2136 Rayburn House Office
Bldg.
Washington, DC 20515-4327
Representative from Texas,
Democrat
Twenty-seventh District

Orton, Bill
1122 Longworth House Office
Bldg.
Washington, DC 20515-4403
Representative from Utah,
Democrat
Third District

Osborne, Jeffrey
c/o Arista
6 W. 57th St.
New York, NY 10019
Singer

Osbourne, Ozzy
1801 Century Park West
Los Angeles, CA 90067
Singer
birthdate 12/3/46

Osby, Greg
c/o Blue Note Records
1750 Vine St.
Hollywood, CA 90028
Hip hop artist

Oscar Mayer
P.O. Box 7188
Madison, WI 53707
James W. McVey, CEO
Hot dog company

Oslin, K. T.
(Kay Toinette)
c/o Stan Moress
21 Music Sq. E.
Nashville, TN 37203
Singer
born 1942

Osmond, Donny
(Donald Clark)
151 El Camino
Beverly Hills, CA 90212
Singer
birthdate 12/9/57

Ottawa Senators
301 Moodie Dr.
Ottawa, Ontario K2H 9C4
  Canada
Professional hockey team

Overachievers Anonymous
1766 Union St., #C
San Francisco, CA 94123
Carol Osborn, Founder

Overeaters Anonymous
383 Van Ness Ave., #1601
Torrance, CA 90501
Jorge N. Sever, Executive
  Director

Owens, Buck
(Alvis Edgar, Jr.)
Buck Owens Productions
3223 N. Sillect Ave.
Bakersfield, CA 93308
Singer, musician, songwriter,
  producer
birthdate 8/12/29

Owens, Major R.
2305 Rayburn House Office
  Bldg.
Washington, DC 20515-3211
Representative from New York,
  Democrat
Eleventh District

Oxley, Michael G.
2233 Rayburn House Office
  Bldg.
Washington, DC 20515-3504
Representative from Ohio,
  Republican
Fourth District

Ozal, Turgut
Cumhurbaskanligi Kosku
Cankaya, Ankara, Turkey
President of Turkey

Ozark Society
P.O. Box 2914
Little Rock, AR 72203
Stewart Noland, President

Ozawa, Seiji
Boston Symphony Orchestra
Symphony Hall
301 Massachusetts Ave.
Boston, MA 02115
Conductor
birthdate 9/1/35

There are no words to express the abyss between isolation and having one ally. It may be conceded to the mathematician that four is twice two. But two is not twice one; two is two thousand times one.

—G. K. CHESTERTON

P C Quest
(Drew Nichols, Kim Whipkey,
Steve Petree, Chad Petree)
1133 Ave. of the Americas
New York, NY 10036
Recording artists

P M Dawn
14 E. Fourth St.
New York, NY 10012
Recording artists

Pacific Stock Exchange
301 Pine St.
San Francisco, CA 94104
Dr. Leopold Korins, CEO &
Chairman

Pacino, Al
9830 Wilshire Blvd.
Beverly Hills, CA 90212
Actor
birthdate 4/25/40

Packard, Ron
2162 Rayburn House Office
Bldg.
Washington, DC 20515-0548
Representative from California,
Republican
Forty-eighth District

Packwood, Bob
259 Senate Russell Office
Bldg.
Washington, DC 20510-3702
Embattled senator from Oregon,
Republican

Paeniu, Bikenibeu
Office of the Prime Minister
Funafuti, Tuvalu
Prime Minister of Tuvalu

Pagan Occult/Witchcraft
Special Interest Group
P.O. Box 52010
Palo Alto, CA 95157
Valerie Voight, Coordinator

Palance, Jack
121 N. San Vicente Blvd.
Beverly Hills, CA 90211
Actor
birthdate 2/18/20

Pallone, Frank, Jr.
420 Cannon House Office
Bldg.
Washington, DC 20515-3006
Representative from New Jersey,
Democrat
Sixth District

Palmer, Robert
2A Chelsea Manor
Blood Street
London, SW3, England
Singer

Paper Bag Institute
505 White Plains Rd., #206
Tarrytown, NY 10591
Brent C. Dixon, President
Association of paper bag
manufacturers

Paramount
5555 Melrose Ave.
Los Angeles, CA 90038
Film production company

Parents Against Molesters
P.O. Box 3557
Portsmouth, VA 23701
Barbara Barker, Executive
Director

Parents Anonymous
520 S. Lafayette Park Pl., #316
Los Angeles, CA 90067
800-421-0353 STRESSLINE
Curtis Richardson, President
Prevents child abuse

Parents of Murdered Children
100 E. 8th St., B-41
Cincinnati, OH 45202
Nancy Ruhe, Executive
Director

Parker Brothers
50 Dunham Rd.
Beverly, MA 01915
John Moore, President
Toy and game manufacturer

Parker, Alan William
9830 Wilshire Blvd.
Beverly Hills, CA 90212
Music-film director, writer
birthdate 2/14/44

Parker, Colonel Tom
P.O. Box 220
Madison, TN 37118
Elvis's mentor

Parker, Mike
1410 Longworth House Office
Bldg.
Washington, DC 20515-2404
Representative from Mississippi,
Democrat
Fourth District

Parker, Samuel B.
c/o ASQ
P.O. Box 1950
Hollywood, CA 90078-1950
Underwater lighting expert

Parker, Sarah Jessica
9830 Wilshire Blvd.
Beverly Hills, CA 90212
Actress
birthdate 3/25/65

Parkinson, Dian
4655 Natick Ave., #1
Sherman Oaks, CA 91403
Former spokesmodel

Partners in Parks
4916 Butterworth Place NW
Washington, DC 20016
Sarah G. Bishop, President
Private sector National Park
preservationists

Parton, Dolly
Crockett Road, Rt. #1
Brentwood, TN 37027
Singer, composer
birthdate 1/19/46

Party, The
P.O. Box 2510
Los Angeles, CA 90078
Recording artists

Pastor, Ed
409 Cannon House Office
Bldg.
Washington, DC 20515-0302
Representative from Arizona,
Democrat
Second District

Pastorelli, Robert
9255 Sunset Blvd., #515
Los Angeles, CA 90069
Actor

Patterson, Percival J.
People's National Party
89 Old Hope Rd.
Kingston 6, Jamaica
Prime Minister of Jamaica

Paul Andrew Dawkins
Children's Project
P.O. Box 11008
Fayetteville, NC 28303
Promotes safety, health, and well-
being of children

Paul, Alexandra
9320 Wilshire Blvd., 3rd Fl.
Beverly Hills, CA 90212
Actress

Pavarotti, Luciano
941 Via Giardini
41040 Saliceta S. Giuliano
Modena, Italy
Opera singer
birthdate 10/12/35

Paxon, L. William
1314 Longworth House Office
Bldg.
Washington, DC 20515-3227
Representative from New York,
Republican
Twenty-seventh District

Payne, Donald M.
417 Cannon House Office
Bldg.
Washington, DC 20515-3010
Representative from New Jersey,
Democrat
Tenth District

Payne, L. F.
1119 Longworth House Office
Bldg.
Washington, DC 20515-4605
Representative from Virginia,
Democrat
Fifth District

PBS
Public Broadcasting Service,
Virginia
1320 Braddock Place
Alexandria, VA 22314
TV network

(New York Office)
1790 Broadway, 16th Fl.
New York, NY 10019

(Los Angeles Office)
4401 Sunset Blvd.
Los Angeles, CA 90027

Pearl Jam
P.O. Box 4450
New York, NY 10101
Alternative rock group

Pearl S. Buck Foundation
P.O. Box 181
Green Hills Farm
Perkasie, PA 18944
Grace C. K. Sum, Executive
Director
Education, medical support, and
emotional support of displaced
children, especially Amerasians

Peck, M. Scott
Biliss Rd.
New Preston, CT 06777
Author

Peeples, Nia
822 S. Robertson Blvd., #200
Los Angeles, CA 90035
Singer, host, actress

Pele Defense Fund
P.O. Box 404
Volcano, HI 86785
Dr. Emmett Aluli, Vice-
President
*Traditional Hawaiian religious
practices and conservation
society*

Pell, Claiborne
335 Senate Russell Office
Bldg.
Washington, DC 20510-3901
*Senator from Rhode Island,
Democrat*

Pelosi, Nancy
240 Cannon House Office
Bldg.
Washington, DC 20515-0508
*Representative from California,
Democrat
Eighth District*

Pena, Federico F.
Department of Transportation
400 7th St., SW
Washington, DC 20590
Secretary of Transportation

Pendergrass, Teddy
Teddy Bear Enterprises
33 Rockhill Rd.
Bala-Cynwyd, PA 19004
Musician
birthdate 3/26/50

Penn & Teller
P.O. Box 1196
New York, NY 10185-0010
Comedian magicians

Penny, Timothy J.
436 Cannon House Office
Bldg.
Washington, DC 20515-2301
*Representative from Minnesota,
Democrat
First District*

**People Against Telephone
Terrorism and Harassment**
18159 Village Mart Dr.
Box 239
Olney, MD 20832
Stacey Blazer, Founder

People for the American Way
2000 M St. NW, #400
Washington, DC 20036
Arthur J. Kropp, President

People Magazine
Time-Warner Inc.
1675 Broadway
Rockefeller Center
New York, NY 10019
Landon Y. Jones, Jr., Editor

**People Organized to Stop
Rape of Imprisoned Persons**
P.O. Box 632
Ft. Bragg, CA 95437
Tom Cahill, Executive
Director

People's News Agency
1354 Montague St., NW
P.O. Box 56466
Washington, DC 20040
A. Brahmananda, Secretary
Alternative news network

PEP
P.O. Box 6306
Captain Cook, HI 96704
Ryan Nearing, President
*Promotes polyfidelity (group
marriage)*

Pepsico
Anderson Hill Rd.
Purchase, NY 10577
D. Wayne Calloway, CEO
Soft drink company

Perkins, Elizabeth
9830 Wilshire Blvd.
Beverly Hills, CA 90212
Actress
born 1961

Perlman, Itzhak
40 W. 57th St.
New York, NY 10019
Violinist
birthdate 8/31/45

Perlman, Rhea
9830 Wilshire Blvd.
Beverly Hills, CA 90212
Actress
birthdate 3/31/48

Permanent Charities
Committee of the
Entertainment
Industries
11132 Ventura Blvd., #401
Studio City, CA 91604-3156
Lisa Paulsen, President

Perot, H. Ross
1700 Lakeside Square
Dallas, TX 75251
Political pot stirrer

Perry, Luke
9830 Wilshire Blvd.
Beverly Hills, CA 90212
Actor

Perry, William
The Pentagon
Washington, DC 20301
Secretary of Defense

Personal Protective Armor
Association
c/o Larry B. Gates
28 Belarco Circle
Burton Hills
Nashville, TN 37215
Bullet-proof vest users

Pesci, Joe
9830 Wilshire Blvd.
Beverly Hills, CA 90212
Actor
birthdate 2/9/43

Pet Lovers Association
P.O. Box 145
Joppa, MD 21085
Eldon Harrison, President
Disposition of dead pets

Peterson's Summer
Opportunities for Kids &
Teenagers
Peterson's Guides
202 Carnegie Ctr., Box 2123
Princeton, NJ 08543

Peterson, Collin C.
1133 Longworth House Office
Bldg.
Washington, DC 20515-2307
Representative from Minnesota,
Democrat
Seventh District

Peterson, Douglas (Pete)
426 Cannon House Office
Bldg.
Washington, DC 20515-0902
Representative from Florida,
Democrat
Second District

Petrenko, Viktor
c/o Galinja Zmijevskaya
Chemomovskaya doroga 1329
270059 Odessa, Ukraine
Figure skater

Petri, Thomas E.
2262 Rayburn House Office
 Bldg.
Washington, DC 20515-4906
Representative from Wisconsin,
 Republican
Sixth District

Petty, Tom
8730 Sunset Blvd., 6th Fl.
Los Angeles, CA 90069
Rock guitarist, bandleader,
 composer
birthdate 10/20/53

Pfeiffer, Michelle
8942 Wilshire Blvd.
Beverly Hills, CA 90211
Actress
birthdate 4/29/57

Phil Collins Information
c/o Brad Lentz
P.O. Box 12250
Overland Park, KS 66212
Fan club

Philadelphia 76ers
P.O. Box 25040
Philadelphia, PA 19147
Professional basketball team

Philadelphia Eagles
Veterans Stadium
Philadelphia, PA 19148
Professional football team

Philadelphia Flyers
Pattison Place
Philadelphia, PA 19148
Professional hockey team

Philadelphia Phillies
P.O. Box 7575
Philadelphia, PA 19101
Professional baseball team

Philbin, Regis
77 W. 66th St.
New York, NY 10023
Talk show host

Phillips, Julianne
232 N. Canon Dr.
Beverly Hills, CA 90210
Actress

Phillips, Lou Diamond
1999 Ave. of the Stars, #2850
Los Angeles, CA 90067
Actor

Phoenix Cardinals
P.O. Box 888
Phoenix, AZ 85001
Professional football team

Phoenix Suns
2910 N. Central Ave.
Phoenix, AZ 85012
Professional basketball team

Phomvihan, Kaysone
Office of the President
Vientiane, Laos
President of Laos

Photographic Society of
 America
3000 United Founders Blvd.,
 #103
Oklahoma City, OK 73112
Terry S. Stull, Contact

Piazza, Mike
L.A. Dodgers
1000 Elysian Park Ave.
Los Angeles, CA 90012
Baseball player

Picaud, Rafael
Body Maxx
8474 W. 3rd St., #110
Los Angeles, CA 90048
Celebrity fitness trainer

Picket Fences
Twentieth Television
P.O. Box 900
Beverly Hills, CA 90213
TV series

Pickett, Owen B.
2430 Rayburn House Office
Bldg.
Washington, DC 20515-4602
Representative from Virginia,
Democrat
Second District

Pickle, J. J.
242 Cannon House Office
Bldg.
Washington, DC 20515-4310
Representative from Texas,
Democrat
Tenth District

Pictopia
Fantagraphics Books Inc.
7563 Lake City Way N.E.
Seattle, WA 98115
International comics anthology

Pill Addicts Anonymous
P.O. Box 278
Reading, PA 19603

Pinchot, Bronson
9200 Sunset Blvd., #428
Los Angeles, CA 90069
Actor
birthdate 5/20/59

Pink Floyd
43 Portland Road
London, W11, England
Rock group

Pioneer Clubs
Box 788
27 W. 130 St. Charles Rd.
Wheaton, IL 60189
Virginia C. Patterson, Ed.D.,
President

Pitt, Brad
9830 Wilshire Blvd.
Beverly Hills, CA 90212
Actor

Pittsburgh Penguins
Civic Arena
Pittsburgh, PA 15219
Professional hockey team

Pittsburgh Pirates
Three Rivers Stadium
Pittsburgh, PA 15212
Professional baseball team

Pittsburgh Steelers
Three Rivers Stadium
Pittsburgh, PA 15212
Professional football team

Plant, Robert Anthony
c/o Atlantic Records
75 Rockefeller Plaza
New York, NY 10019
Singer, composer

Plastic Bottle Institute
1275 K St. NW, #400
Washington, DC 20005
John Malloy, Director
Plastic bottle promoters

Platters, The
P.O. Box 39
Las Vegas, NV 89101
Pop group

Play Schools Association
9 E. 38th St., 8th Fl.
New York, NY 10016
Joseph Corrado, Executive
Director
Play activities as educational
therapy

Playskool Inc.
110 Pitney Rd.
Lancaster, PA 17602
S. Erman, Director
Toy manufacturer

Plimpton, Martha
8942 Wilshire Blvd.
Beverly Hills, CA 90211
Actress

Pockets
Board of Discipleship
1908 Grand Ave., Box 189
Nashville, TN 37212
Christian magazine

Pointer Sisters
151 El Camino
Beverly Hills, CA 90212
Pop group

Points of Light Foundation
1737 H St. NW
Washington, DC 20006
Richard F. Schubert, President
and CEO
Promotes volunteerism

Poison
1750 N. Vine St.
Hollywood, CA 90028
Rock group

Poitier, Sidney
9830 Wilshire Blvd.
Beverly Hills, CA 90212
Actor, director
birthdate 2/20/27

Police, The
194 Kensington Park Rd.
London, W11 2ES England
Defunct rock group

Pollan, Tracy
232 N. Canon Dr.
Beverly Hills, CA 90210
Actress

**Polly Klaas Foundation for
Missing and Exploited
Children**
P.O. Box 800
Petaluma, CA 94953
Cheryl Friedman, Contact

PolyGram Label Group
Worldwide Plaza
825 8th Ave.
New York, NY 10019
Rick Dobbis, President/CEO
*Record label, includes Polydor,
London, Smash, PolyGram
Jazz, Victory, Delicious Vinyl,
Verve*

(Los Angeles Office)
11150 Santa Monica Blvd.,
#1000
Los Angeles, CA 90025

PolyGram Records
901 18th Ave. S.
Nashville, TN 37212
Paul Lucks, Vice-President/
General Manager
Record label

Pombo, Richard W.
1519 Longworth House Office
Bldg.
Washington, DC 20515-0511
*Representative from California,
Republican
Eleventh District*

Pomeroy, Earl
318 Cannon House Office
Bldg.
Washington, DC 20515-3401
*Representative from North Dakota,
Democrat At Large*

Pony Baseball/Softball
P.O. Box 225
Washington, PA 15301
Roy Gillespie, President

Pop Warner Football
920 Town Center Dr., #I-25
Langhorne, PA 19047
Jon C. Butler, Executive
Director

Pop, Iggy
(James Newell Osterberg)
c/o Floyd Peluce
449 S. Beverly Dr., #102
Beverly Hills, CA 90212
Composer, singer, musician

Popcorn Institute
401 N. Michigan Ave.
Chicago, IL 60611-4267
William E. Smith, Executive
  Director
Popcorn promoters

Population Council
1 Dag Hammarskjold Plaza
New York, NY 10017
Margaret Catley-Carlson,
  President

Porizkova, Paulina
9830 Wilshire Blvd.
Beverly Hills, CA 90212
Model, actress

Porter, Jerry
Metrospace
Brentwood Financial Plaza
11726 San Vicente, #500
Los Angeles, CA 90048
Commercial realtor

Porter, John E.
1026 Longworth House Office
  Bldg.
Washington, DC 20515-1310
Representative from Illinois,
  Republican
Tenth District

Portland Trail Blazers
700 NE Multnomah St.
Portland, OR 97232
Professional basketball team

Portman, Rob
238 Cannon House Office
  Bldg.
Washington, DC 20515-3502
Representative from Ohio,
  Republican
Second District

Poshard, Glen
107 Cannon House Office
  Bldg.
Washington, DC 20515-1319
Representative from Illinois,
  Democrat
Nineteenth District

Postpartum Support,
  International
927 N. Kellogg Ave.
Santa Barbara, CA 93111
Jane Honikman, President

Potsmokers Anonymous
208 W. 23rd St., #1414
New York, NY 10011-2139
Francis Duffy, Director

Potts, Annie
9830 Wilshire Blvd.
Beverly Hills, CA 90212
Actress
birthday 10/28

Poundstone, Paula
151 El Camino
Beverly Hills, CA 90212
Comedienne

Povich, Maury
5555 Melrose Ave.
Los Angeles, CA 90038
Talk show host

Prager, Dennis
10573 W. Pico Blvd., #167
Los Angeles, CA 90064-2300
Radio talk show host

Premadasa, Ranasinghe
Office of the President
Republic Square
Colombo 1, Sri Lanka
President of Sri Lanka

Premiere
Murdoch Publications, Inc.
2 Park Ave., 4th Fl.
New York, NY 10016
Susan Lyne, Editor
*Movie and entertainment
magazine*

Presley, Priscilla Beaulieu
151 El Camino
Beverly Hills, CA 90212
Actress, famous ex-wife
birthdate 5/24/45

Pressler, Larry
283 Senate Russell Office
Bldg.
Washington, DC 20510-4102
*Senator from South Dakota,
Republican*

Pressman Toy Corporation
200 Fifth Ave., #1052
New York, NY 10010
James R. Pressman, President
Toy manufacturer

Price, David E.
2458 Rayburn House Office
Bldg.
Washington, DC 20515-3304
*Representative from North
Carolina, Democrat
Fourth District*

Price, Ray
P.O. Box 1986
Mount Pleasant, TX 75456
Singer
birthdate 1/12/26

Price, Rt. Hon. George Cadle
c/o House of Representatives
Belmopan, Belize
Prime Minister of Belize

Pride, Charley
c/o Chardon Inc.
3198 Royal Lane, #204
Dallas, TX 75229
Singer
birthdate 3/18/39

Priestley, Jason
9560 Wilshire Blvd., 5th Fl.
Beverly Hills, CA 90212
Actor

Prime Suspect
Rysher Entertainment
3400 Riverside Dr., 6th Fl.
Burbank, CA 91505
TV series

Prime Ticket Network
10000 Santa Monica Blvd.
Los Angeles, CA 90067

**Prince
(the artist formerly known as
Prince)**
(Prince Rogers Nelson)
3300 Warner Blvd.
Burbank, CA 91510
Singer
birthdate 6/7/58

Prince Rainier, III
Plais de Monaco
Boit Postal 518
98015 Monte Carlo
Monaco
Ruler of Monaco

Prism
Lauderdale Publishing, Inc.
2455 E. Sunrise Blvd.
Ft. Lauderdale, FL 33304
Written by and for gifted children

Pro-Choice Defense League
131 Fulton Ave.
Hempstead, NY 11550
Bill Baird, Director

Professional Bowlers Association of America
1720 Merriman Rd.
P.O. Box 5118
Akron, OH 44334
Michael J. Connor,
Commissioner

Professional Comedians' Association
581 9th Ave., #3C
New York, NY 10036
Kate Magill, Executive Officer

PGA Professional Golfer's Association of America
100 Ave. of the Champions
Palm Beach Gardens, FL 33418
Jim Qwtrey, Executive Director and CEO

Project Children
P.O. Box 933
Greenwood Lake, NY 10925
Denis Mulcahy, Founder & Chairman
Vacations for kids from N. Ireland in the U.S.

Project Cuddle
1075 Corona Lane
Costa Mesa, CA 92626
Debbie Magnusen, Executive Officer
Seeks to improve the lives of drug exposed children

Prostitutes Anonymous
11225 Magnolia Blvd., Box 181
N. Hollywood, CA 91601
Jody Williams, Contact

Pryce, Deborah
128 Cannon House Office Bldg.
Washington, DC 20515-3515
Representative from Ohio, Republican
Fifteenth District

Pryor, David H.
267 Senate Russell Office Bldg.
Washington, DC 20510-0402
Senator from Arkansas, Democrat

Public Enemy
c/o Columbia Records
2100 Colorado Blvd.
Santa Monica, CA 90404
Rock group

Puppeteers of America
5 Cricklewood Path
Pasadena, CA 91107
Gayle G. Schluter, Chairperson

Purple Cow Newspaper for Teens
Hudson Brooke Publishing
1780 Century Circle, #2
Atlanta, GA 30345

Pyrotechnics Guild International
221 Spring Ave.
Lutherville, MD 21093
John W. Leonard, President

Real letter-writing makes writing into a different process because the letter is to somebody—a significant other—and not just a pronouncement to an imaginary world, a generalized other.

—ED POWELL, *The Letter Exchange*

Qaddafi, Colonel Muammar el
Office of the President
Tripoli, Libya
Head of State of Libya

Quaid, Dennis
8942 Wilshire Blvd
Beverly Hills, CA 90211
Actor
birthdate 4/9/54

Quayle, Dan
201 N. Illinois St., #2240
Indianapolis, IN 46204
Former Vice-President

Quebec Nordiques
2205 Ave. du Colisee
Quebec, Quebec G1L 4W7
   Canada
Professional hockey team

Quillen, James H.
102 Cannon House Office
   Bldg.
Washington, DC 20515-4201
Representative from Tennessee,
   Republican
First District

Quinn, Aidan
9830 Wilshire Blvd.
Beverly Hills, CA 90212
Actor
birthdate 3/8/59

Quinn, Jack
331 Cannon House Office
   Bldg.
Washington, DC 20515-3230
Representative from New York,
   Republican
Thirtieth District

Quinn, Martha
8730 Sunset Blvd., #220
Los Angeles, CA 90069
Host
birthdate 5/11/59

QVC
1045 Xenium Lane
Minneapolis, MN 55441
Shopping network

R

An intention to write never turns into a letter. A letter must happen to one like a surprise, and one may not know where in the day there was room for it to come into being. So it is that my daily intentions have nothing to do with this fulfillment of today.

—RAINER MARIA RILKE,
letter to F. von Bülow

Rabbani, Burhanuddin
People's Democratic Party of
Afghanistan
Kabul, Afghanistan
President of Afghanistan

Rabbitt, Eddie
c/o Moress, Nanas, Golden
Entertainment
12424 Wilshire Blvd.
Los Angeles, CA 90025
Singer, songwriter
birthdate 11/27/41

Rabin, Yitzhak
Office of the Prime Minister
Hakirya, Ruppin St.
Jerusalem, Israel
Prime Minister of Israel

Rachins, Alan
9000 Sunset Blvd., #1200
Los Angeles, CA 90069
Actor
birthdate 10/10/47

Racicot, Mark
State Capitol
Helena, MT 59620
Governor of Montana

Raffi
(Cavoukian)
c/o Jensen Communications
120 S. Victory Blvd., #201
Burbank, CA 91502
Singer

Rafsanjani, Hashemi
c/o Islamic Republican Party
Dr. Al Shariati Ave.
Teheran, Iran
President of Iran

Rahal, Nick J.
2269 Rayburn House Office
Bldg.
Washington, DC 20515-4803
*Representative from West Virginia,
Democrat
Third District*

**Rainbows for All God's
Children**
111 Tower Rd.
Schaumburg, IL 60173
Suzy Yehl Marta, Executive
Director
*Support program for kids who
have suffered a significant
loss*

Rainforest Action Network
450 Sansome St., #700
San Francisco, CA 94111
Randall Hayes, Director

Raitt, Bonnie
P.O. Box 626
Los Angeles, CA 90078
Singer
birthdate 11/8/49

Ramaema, Colonel E. P.
The Military Council
Maseru, Lesotho
Head of Government of Lesotho

Ramos, Fidel V.
Office of the President
Malacanong
Manila, Philippines
President of the Philippines

Rampal, Jean-Pierre Louis
15 Avenue Mozart
75016 Paris France
Flutist
birthdate 1/7/22

Ramstad, Jim
322 Cannon House Office
   Bldg.
Washington, DC 20515-2303
Representative from Minnesota,
   Republican
Third District

Ramushwana, Col. Gabriel
   Mutheiwana
Council of National Unity
Thohoyandouw, Venda, South
   Africa
Chairman of the Council of
   National Unity of Venda

Randolph, Carol
Court TV
600 3rd Ave.
New York, NY 10016
Reporter

Randy Travis Fan Club
1604 16th Ave., S.
Nashville, TN 37212

Rangel, Charles B.
2252 Rayburn House Office
   Bldg.
Washington, DC 20515-3215
Representative from New York,
   Democrat
Fifteenth District

Ranger Rick's Nature Club
National Wildlife Federation
8925 Leesburg Pike
Vienna, VA 22184
Gerald Bishop, Editor

Rao, P. V. Narasimha
Lok Sabha
New Delhi, India
Prime Minister of India

Raphael, Sally Jessy
Multimedia Entertainment
45 Rockefeller Plaza, 35th Fl.
New York, NY 10111
Talk show host

Ratsiraka, Didier
Presidence de la Republique
Antananarivo, Madagascar
Head of State of Madagascar

RAVE
Entertainment Media Group
228 E. 45th St., 4th Fl.
New York, NY 10017
Magazine about comedians

Ravenal, Arthur, Jr.
231 Cannon House Office
   Bldg.
Washington, DC 20515-4001
Representative from South
   Carolina, Republican
First District

Rawlings, Flight Lt. Jerry John
Office of the Head of State
The Castle
Accra, Ghana
President of Ghana

Real Stuff
Fantagraphics Books, Inc.
7563 Lake City Way N.E.
Seattle, WA 98115
Comic

Real Talk
Boces Geneseo Migrant
Center
210 Holcomb Bldg.
Geneseo, NY 14454
Mary Fink, Editor
Magazine for migrant farmworker kids

Reba McEntire International Fan Club
P.O. Box 121996
Nashville, TN 37212

RECAP
3205 Northwood Dr., #209
Concord, CA 94520
R. Wayne Griffiths, Executive Director
Men who seek to restore their foreskin

Recycled Paperboard Technical Association
350 S. Kalamazoo Mall, #207
Kalamazoo, MI 49007
J. D. Hamelink, Executive Director

Red Hot Chili Peppers
75 Rockefeller Plaza, 20th Fl.
New York, NY 10019
Rock group

Redding, Otis
c/o Atlantic Records
75 Rockefeller Plaza
New York, NY 10019
Singer

Redford, Robert
9830 Wilshire Blvd.
Beverly Hills, CA 90212
Actor, director, producer
birthdate 8/18/37

Reed, Jack
1510 Longworth House Office Bldg.
Washington, DC 20515-3902
Representative from Rhode Island, Democrat

Reed, Lou
38 E. 68th St.
New York, NY 10021
Musician

Reeves, Keanu
9830 Wilshire Blvd.
Beverly Hills, CA 90212
Actor

Regalbuto, Joe
606 N. Larchmont Blvd., #309
Los Angeles, CA 90004
Actor
birthdate 8/24

Regula, Ralph
2309 Rayburn House Office Bldg.
Washington, DC 20515-3516
Representative from Ohio, Republican
Sixteenth District

Rehnquist, William H.
U.S. Supreme Court Bldg.
One First St. NE
Washington, DC 20543
Chief Justice of the Supreme Court

Reich, Robert B.
Department of Labor
200 Constitution Ave., NW
Washington, DC 20210
Secretary of Labor

Reid, Harry M.
324 Senate Hart Office Bldg.
Washington, DC 20510-2803
Senator from Nevada, Democrat

Reid, L. A.
(Antonio)
Kear Music, c/o Carter Tuner
9229 Sunset Blvd.
West Hollywood, CA 90069
Musician, songwriter

Reinhold, Judge
8942 Wilshire Blvd.
Beverly Hills, CA 90211
Actor
birthdate 5/21/56

Reiser, Paul
c/o Mad About You
Tri-Star Television
9336 W. Washington Blvd.
Culver City, CA 90232
Comedian, actor, producer

R.E.M.
P.O. Box 8032
Athens, GA 30603
Rock group

Ren & Stimpy Show, The
Nickelodeon
1515 Broadway
New York, NY 10036
Animated series

Renaissance Education
Coalition
P.O. Box 60552
King of Prussia, PA 19406
Brenda Davidson, Director
Association of transvestites and transsexuals

Renaissance Society of
America
24 W. 12th St.
New York, NY 10011
Margaret L. King, Executive
Director

Rene Guyon Society
256 S. Robertson Blvd.,
#5020P
Beverly Hills, CA 90211
Tim O'Hara, Spokesperson
"Those advocating consenting child bisexuality" by age eight

Rene, France-Albert
The State House
Victoria, Mahe
Seychelles
President of the Seychelles

Renegade
Stu Segall Productions
4705 Ruffin Rd.
San Diego, CA 92123
TV series

Reno, Janet
Department of Justice
Constitution Ave. and 10th St.,
NW
Washington, DC 20530
Attorney General

Reprise Records
3300 Warner Blvd.
Burbank, CA 91510
Mo Ostin, Chairman
Record label

Rescue 911
c/o Arnold Shapiro
Productions
100 Wilshire Blvd., #1800
Santa Monica, CA 90401
TV series

Retail Bakers of America
14239 Bark Center Dr.
Laurel, MD 20707
Peter Houstle, Executive Vice-
President

Retro Rock
44 E. 5th St.
Brooklyn, NY 11218
Heidi Stock, Editor
Magazine

Reynolds, Albert
(Republic of Ireland, Eire)
Abbeville, Kinsealy
County Dublin, Ireland
Prime Minister of Ireland

Reynolds, Mel
514 Cannon House Office
   Bldg.
Washington, DC 20515-1302
Representative from Illinois,
   Democrat
Second District

Rhino Records
2225 Colorado Ave.
Santa Monica, CA 90404
Richard Foos, President
Record label

Rhythm and Blues Rock and
   Roll Society
P.O. Box 1949
New Haven, CT 06510
William J. Nolan, Director

Ricardo, Joaquin Balaguer
Oficina del Presidente
Santo Domingo, D.N.,
   Dominican Republic
President of the Dominican
   Republic

Rice, Tim
500 S. Buena Vista St.
Burbank, CA 91521
Lyricist

Rich, Charlie
6584 Poplar, #460
Memphis, TN 38138
Singer
birthdate 12/14/32

Richards, Ann
State Capitol
Austin, TX 78711
Governor of Texas

Richards, Keith
Raindrop Services
1776 Broadway
New York, NY 10019
Musician
birthdate 12/18/43

Richardson, Bill
2349 Rayburn House Office
   Bldg.
Washington, DC 20515-3103
Representative from New Mexico,
   Democrat
Third District

Richardson, Miranda
121 N. San Vicente Blvd.
Beverly Hills, CA 90211
Actress

Richie Rich
Harvey Comics Entertainment,
   Inc.
100 Wilshire Blvd., #500
Santa Monica, CA 90401
Comic

Richie, Lionel
P.O. Box 1862
Encino, CA 91426
Singer, songwriter, producer
birthdate 6/20/50

Ricky Skaggs International Fan
   Club
P.O. Box 121799
Nashville, TN 37212

Ridge, Thomas J.
1714 Longworth House Office
   Bldg.
Washington, DC 20515-3821
Representative from Pennsylvania,
   Republican
Twenty-first District

Riegle, Donald W.
105 Senate Dirksen Office
  Bldg.
Washington, DC 20510-2201
Senator from Michigan, Democrat

Right On!
Sterling's Magazines Inc.
355 Lexington Ave., 13th Fl.
New York, NY 10017
Cynthia Horner, Editor
Articles on black entertainers

Righteous Brothers
5218 Almont St.
Los Angeles, CA 90032
Pop duo

Riley, Richard W.
Department of Education
400 Maryland Ave., SW
Washington, DC 20202
Secretary of Education

Riordan, Richard
300 S. Grand Ave., 29th Fl.
Los Angeles, CA 90071
Mayor of Los Angeles

Rivera, Geraldo
555 W. 57th St.
New York, NY 10019
Talk show host
birthdate 7/4/43

Rivers, Joan
524 W. 57th St.
New York, NY 10019
Talk show host
birthdate 6/8/33

RJR Nabisco Inc.
9 W. 57th St., 48th Fl.
New York, NY 10019
Louis V. Gerstner, Jr., CEO
*Cookies, crackers, nuts, and snack
  food manufacturer*

Robb, Charles S.
493 Senate Russell Office
  Bldg.
Washington, DC 20510-4603
Senator from Virginia, Democrat

Roberta Jo Society
Box 916
Circleville, OH 43113
Robin Steely, Executive
  Director
*Research and information
  clearinghouse for missing
  children*

Roberts, Barbara
State Capitol
Salem, OR 97310
Governor of Oregon

Roberts, Cokie
ABC World News Tonight
47 W. 66th St.
New York, NY 10023
Broadcast journalist

Roberts, Julia
8942 Wilshire Blvd.
Beverly Hills, CA 90211
Actress
born 1967

Roberts, Pat
1126 Longworth House Office
  Bldg.
Washington, DC 20515-1601
*Representative from Kansas,
  Republican
First District*

Robinson, Holly
1999 Ave. of the Stars, #2850
Los Angeles, CA 90067
Actress
born 1965

Robinson, Smokey
6244 Sunset Blvd., #18
Los Angeles, CA 90028
Singer, composer
birthdate 2/19/40

Rock & Roll Confidential
Box 1073
Maywood, NJ 07607
Dave Marsh, Editor
Magazine

Rock and Roll Hall of Fame Foundation
c/o Suzan Evans
Atlantic Records
75 Rockefeller Plaza, 2nd Fl.
New York, NY 10019

Rock Legend
Dream Guys Inc.
Box 7042
New York, NY 10021
Roseann Hirsch, Publisher
Magazine

Rockefeller, John D., IV
109 Senate Hart Office Bldg.
Washington, DC 20510-4802
Senator from West Virginia, Democrat

Rockpress
P.O. Box 99090
San Diego, CA 92169
Rock music book publishing company

Rodale Institute
222 Main St.
Emmaus, PA 18098
John Haberern, President
Student program for farm preservation

Rodriguez, Carlos Andres Perez
c/o Oficina del Presidente
Palacio de Miraflores
Caracas, Venezuela
President of Venezuela

Rodriguez, General Andres
Casa Presidencial
Avenida Mariscal Lopez
Asuncion, Paraguay
President of Paraguay

Roemer, Tim
415 Cannon House Office Bldg.
Washington, DC 20515-1403
*Representative from Indiana, Democrat
Third District*

Rogers, Harold
2468 Rayburn House Office Bldg.
Washington, DC 20515-1705
*Representative from Kentucky, Republican
Fifth District*

Rogers, Kenny
Box 100, Rt. #1
Colbert, GA 30628
Singer
birthdate 8/21/38

**Rogers, Roy
(Leonard Slye)**
15650 Seneca Rd.
Victorville, CA 92392
Singing cowboy on the comeback trail
birthdate 11/5/12

Rohrbacher, Dana
1027 Longworth House Office Bldg.
Washington, DC 20515-0545
*Representative from California, Republican
Forty-fifth District*

Roller Hockey Federation
P.O. Box 6579
Lincoln, NE 68506
George Pickard, Executive Director

Rolling Stone
1290 Ave. of the Americas
New York, NY 10104
Jann S. Wenner, Editor and Publisher
Magazine

Rolling Stones Fan Club
c/o Bill German
P.O. Box 6152
New York, NY 10128

Rolling Stones, The
1776 Broadway, #507
New York, NY 10019
Grandaddies of rock and roll

Romance Writers of America
13700 Veterans Memorial Dr.,
  #315
Houston, TX 77014
Linda Fisher, Contact

Romer, Roy
136 State Capitol
Denver, CO 80203
Governor of Colorado

Ronnie Milsap Fan Club
P.O. Box 23109
Nashville, TN 37202

Ronstadt, Linda
644 N. Doheny Dr.
West Hollywood, CA 90069
Singer
birthdate 7/15/46

Ros-Lehtinen, Ileana
127 Cannon House Office
  Bldg.
Washington, DC 20515-0918
Representative from Florida,
  Republican
Eighteenth District

Rose, Charlie
2230 Rayburn House Office
  Bldg.
Washington, DC 20515-3307
Representative from North
  Carolina, Democrat
Seventh District

Roseanne
(formerly Barr, formerly
  Arnold)
151 El Camino
Beverly Hills, CA 90212
Actress, comedienne
birthdate 11/3/52

Roseanne
c/o Carsey-Werner Company
4024 Radford Ave., #3
Studio City, CA 91604
TV series

Ross, Diana
RTC Management
P.O. Box 1683
New York, NY 10185
Singer
birthdate 3/26/44

Ross, Gary A.
9830 Wilshire Blvd.
Beverly Hills, CA 90212
Screenwriter

Rostenkowski, Dan
2111 Rayburn House Office
  Bldg.
Washington, DC 20515-1305
Representative from Illinois,
  Democrat
Fifth District

Rotary International
1 Rotary Center
1560 Sherman Ave.
Evanston, IL 60201
Spencer Robinson, General
  Secretary

Roth, David Lee
c/o Warner Bros.
3300 Warner Blvd.
Burbank, CA 91510
Singer
birthdate 10/10/55

Roth, Toby
2234 Rayburn House Office
Bldg.
Washington, DC 20515-4908
Representative from Wisconsin,
Republican
Eighth District

Roth, William V.
104 Senate Hart Office Bldg.
Washington, DC 20510-0801
Senator from Delaware,
Republican

Roukema, Marge
2244 Rayburn House Office
Bldg.
Washington, DC 20515-3005
Representative from New Jersey,
Republican
Fifth District

Rowland, J. Roy
2134 Rayburn House Office
Bldg.
Washington, DC 20515-1008
Representative from Georgia,
Democrat
Eighth District

Roxette
(Marie Fredrikson, Per Gessle)
1800 North Vine St.
Hollywood, CA 90028
Singing duo

Roybal-Allard, Lucille
324 Cannon House Office
Bldg.
Washington, DC 20515-0533
Representative from California,
Democrat
Thirty-third District

Royce, Edward R.
1404 Longworth House Office
Bldg.
Washington, DC 20515-0539
Representative from California,
Republican
Thirty-ninth District

Rubinstein, Zelda
8730 Sunset Blvd., #220
Los Angeles, CA 90069
Actress

Rudner, Rita
8942 Wilshire Blvd.
Beverly Hills, CA 90211
Comedienne

Ruehl, Mercedes
8942 Wilshire Blvd.
Beverly Hills, CA 90211
Actress

Rugrats
Klasky Csupo Inc.
1258 N. Highland Ave.
Hollywood, CA 90038
Animated series

Run D.M.C.
296 Elizabeth St.
New York, NY 10012
Rappers

Rundgren, Todd
c/o Bearsville
Warner Records
3300 W. Warner Blvd.
Burbank, CA 91505
Musician, record producer

Rush, Bobby L.
1725 Longworth House Office
Bldg.
Washington, DC 20515-1301
Representative from Illinois,
Democrat
First District

Russell, Kurt
9830 Wilshire Blvd.
Beverly Hills, CA 90212
Actor
birthdate 3/17/51

Russo, Rene
400 S. Beverly Dr., #216
Beverly Hills, CA 90212
Actress

Ruutel, Arnold
Office of the President
Tallin, Republic of Estonia
President of Estonia

Ryan, Meg
8942 Wilshire Blvd.
Beverly Hills, CA 90211
Actress
birthdate 11/19/63

Ryder, Winona
8942 Wilshire Blvd.
Beverly Hills, CA 90211
Actress
born 1971

Probably the disembodied abstractness of a letter permits the reader to impute to the writer whatever qualities the reader is already listening for . . .

—SHANA ALEXANDER, "The Feminine Eye"

666: Mark of the Beast
Fleetway/Quality
Box 4569
Toms River, NJ 08754
Comic

7-Eleven
(Southland Corp.)
2828 N. Haskell Ave.
Dallas, TX 75221
Jere W. Thompson, CEO
Convenience store chain

al-Sabah, Sheikh Jaber al-Ahmad
Sief Palace
Amiry Diwan, Kuwait
Emir of Kuwait

78 Quarterly
Box 283
Key West, FL 33041
Blues, jazz magazine

Sabo, Martin Olav
2336 Rayburn House Office
Bldg.
Washington, DC 20515-2305
Representative from Minnesota, Democrat
Fifth District

Sacramento Kings
One Sports Pkwy.
Sacramento, CA 95834
Professional basketball team

Sagal, Katey
400 S. Beverly Dr., #216
Beverly Hills, CA 90212
Actress

Saibou, General Ali
Office of the Chairman of the
    Hight Council for National
    Orientation
Niamey, Niger
President of Niger

Said, Qaboos bin
The Palace
Muscat, Sultanate of Oman
Sultan of Muscat

Sailplane Homebuilders
    Association
c/o A. McCarty
545 McCarty Dr.
Furlong, PA 18925

Saldana, Theresa
15301 Ventura Blvd., #345
Sherman Oaks, CA 91403
Actress, activist

Salen, Ali Abdullah
Office of the President
San'a', Republic of Yemen
President of Yemen

Salvation Army
615 Slaters Lane
P.O. Box 269
Alexandria, VA 22313
Commissioner James Osborne,
    Commander

San Antonio Spurs
600 E. Market St.
San Antonio, TX 78205
Professional basketball team

San Diego Chargers
P.O. Box 20666
San Diego, CA 92120
Professional football team

San Diego Padres
P.O. Box 2000
San Diego, CA 92112
Professional baseball team

San Francisco 49ers
4949 Centennial Blvd.
Santa Clara, CA 95054
Professional football team

San Francisco Giants
Candlestick Park
San Francisco, CA 94124
Professional baseball team

San Jose Sharks
10 Almaden Blvd.
San Jose, CA 95113
Professional hockey team

Sanders, Bernard
213 Cannon House Office
    Bldg.
Washington, DC 20515-4501
Representative from Vermont,
    Independent At Large

Sanders, Steve
Oak Ridge Boys
329 Rockland Rd.
Hendersonville, TN 37075
Musician

Sangmeister, George E.
1032 Longworth House Office
    Bldg.
Washington, DC 20515-1311
Representative from Illinois,
    Democrat
Eleventh District

Santana
P.O. Box 26671
San Francisco, CA 94126
Rock group

Santana, Carlos
P.O. Box 881630
San Francisco, CA 94188
Guitarist
birthdate 7/20/47

Santorum, Richard J.
1222 Longworth House Office
    Bldg.
Washington, DC 20515-3818
Representative from Pennsylvania,
    Republican
Eighteenth District

Sara Lee Corporation
3 First National Plaza
Chicago, IL 60602
John H. Bryan, Jr., CEO
Goodies manufacturer

Sarbanes, Paul S.
309 Senate Hart Office Bldg.
Washington, DC 20510-2002
Senator from Maryland, Democrat

Sarpalius, Bill
126 Cannon House Office
    Bldg.
Washington, DC 20515-4313
Representative from Texas,
    Democrat
Thirteenth District

Sasser, Jim
363 Senate Russell Office
    Bldg.
Washington, DC 20510-4201
Senator from Tennessee, Democrat

Sassou-Nguessou, Colonel Denis
Office du President
Comite Miltaire du Parti
   Congolais du Travail
Brazzaville, Congo People's
   Republic
President of the Congo

Sassy
Lang Communications
230 Park Ave., 7th Fl.
New York, NY 10013
Mary Kaye Schilling, Editor
Teen magazine

Saturday Night Live
c/o NBC Productions
30 Rockefeller Plaza
New York, NY 10112
TV series

Savage, Ben
c/o Burton
1450 Belfast Dr.
Los Angeles, CA 90069
Actor

Save America's Forest
4 Library Ct., SE
Washington, DC 20003
Carl Ross, Co-Director

Save the Children Foundation
54 Wilton Rd.
Westport, CT 06880
James J. Bausch, President

Save-the-Redwoods League
114 Sansome St., #605
San Francisco, CA 94104
John B. Dewitt, Executive
   Director

Saved by the Bell: The College Years
NBC Productions
330 Bob Hope Dr.
Burbank, CA 91523
TV series

Sawyer, Amos
Office of the President
Monrovia, Liberia
President of Liberia

Sawyer, Thomas C.
1414 Longworth House Office
   Bldg.
Washington, DC 20515-3514
*Representative from Ohio,
   Democrat
Fourteenth District*

Saxton, Jim
438 Cannon House Office
   Bldg.
Washington, DC 20515-3003
*Representative from New Jersey,
   Republican
Third District*

Sbarge, Raphael
9320 Wilshire Blvd., 3rd Fl.
Beverly Hills, CA 90212
Actor

Scalfaro, Oscal Luigi
Palazzo del Quirinale
00187 Rome, Italy
President of Italy

Scalia, Antonin
U.S. Supreme Court Bldg.
One First St. NE
Washington, DC 20543
Supreme Court justice

Schaefer, Dan
2448 Rayburn House Office
   Bldg.
Washington, DC 20515-0606
*Representative from Colorado,
   Republican
Sixth District*

Schaefer, William Donald
State House
Annapolis, MD 21404
Governor of Maryland

Schafer, Ed
600 E. Blvd., State Capitol,
Ground Fl.
Bismarck, ND 58505
Governor of North Dakota

Schenk, Lynn
315 Cannon House Office
Bldg.
Washington, DC 20515-0549
Representative from California,
Democrat
Forty-ninth District

Schiff, Steven H.
1009 Longworth House Office
Bldg.
Washington, DC 20515-3101
Representative from New Mexico,
Republican
First District

Schiffer, Claudia
5 Union Sq., #500
New York, NY 10003
Model

Schizophrenics Anonymous
1209 California Rd.
Eastchester, NY 10709
Elizabeth A. Plante, Director

Schluter, Poul Holskov
Prime Minister's Office
Christianborg, Prins Jorgens
Gaardii
1218 Copenhagen K, Denmark
Prime Minister of Denmark

Scholastic Rowing Association
of America
c/o Msgr. Glendon E.
Robertson
120 United States Ave.
Gibbsboro, NJ 08026

Schroeder, Patricia
2208 Rayburn House Office
Bldg.
Washington, DC 20515-0601
Representative from Colorado,
Democrat
First District

Schumer, Charles E.
2412 Rayburn House Office
Bldg.
Washington, DC 20515-3209
Representative from New York,
Democrat
Ninth District

Schwarzenegger, Arnold
Oak Productions
321 Hampton Dr., #20
Venice, CA 90201
Actor/Special Olympics trainer
birthdate 7/30/47

Science Fiction and Fantasy
Writers of America
5 Winding Brook Drive, #18
Guilderland, NY 12084-9719
Peter Dennis Pautz, Executive
Secretary

Science Fiction Pen Pal Center
P.O. Box 2522
Renton, WA 98056
Deena Brooks, President

Science-by-Mail
Museum of Science
Science Park
Boston, MA 02114
Joan Stanley, Program
Manager
Kids corresponding with scientists

Scoon, Sir Paul
Governor General's House
St. George's Grenada
Governor General of Grenada

Scott, Robert C.
501 Cannon House Office
   Bldg.
Washington, DC 20515-4603
Representative from Virginia,
   Democrat
Third District

Scotti Brothers Records
2114 Pico Blvd.
Santa Monica, CA 90405
Myron Roth, President
Record label

Seagal, Steven
9830 Wilshire Blvd.
Beverly Hills, CA 90212
Actor

SeaQuest DSV
Universal Television
70 Universal City Plaza
Universal City, CA 91608
TV series

**Search Reports Inc./Central
   Registry of the Missing**
345 Boulevard
Hasbrouck Heights, NJ 07604
Charles A. Sutherland,
   President

Seattle Mariners
P.O. Box 4100
Seattle, WA 98104
Professional baseball team

Seattle Seahawks
11220 NE 53d St.
Kirkland, WA 98033
Professional football team

Seattle SuperSonics
190 Queen Anne Ave. N.
Seattle, WA 98109
Professional basketball team

Seconds Magazine
Seconds, Inc.
24 Fifth Ave., #405
New York, NY 10011
Steven Blush, Editor
Music magazine

Seeger, Michael
P.O. Box 1592
Lexington, VA 24450
Musician, singer, folklorist

Seeger, Peter
c/o Harold Leventhal
250 W. 57th St.
New York, NY 10107
Songwriter
birthdate 5/3/19

**Sega, Inc.
(Sega-Genesis)**
573 Forbes Blvd.
S. San Francisco, CA 94080
Thomas Kalinske, President
Software and hardware
   manufacturer of video games

Seger, Bob
1750 Vine St.
Los Angeles, CA 90028
Musician

Seignoret, Sir Clarence
The President's Office
Roseau, Commonwealth of
   Dominica, West Indies
President of Dominica

Seinfeld, Jerry
9830 Wilshire Blvd.
Beverly Hills, CA 90212
Comedian, actor
born 1954

Seko, Mobutu Sese
Presidence de la Republique
Kinshasa, Zaire
President of Zaire

Seles, Monica
c/o International Mgmt.
  Group
One Erieview Plaza, #1300
Cleveland, OH 44114
Tennis player

Sellecca, Connie
151 El Camino
Beverly Hills, CA 90212
Actress
birthdate 5/25/55

Selleck, Tom
9830 Wilshire Blvd.
Beverly Hills, CA 90212
Actor
birthdate 1/29/45

Senate Staff Club
P.O. Box 10
Washington, DC 20510
Sandra Gibbons, President

Sensenbrenner, F. James
2332 Rayburn House Office
  Bldg.
Washington, DC 20515-4909
Representative from Wisconsin,
  Republican
Ninth District

Seraphine, Danny Peter
c/o Warner Bros.
75 Rockefeller Plaza
New York, NY 10019
Drummer

Serrano, Jose E.
336 Cannon House Office
  Bldg.
Washington, DC 20515-3216
Representative from New York,
  Democrat
Sixteenth District

Sesame Street
c/o Children's Television
  Workshop
One Lincoln Plaza
New York, NY 10023
TV series

Sesame Street Magazine
Children's Television
  Workshop
One Lincoln Plaza
New York, NY 10023
Nina Link, Editor

Seven-Up Company
8144 Walnut Hill Lane
Dallas, TX 75231
John R. Albers, CEO
Soft drink company

Seventeen
K-III Magazines
717 Fifth Ave.
New York, NY 10022
Janice Grossman, Publisher
Teen magazine

Sex Addicts Anonymous
P.O. Box 3038
Minneapolis, MN 55403

Sexaholics Anonymous
P.O. Box 300
Simi Valley, CA 93062
Stop sexually self-destructive
  thinking

Seymour, Jane
9320 Wilshire Blvd., 3rd Fl.
Beverly Hills, CA 90212
Actress
birthdate 2/15/51

Shaffer, Paul
Worldwide Pants Inc.
1697 Broadway
New York, NY 10019
Musician, bandleader
birthdate 11/28/49

Shalala, Donna E.
Department of Health and
Human Services
200 Independence Ave., SW
Washington, DC 20201
*Secretary of Health and Human
Services*

Shandling, Garry
9200 Sunset Blvd., #428
Los Angeles, CA 90069
Comedian, actor
birthdate 11/29/49

Shangkun, General Yang
Office of the President
Beijing, People's Republic of
China
President of China

Shanti Project
525 Howard St.
San Francisco, CA 94105
Eric E. Rofes, Director
*Counseling for AIDS patients and
loved ones*

Shapiro, Robert
2121 Ave. of the Stars, 19th Fl.
Los Angeles, CA 90067
*Criminal defense attorney; lead
attorney on O.J. Simpson
case*

Sharp, Philip R.
2217 Rayburn House Office
Bldg.
Washington, DC 20515-1402
*Representative from Indiana,
Democrat
Second District*

Sharper Image Corporation
650 David St.
San Francisco, CA 94111
Richard Thalheimer,
Chairman, President and
CEO
Gadget and high-tech "toy" store

Shatner, William
100 Wilshire Blvd., #1800
Santa Monica, CA 90401
Actor
birthdate 3/22/31

Shaud, Grant
121 N. San Vicente Blvd.
Beverly Hills, CA 90211
Actor

Shaw, E. Clay
2267 Rayburn House Office
Bldg.
Washington, DC 20515-0922
*Representative from Florida,
Republican
Twenty-second District*

Shays, Christopher
1034 Longworth House Office
Bldg.
Washington, DC 20515-0704
*Representative from Connecticut,
Republican
Fourth District*

Shea, John
151 El Camino
Beverly Hills, CA 90212
Actor
birthdate 4/14/49

Sheen, Charlie
8942 Wilshire Blvd.
Beverly Hills, CA 90211
Actor
birthdate 9/3/65

Sheffer, Craig
9830 Wilshire Blvd.
Beverly Hills, CA 90212
Actor

Shelby, Richard C.
509 Senate Hart Office Bldg.
Washington, DC 20510-0103
Senator from Alabama, Democrat

Shepherd, Karen
414 Cannon House Office
   Bldg.
Washington, DC 20515-4402
Representative from Utah,
   Democrat
Second District

Sheridan, Nicollette
8942 Wilshire Blvd.
Beverly Hills, CA 90211
Actress

Shevardnadze, Edouard A.
c/o State Council
Tbilisi, Republic of Georgia
Chairman, Republic of Georgia

Shoe Tree
National Association for Young
   Writers
Box 228
Sandusky, MI 48471
Sheila Cowing, Editor
Fiction, poetry, nonfiction and art
   by and for children

Shoplifters Anonymous
380 N. Broadway, #206
Jericho, NY 11753
Peter D. Berlin, Executive
   Officer

Shore, Pauly
c/o 3 Artists
7920 Sunset Blvd.
Los Angeles, CA 90069
Comedian, actor

Show Music
Goodspeed Opera House
Box 466
East Haddam, CT 06423
Musical theater magazine

Show, Grant
9830 Wilshire Blvd.
Beverly Hills, CA 90212
Actor

Showtime Networks
1633 Broadway
New York, NY 10019

Shue, Andrew
c/o Spelling Television
5700 Wilshire Blvd.
Los Angeles, CA 90036
Actor

Shue, Elizabeth
9830 Wilshire Blvd.
Beverly Hills, CA 90212
Actress

Shuster, Bud
2188 Rayburn House Office
   Bldg.
Washington, DC 20515-3809
Representative from Pennsylvania,
   Republican
Ninth District

Shwe, General Than
Office of the Prime Minister
Yangon, Myanmar
Head of State of Myanmar

Sierra Club
730 Polk St.
San Francisco, CA 94109
Michael Fischer, Executive
   Director

Sills, Beverly
c/o Edgar Vincent
157 W. 57th St.
New York, NY 10019
Opera company director,
   coloratura soprano
birthdate 5/25/29

Silverman, Jonathan
8942 Wilshire Blvd.
Beverly Hills, CA 90211
Actor

Simmonds, Kennedy Alphonse
Office of the Prime Minister
Basseterre, St. Kitts, West
    Indies
*Prime Minister of St. Kitts and
    Nevis*

Simmons, Gene
c/o Polygram
825 8th Ave.
New York, NY 10019
Musician
birthdate 8/25/49

Simon, Paul
1619 Broadway, #500
New York, NY 10019
Singer, songwriter
birthdate 11/5/42

Simon, Paul
462 Senate Dirksen Office
    Bldg.
Washington, DC 20510-1302
Senator from Illinois, Democrat

Simpson, Alan K.
261 Senate Dirksen Office
    Bldg.
Washington, DC 20510-5002
*Senator from Wyoming,
    Republican*

Simpson, O. J.
Los Angeles County Jail
441 Bouchet St.
Los Angeles, CA 90012
Former football star

Simpsons Illustrated
Welsh Publishing Group
300 Madison Ave.
New York, NY 10017
Comic

**Simpsons, The
(Homer, Marge, Lisa, Maggie,
    and Bart)**
Twentieth Television
P.O. Box 900
Beverly Hills, CA 90213
TV series

Sinatra Society of America
P.O. Box 269
Newtonville, NY 12128
Fan club

Sinatra, Frank
3701 Wilshire Blvd.
Los Angeles, CA 90010
Singer
birthdate 12/12/15

Single Mothers by Choice
P.O. Box 1642
Gracie Square Station
New York, NY 10028
Jane Mattes, Chairperson

Sire Records
75 Rockefeller Plaza, 21st Fl.
New York, NY 10019
Sandy Alouete, Label Manager
Record label

(California Office)
3300 Warner Blvd.
Burbank, CA 91510

Sisisky, Norman
2352 Rayburn House Office
    Bldg.
Washington, DC 20515-4604
*Representative from Virginia,
    Democrat
Fourth District*

Sisters
Warner Bros. Television
4000 Warner Blvd.
Burbank, CA 91522
TV series

Sixteen
Sixteen Magazines, Inc.
157 W. 57th St.
New York, NY 10019
Randi Reisfield, Editor
Teen magazine

Skaggs, David E.
1124 Longworth House Office
Bldg.
Washington, DC 20515-0602
Representative from Colorado,
Democrat
Second District

Skaggs, Ricky
54 Music Sq. E., #100
Nashville, TN 37203
Musician

Skate Sailing Association of
America
c/o Richard Friary
1252 Crim Rd.
Bridgewater, NJ 08807

Skeen, Joe
2367 Rayburn House Office
Bldg.
Washington, DC 20515-3102
Representative from New Mexico,
Republican
Second District

Skelton, Ike
2227 Rayburn House Office
Bldg.
Washington, DC 20515-2504
Representative from Missouri,
Democrat
Fourth District

Skerritt, Tom
151 El Camino
Beverly Hills, CA 90212
Actor
birthdate 8/25/33

Ski for Light
1455 W. Lake St.
Minneapolis, MN 55408
Judy Dixson, President
Cross-country skiing for the
physically challenged

Skid Row
9229 Sunset Blvd., #710
Los Angeles, CA 90069
Rock group

Slater, Christian
9830 Wilshire Blvd.
Beverly Hills, CA 90212
Actor

Slattery, Jim
2243 Rayburn House Office
Bldg.
Washington, DC 20515
Representative from Kansas,
Democrat
Second District

Slaughter, Louise M.
2421 Rayburn House Office
Bldg.
Washington, DC 20515-3228
Representative from New York,
Democrat
Twenty-eighth District

Slick, Grace Wing
Starship
1319 Broadway
Sausalito, CA 94965
Singer

Slow Food Foundation
107 Waverly Pl., #1R
New York, NY 10011-9172
Flavio Accornero, President
Stop rushing!!!

Small Luxury Hotels of the
World
337 S. Robertson Blvd., #202
Beverly Hills, CA 90211
Roberta Dorinson, Director

Smith, Christopher H.
2353 Rayburn House Office
Bldg.
Washington, DC 20515-3004
Representative from New Jersey,
Republican
Fourth District

Smith, Lamar
2443 Rayburn House Office
Bldg.
Washington, DC 20515-4321
Representative from Texas,
Republican
Twenty-first District

Smith, Neal
2373 Rayburn House Office
Bldg.
Washington, DC 20515-1504
Representative from Iowa,
Democrat
Fourth District

Smith, Nick
1708 Longworth House Office
Bldg.
Washington, DC 20515-2207
Representative from Michigan,
Republican
Seventh District

Smith, Robert C.
332 Senate Dirksen Office
Bldg.
Washington, DC 20510-2903
Senator from New Hampshire,
Republican

Smith, Robert F.
108 Cannon House Office
Bldg.
Washington, DC 20515-3702
Representative from Oregon,
Republican
Second District

Smith, Will
(also known as Fresh Prince)
1133 Ave. of the Americas
New York, NY 10036
Actor, former rapper

Smothers Brothers
(Dick and Tom)
8489 W. Third St., #1020
Los Angeles, CA 90048
Comic musicians

Smurf Collector's Club
International
24 Cabot Rd., W., Dept. E
Massapequa, NY 11758
Suzanne Lipschitz, Founder

Snack Food Association
1711 King St., #1
Alexandria, VA 22314
James W. Shufelt, President

Snegur, Mircea
Office of the President
Kishinev, Republica
Moldoveneasca
President of Moldovia

Snow
c/o East West
75 Rockefeller Plaza
New York, NY 10019
Rappers

Snow, Olympia J.
2268 Rayburn House Office
Bldg.
Washington, DC 20515-1902
Representative from Maine,
Republican
Second District

Soap Opera People
Tempo Publishing
475 Park Ave. S.
New York, NY 10016
David Zentner, Publisher
Fan magazine

Soares, Mario
Presidencia da Republica
Palacio de Belem
1300 Lisbon
Portugal
President of Portugal

Soccer Association for Youth
4903 Vine St.
Cincinnati, OH 45217
James H. Gruenwald,
   Executive Director

Society for Business Ethics
Loyola University of Chicago
Department of Philosophy
6525 N. Sheridan Rd.
Chicago, IL 60626
Patricia Werhane, Contact

Society for Calligraphy
P.O. Box 64174
Los Angeles, CA 90064
Sue Perez, Contact

Society for Human Resource Management
606 N. Washington St.
Alexandria, VA 22314
Michael R. Losey, CEO

Society for Research in Child Development
University of Chicago Press
5720 Woodlawn Ave.
Chicago, IL 60637
Barbara Kahn, Business
   Manager

Society for the Eradication of Television
Box 10491
Oakland, CA 94610-0491
Steve Wagner, Director

Society for the Furtherance and Study of Fantasy and Science Fiction
Box 1624
Madison, WI 53701-1624
Pat Hario, Treasurer

Society for the Preservation and Advancement of the Harmonica
P.O. Box 865
Troy, MI 48099
Gordon M. Mitchell, President

Society for the Second Self
P.O. Box 4067
Visalia, CA 93278
Donna Martin, Director
Heterosexual cross-dressers

Society for the Study of Myth and Tradition
656 Broadway
New York, NY 10012
Joseph Kulin, Executive
   Publisher

Society for Young Victims
Missing Children Center
66 Broadway
Paramount Plaza
Newport, RI 02840
June Vlasaty, Executive
   Director

Society of Composers
P.O. Box 296
Old Chelsea Station
New York, NY 10013-0296
Martin Gonzalez, Executive
   Secretary

Society of Photographer and Artist Representatives
60 E. 42nd Street, #1166
New York, NY 10165
Harriet Kasak, President

Society of the Philosophy of Sex and Love
c/o Professor Carol Caraway
Indiana University of
   Pennsylvania
Philosophy and Religion
Indiana, PA 15705

SCROOGE
Society to Curtail Ridiculous,
 Outrageous and
 Ostentatious
 Gift Exchange
1447 Westwood Rd.
Charlottesville, VA 22901
Charles G. Langham,
 Executive Director
Strives to de-emphasize the
 commercialization of
 Christmas

Society to Preserve and
 Encourage Radio Drama,
 Variety and Comedy
P.O. Box 7177
Van Nuys, CA 91409-9712
Bob Steinmetz, President

Socks
The White House
1600 Pennsylvania Ave.
Washington, DC 20500
First cat

Soglo, Nicephore
Office of the President
Cotonou, Benin
President of Benin

Solomon, Gerald B. H.
2265 Rayburn House Office
 Bldg.
Washington, DC 20515-3222
Representative from New York,
 Republican
Twenty-second District

Sondheim, Stephen
c/o F. Roberts
65 E. 55th St., #702
New York, NY 10022
Composer, lyricist

Songwriter's Market
Writer's Digest Books
1507 Dana Ave.
Cincinnati, OH 45207
Lists publishers, record companies,
 producers, etc.

Songwriters Guild of America
276 5th Ave.
New York, NY 10001
Lewis M. Bachman, Executive
 Director

Sons and Daughters of the
 Soddies
c/o Vivian D. Phillips
P.O. Box 393
Colby, KS 67701-0393
Descendants of pioneers who lived
 in sod houses

Sony Classical
1285 Ave. of the Americas
New York, NY 10019
Gunther Breest, President
Record label

Sony Music Nashville
(also Columbia Nashville, Epic
 Nashville)
34 Music Square E.
Nashville, TN 37203
Roy Wunsch, President
Record label

Source, The
Source Publications, Inc.
594 Broadway
New York, NY 10012
Jon Schechter, Editor
Rap magazine

Souter, David H.
U.S. Supreme Court Bldg.
One First St. NE
Washington, DC 20543
Supreme Court justice

Spader, James
8942 Wilshire Blvd.
Beverly Hills, CA 90212
Actor
born 1961

Special Olympics International
1350 New York Ave., NW,
#500
Washington, DC 20005
Sargent Shriver, Board
Chairman

Special Wish Foundation, A
c/o Ramona Fickle
2244 S. Hamilton Rd., #202
Columbus, OH 43232
*Grants wishes of kids who are
threatened with life-threatening
disorders*

**Specialty Coffee Association
of America**
1 World Trade Center, #800
Long Beach, CA 90831
Ted R. Linple, Executive
Director

Spectacular Spider-Man
Marvel Entertainment Group
387 Park Ave. S.
New York, NY 10016
Comic

Specter, Arlen
530 Senate Hart Office Bldg.
Washington, DC 20510-3802
*Senator from Pennsylvania,
Republican*

Spelling, Tori
8942 Wilshire Blvd.
Beverly Hills, CA 90211
Actress

Spence, Floyd D.
2405 Russell House Office
Bldg.
Washington, DC 20515-4002
*Representative from South
Carolina, Republican
Second District*

Spielberg, Steven
Amblin Entertainment
100 Universal City Plaza, #477
Universal City, CA 91608
Film director, producer
birthdate 12/18/47

**Spill Control Association of
America**
400 Renaissance Center, #1900
Detroit, MI 48243
Marc K. Shaye, General
Counsel

Spin
Spin Publications
6 W. 18th St.
New York, NY 10011
Bob Guccione, Jr., Editor
Music magazine

Spirit: The Origin Years
Kitchen Sink Press
2 Swamp Rd.
Princeton, WI 54968
Comic

Splatter Effect
Box 2
Bound Brook, NJ 08805
Spiros P. Ballas II, Editor
Music magazine

Sports Illustrated
Time & Life Bldg.
Rockefeller Center
New York, NY 10020

Spratt, John M., Jr.
1536 Longworth House Office
Bldg.
Washington, DC 20515-4005
*Representative from South
Carolina, Democrat
Fifth District*

Springer, Jerry
Multimedia Entertainment
45 Rockefeller Plaza, 35th Fl.
New York, NY 10111
Talk show host

Springfield, Rick
9200 Sunset Blvd., PH15
Los Angeles, CA 90069
Singer, actor
birthdate 8/23/49

Springsteen, Bruce
c/o Premier Talent Agency
3 E. 54th St.
New York, NY 10022
"The Boss"
birthdate 9/23/49

St. Louis Blues
5700 Oakland Ave.
St. Louis, MO 63110
Professional hockey team

St. Louis Cardinals
Busch Stadium
St. Louis, MO 63102
Professional baseball team

Stack, Robert
415 N. Camden Dr., #121
Beverly Hills, CA 90210
Actor
birthdate 1/13/19

Stallone, Sylvester
8800 Sunset Blvd., #214
Los Angeles, CA 90069
Actor
birthdate 7/6/46

Stamos, John
151 El Camino
Beverly Hills, CA 90212
Actor, singer
birthdate 8/19/63

Stansfield, Lisa
c/o Arista Records
6 W. 57th St.
New York, NY 10019
Singer

Star Trek
DC Comics Inc.
1325 Ave. of the Americas
New York, NY 10019
Comic

Star Trek: Deep Space Nine
Paramount
5555 Melrose Ave.
Los Angeles, CA 90038
TV series

Star Trek: The Next Generation
DC Comics Inc.
1325 Ave. of the Americas
New York, NY 10019
Comic

Stark, Pete
239 Cannon House Office Bldg.
Washington, DC 20515-0513
Representative from California, Democrat
Thirteenth District

Starlight Foundation
12233 W. Olympic Blvd.
Los Angeles, CA 90064
Holly Rasey, COO
Wishes for terminally ill kids

Starr, Ringo (Richard Starkey)
2 Glynde Mews
London SW3 1SB England
Musician
birthdate 7/7/40

Statler Brothers
P.O. Box 2703
Staunton, VA 24401
Country and western group

Statue of Liberty/Ellis Island Foundation
52 Vanderbilt Ave.
New York, NY 10017-3898
Stephen A. Briganti, President

Stearns, Clifford B.
332 Cannon House Office
  Bldg.
Washington, DC 20515-0906
Representative from Florida,
  Republican
Sixth District

Stenholm, Charles W.
1211 Longworth House Office
  Bldg.
Washington, DC 20515-4317
Representative from Texas,
  Democrat
Seventeenth District

Step by Step
Warner Bros. Television
4000 Warner Blvd.
Burbank, CA 91522
TV series

Stepfamily Foundation
333 West End Ave.
New York, NY 10023
Jeanette Lofas, President

Sterling Silversmiths Guild of
  America
312-A Wyndhurst Ave.
Baltimore, MD 21210
Robert M. Johnston, Executive
  Vice-President

Stern, Howard
K-ROCK-FM (WXRK)
600 Madison Ave.
New York, NY 10022
DJ
born 1954

Stern, Isaac
40 W. 57th St.
New York, NY 10019
Violinist
birthdate 7/21/20

Stevens, John Paul
U.S. Supreme Court Bldg.
One First St. NE
Washington, DC 20543
Supreme Court justice

Stevens, Ted
522 Senate Hart Office Bldg.
Washington, DC 20510-0201
Senator from Alaska, Republican

Stevenson, Parker
9320 Wilshire Blvd., 3rd Fl.
Beverly Hills, CA 90212
Actor
birthdate 6/4/52

Stewart, Patrick
8942 Wilshire Blvd.
Beverly Hills, CA 90211
Actor

Stewart, Rod
c/o Warner Bros.
3300 Warner Blvd.
Burbank, CA 91510
Singer
birthdate 1/10/45

Sting
(Gordon Matthew Sumner)
The Bugle House
21 A Noel St.
London W1 England
Singer
birthdate 10/2/51

Stokes, Louis
2365 Rayburn House Office
  Bldg.
Washington, DC 20515-3511
Representative from Ohio,
  Democrat
Eleventh District

Stone, Sharon
P.O. Box 7304
N. Hollywood, CA 91603-7304
Actress

Stop Abuse by Counselors
P.O. Box 68292
Seattle, WA 98168
Shirley Siegel, Coordinator

Stop War Toys Campaign
c/o War Resisters League
339 Lafayette St.
New York, NY 10012

Strait, George
c/o Erv Woolsey
1000 18th Ave. S.
Nashville, TN 37212
Singer

Strasky, Jan
Kancelar prezidenta republiky
11908 Prah-Hradcany
Prague, The Czech Republic
Prime Minister of The Czech Republic

Straw, Syd
Monterey Peninsula Artists
P.O. Box 7308
Carmel, CA 93921
Singer

Strawberry, Darryl
San Francisco Giants
Candlestick Park
San Francisco, CA 94124
Baseball player

Stray Cats
113 Wardour Street
London, W1, England
Rock group

Streep, Meryl
9830 Wilshire Blvd.
Beverly Hills, CA 90212
Actress
birthdate 6/22/49

Street, Peekaboo
U.S. Olympic Committee
1750 E. Boulder St.
Colorado Springs, CO 80909
Skier

Streisand, Barbra
(Barbara Joan)
9830 Wilshire Blvd.
Beverly Hills, CA 90212
Singer, actress, director, producer
birthdate 4/24/42

Strickland, Ted
1429 Longworth House Office
Bldg.
Washington, DC 20515-3506
Representative from Ohio,
Democrat
Sixth District

Studds, Gerry E.
237 Cannon House Office
Bldg.
Washington, DC 20515-2110
Representative from
Massachusetts, Democrat
Tenth District

Student Conservation
Association
Box 550
Charlestown, NH 03603
Scott D. Izzo, President

Student Letter Exchange
630 3rd Ave.
New York, NY 10017
Wayne J. Dankert, General
Manager

S.A.D.D.
Students Against Driving
Drunk
P.O. Box 800
Marlborough, MA 01752
William F. Cullinane,
Executive Director

Stump, Bob
211 Cannon House Office
Bldg.
Washington, DC 20515-0303
Representative from Arizona,
Republican
Third District

Stuntmen's Association of Motion Pictures
4810 Whitsett Ave.
N. Hollywood, CA 91607
Carl Ciarfalio, President

Stuntwomen's Association of Motion Pictures
5125 Lankershim Blvd., #8
N. Hollywood, CA 91601
Mary Peters, President

Stupak, Bart
317 Cannon House Office Bldg.
Washington, DC 20515-2201
Representative from Michigan, Democrat
First District

Sub-Pop
P.O. Box 2391
Olympia, WA 98507
Bruce Pairtt, Editor
Music magazine

Suharto
Office of the President
15 Jalan Merdeka Utara
Jakarta, Indonesia
President of Indonesia

Sullivan, Mike J.
State Capitol
Cheyenne, WY 82002
Governor of Wyoming

Sundance Institute
R.R. 3, Box 624A
Sundance, UT 84604
Suzanne Weil, Executive Director
Institute for film studies founded by Robert Redford

Sundlun, Bruce
State House
Providence, RI 02903
Governor of Rhode Island

Sundquist, Don
339 Cannon House Office Bldg.
Washington, DC 20515-4207
Representative from Tennessee, Republican
Seventh District

Sunshine Foundation
2001 Bridge St.
Philadelphia, PA 19124
Bill Sample, President
Wishes for ill children

Super Dave
(Bob Einstein)
8955 Beverly Blvd.
Los Angeles, CA 90048
Comic stuntman

Super Teen
Sterling's Magazines Inc.
355 Lexington Ave., 13th Fl.
New York, NY 10017
Magazine

Superstars
Sixteen Magazines Inc.
157 W. 57th St.
New York, NY 10019
Katherine Young, Publisher
Fan magazine

Sutherland, Kiefer
9830 Wilshire Blvd.
Beverly Hills, CA 90212
Actor
birthdate 12/20/66

Swamp Thing
DC Comics Inc.
1325 Ave. of the Americas
New York, NY 10019
Comic

Swayze, Patrick
8942 Wilshire Blvd.
Beverly Hills, CA 90212
Actor, dancer
birthdate 8/18/54

Sweetin, Jodie
c/o Full House
4000 Warner Blvd.
Burbank, CA 91522
Actress

Swensen's
P.O. Box 9008
Andover, MA 01810
Richard Smith, Chairman
Ice cream store chain

Swett, Dick
230 Cannon House Office
  Bldg.
Washington, DC 20515-2902
*Representative from New
  Hampshire, Democrat
Second District*

Swift, Al
1502 Longworth House Office
  Bldg.
Washington, DC 20515-4702
*Representative from Washington,
  Democrat
Second District*

Symington, Fife
State House
Phoenix, AZ 85007
Governor of Arizona

Synar, Mike
2329 Rayburn House Office
  Bldg.
Washington, DC 20515-3602
*Representative from Oklahoma,
  Democrat
Second District*

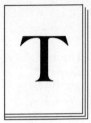

Letters blur the lines between two separate lives.

—VICKI RENTZ

10,000 Maniacs
9830 Wilshire Blvd.
Beverly Hills, CA 90212
Rock group

13 Engines
Collins Mgmt.
5 Bigelow St.
Cambridge, MA 02139
Rock group

13 Stitches
Rustron Music Mgmt.
1156 Park Lane
W. Palm Beach, FL 33417
Rock group

2 AM Magazine
Box 6754
Rockford, IL 22209
Gretta Anderson, Editor
*Horror, fantasy, science fiction
  magazine*

2 Die 4
c/o Morgan Creek
1875 Century Park E., #600
Los Angeles, CA 90067
Rock group

2 Live Crew
c/o Luke Records
8400 N.E. 2nd Ave.
Liberty City, FL 33138
Rock group

25 G's Max
1655 Cherokee, #200
Hollywood, CA 90028
Music video production company

2AZZ1
P.O. Box 2512
Toluca Lake, CA 91610
Pop duo

3-2-1 Contact
Children's Television
  Workshop
1 Lincoln Plaza
New York, NY 10023
Jonathan Rosenbloom, Editor
  in Chief
Science magazine for kids

Tabone, Censu
Office of the President
The Palace
Valletta, Malta
President of Malta

Taco Bell Corporation
17901 Von Karman
Irvine, CA 92714
John E. Martin, President
Fast-food chain

Tai Chi Chuan/Shaolin Chuan Association
33W624 Roosevelt Rd.
P.O. Box 430
Geneva, IL 60134
Bonnie Dodaro, Contact

Tale of the Ninja Warrior
CFW Enterprises
4201 Vanowen Pl.
Burbank, CA 91505
Comic

Talent, James M.
1022 Longworth House Office
Bldg.
Washington, DC 20515-2502
Representative from Missouri,
Republican
Second District

Talking Heads
1775 Broadway, #700
New York, NY 10019
Rock group

Tampa Bay Buccaneers
1 Buccaneer Pl.
Tampa, FL 33607
Professional football team

Tampa Bay Lightning
501 E. Kennedy Blvd.
Tampa, FL 33601
Professional hockey team

Tandem Club of America
35 E. Centennial Dr.
Medford, NJ 08055
Malcolm Boyd, Treasurer
Bicyclists

Tang, Tommy
7473 Melrose Ave.
Los Angeles, CA 90046
Restaurant owner

Tanner, John S.
1427 Longworth House Office
Bldg.
Washington, DC 20515-4208
Representative from Tennessee,
Democrat
Eighth District

Tanumafili, Malietoa II
Government House
Vailima, Apia
Western Samoa, South Pacific
Head of State of Western Samoa

Tapori
Fourth World Movement
7600 Willow Hill Dr.
Landover, MD 20785
Friendship magazine

Tattoo Club of America
c/o Spider Webb's Studio
Captains Cove Seaport
1 Bastwick Ave.
Bridgeport, CT 06605
Joe O'Sullivan, Secretary

Tauzin, W. J. (Billy)
2330 Rayburn House Office
Bldg.
Washington, DC 20515-1803
Representative from Louisiana,
Democrat
Third District

Taya, Col. Maaouye Ould Sidi Ahmed
Presidence de la Republique
B.P. 184, Nouakchott
Mauritania
Chief of State and Head of
Government of Mauritania

Taylor, Charles H.
516 Cannon House Office
  Bldg.
Washington, DC 20515-3311
*Representative from North
  Carolina, Republican
  Eleventh District*

Taylor, Gene
215 Cannon House Office
  Bldg.
Washington, DC 20515-2405
*Representative from Mississippi,
  Democrat
  Fifth District*

Taylor, James
644 N. Doheny Dr.
West Hollywood, CA 90069
Musician
birthdate 3/12/48

Taylor, Meshach
10100 Santa Monica Blvd.,
  25th Fl.
Los Angeles, CA 90067
Actor

Taz-Mania
Warner Bros. Animation
15303 Ventura Blvd., #1100
Sherman Oaks, CA 91403
Animated series

TBS
One CNN Center
P.O. Box 105366
Atlanta, GA 30348

Team Titans
DC Comics, Inc.
1325 Ave. of the Americas
New York, NY 10019
Comic

Teannaki, Teato
Office of the President
Tarawa, Kiribati
President of Kiribati

Tears for Fears
50 New Bond Street
London, W1, England
Rock group

**Teen Association of Model
  Railroaders**
c/o John Reichel
1800 E. 38th St.
Oakland, CA 94602

Teen Beat
Macfadden Holdings
233 Park Ave. S.
New York, NY 10003
Sheila Steinbach, Editor
Magazine

Teen Machine
Sterling's Magazines
355 Lexington Ave.
New York, NY 10017
Marie Therese Morreale,
  Editor
Magazine

Teen Magazine
Petersen Publishing Co.
8490 Sunset Blvd.
Los Angeles, CA 90069
Roxanne Cameron, Editor

Teen Throbs
Tempo Publishing
475 Park Ave. S.
New York, NY 10016
David Zentner, Publisher
Magazine

**Teenage Mutant Ninja Turtles
  (Michelangelo, Donatello,
  Leonardo, and Raphael)**
c/o New Line Cinema
116 N. Robertson Blvd., #200
Los Angeles, CA 90048

Tejeda, Frank
323 Cannon House Office
  Bldg.
Washington, DC 20515-4328
Representative from Texas,
  Democrat
Twenty-eighth District

Ten-hui, Li
Office of the President
Taipei, Taiwan, Republic of
  China
President of Taiwan

Tender Treasures
3706 Ocean View Blvd.
Montrose, CA 91020
Marilyn Beck, Owner
Children's clothing store

Tenuta, Judy
9320 Wilshire Blvd., 3rd Fl.
Beverly Hills, CA 90212
Comedienne

Terror, Inc.
Marvel Entertainment Group
387 Park Ave. S.
New York, NY 10016
Comic

Tesh, John
5555 Melrose Ave.
Los Angeles, CA 90038
"Entertainment Tonight" host,
  musician

Texas Rangers
P.O. Box 90111
Arlington, TX 76004
Professional baseball team

al-Thani, Sheikh Khalifa bin
  Hamad
The Royal Palace
Doha, Qatar
Emir of Qatar

Theatre Communications
  Group
355 Lexington Ave.
New York, NY 10017
Peter Zeisler, Director
Service organization for non-profit
  professional theaters

Thiessen, Tiffany-Amber
c/o Gold/Marshak
3500 West Olive Ave.
Burbank, CA 91505
Actress

Thigpen, Lynne
10100 Santa Monica Blvd.,
  25th Fl.
Los Angeles, CA 90067
Actress, Acme Detective "Carmen
  Sandiego"

Thomas, Bill
2209 Rayburn House Office
  Bldg.
Washington, DC 20515-0521
Representative from California,
  Republican
Twenty-first District

Thomas, Clarence
U.S. Supreme Court Bldg.
One First St. NE
Washington, DC 20543
Supreme Court justice

Thomas, Craig
1019 Longworth House Office
  Bldg.
Washington, DC 20515-5001
Representative from Wyoming,
  Republican At Large

Thomas, Jay
9229 Sunset Blvd., #710
Los Angeles, CA 90069
DJ, actor

Thompson, Bennie G.
1408 Longworth House Office
  Bldg.
Washington, DC 20515-2402
Representative from Mississippi,
  Democrat
Second District

Thompson, Tommy G.
State Capitol
Madison, WI 53707
Governor of Wisconsin

Thorne-Smith, Courtney
10100 Santa Monica Blvd.,
  25th Fl.
Los Angeles, CA 90067
Actress

Thornton, Ray
1214 Longworth House Office
  Bldg.
Washington, DC 20515-0402
Representative from Arkansas,
  Democrat
Second District

Thrasher Magazine
High Speed Productions, Inc.
1303 Underwood Ave.
San Francisco, CA 94124
Kevin J. Thatcher, Editor
Skateboarding, rock 'n' roll, etc.

Three Stooges Journal, The
Three Stooges Fan Club
Box 747
Gwynedd Valley, PA 19437
Fan magazine

Thurman, Karen L.
130 Cannon House Office
  Bldg.
Washington, DC 20515-0905
Representative from Florida,
  Democrat
Fifth District

Thurmond, Strom
217 Senate Russell Office
  Bldg.
Washington, DC 20510-4001
Senator from South Carolina,
  Republican

Timakata, Fred
Office of the President
Port Vila, Vanuatu
President of Vanuatu

Time Trax
Warner Bros. Television
4000 Warner Blvd.
Burbank, CA 91522
TV series

Time Warner Inc.
75 Rockefeller Plaza
New York, NY 10019
Largest media and entertainment
  company in the world

Tiny Toon Adventures
Warner Bros. Animation
15303 Ventura Blvd., #1100
Sherman Oaks, CA 91403
Animated series

Tippers International
P.O. Box 2351
Oshkosh, WI 54903
John F. Schein, President
Seeks to restore tipping to its
  original concept, a rating
  for services rendered

TLC
6 W. 57th St.
New York, NY 10019
Recording artists

TNT
One CNN Plaza
P.O. Box 105366
Atlanta, GA 30348
Cable network

Toastmasters International
P.O. Box 952
Mission Viejo, CA 92690
Terrence J. McCann,
  Executive Director

Tobacco Institute
1875 Eye St. NW, #800
Washington, DC 20006
Samuel Chilcote, President
Pro-smoking for financial gain

**Tobacco Products Liability
  Project**
Northeastern University
  School of Law
400 Huntington Ave.
Boston, MA 02115
Prof. Richard Daynard,
  Chairperson

Tom & Jerry
Harvey Comics Entertainment,
  Inc.
100 Wilshire Blvd., #500
Santa Monica, CA 90401
Comic

**Tom Petty and The
  Heartbreakers**
1755 Broadway, 8th Fl.
New York, NY 10019
Rock group

Tomei, Marisa
151 El Camino
Beverly Hills, CA 90212
Actress

Tomlin, Lily
151 El Camino
Beverly Hills, CA 90211
*Actress, comedienne, writer,
  producer*
birthdate 9/1/39

Tomorrow's Business Leader
Future Business Leaders of
  America
2800 Shirlington Rd.
Arlington, VA 22206
Magazine

Tong, Goh Chok
Prime Minister's Office
Istana, Singapore 0923
Prime Minister of Singapore

**Tonight Show with Jay Leno,
  The**
330 Bob Hope Dr.
Burbank, CA 91523
TV talk show

Tonka Corporation
6000 Clearwater Dr.
Minnetonka, MN 55343
Stephen G. Shank, CEO
*Toy company, manufactures
  famous trucks and games*

Tony the Tiger
c/o Kellogg Co.
235 Porter
Battle Creek, MI 49017
Kellogg's mascot

Tootsie Roll
7401 Cicero Ave.
Chicago, IL 60629
M. J. Gordon, President
Candy company

Top Cops
Grosso-Jacobson Productions
8981 Sunset Blvd., #102
Los Angeles, CA 90069
TV series

Torkildsen, Peter G.
120 Cannon House Office
  Bldg.
Washington, DC 20515-2106
*Representative from
  Massachusetts, Republican
Sixth District*

Toronto Blue Jays
300 Bremner Blvd.
Toronto, Ontario
M5V 3B3 Canada
Professional baseball team

Toronto Maple Leafs
60 Carlton St.
Toronto, Ontario M5B 1L1
Canada
Professional hockey team

Torres, Esteban E.
1740 Longworth House Office
Bldg.
Washington, DC 20515-0534
Representative from California,
Democrat
Thirty-fourth District

Torricelli, Robert G.
2159 Rayburn House Office
Bldg.
Washington, DC 20515-3009
Representative from New Jersey,
Democrat
Ninth District

Toto
P.O. Box 7308
Carmel, CA 93921
Pop group

Touchstone Pictures
500 S. Buena Vista St.
Burbank, CA 91521
Film production company

Toughlove International
P.O. Box 1069
Doylestown, PA 18901
"Tough" help for troubled teens

**Toure, Lt. Co. Amadou
Toumani**
c/o Cabinet du President
Comite militaire du liberation
nationale
B.P. 1463, Bamako, Mali
Head of transitional government
of Mali

Towns, Edolphus
2232 Rayburn House Office
Bldg.
Washington, DC 20515-3210
Representative from New York,
Democrat
Tenth District

**Toy Manufacturers of
America, Inc.**
200 Fifth Ave.
New York, NY 10010
Walter Armatys, Executive
Director

Toys
Western Publishing Co.
1220 Mound Ave.
Racine, WI 53404
Magazine

Toys "Я" Us
395 W. Passaic St.
Rochelle Park, NJ 07662
Charles Lazarus, CEO
Toy store chain

Trabulus, Dr. Josh
435 N. Roxbury Dr., #300
Beverly Hills, CA 90210
Medical doctor

Traficant, James A., Jr.
2446 Rayburn House Office
Bldg.
Washington, DC 20515-3517
Representative from Ohio,
Democrat
Seventeenth District

Traveling Wilburys
c/o Warner Bros.
3300 Warner Blvd.
Burbank, CA 91510
"Star" group

Travis, Randy
P.O. Box 121712
Nashville, TN 37212
Singer
birthdate 5/4/59

Travolta, John
c/o Krane
7944 Woodrow Wilson Dr.
Los Angeles, CA 90046
Actor
birthdate 2/18/54

**Treasure Hunting Research
and Information Center**
P.O. Box 761
Patterson, LA 70392
John H. Reed, Director

Tree People
12601 Mulholland Dr.
Beverly Hills, CA 90210
Andy Lipkis, President
Tree planting organization

Tri-M Music Honor Society
c/o MENC
1902 Association Dr.
Reston, VA 22091
Sandra Fridy, Contact
*Honor society for music students
in junior and senior high
school*

TriStar Pictures
10202 W. Washington Blvd.
Culver City, CA 90232
Film production company

**Trovoada, Miguel Anjos de
Cunha Lisboa**
Office of the President
Sao Tome
Sao Tome and Principe
*President of Sao Tome and
Principe*

Trujillo, Cesar Gaviria
Office of the President
Casa de Narino
Carrera 8A, No 7-26
Bogota, Colombia
President of Colombia

Trust for the Public Land
116 New Montgomery St.,
4th Fl.
San Francisco, CA 94105
Martin J. Rosen, President

Tucker, Jim Guy
State Capitol
Little Rock, AR 72201
Governor of Arkansas

Tucker, Tanya
P.O. Box 15245
Nashville, TN 37215
Singer
birthdate 10/10/58

Tucker, Walter R. III
419 Cannon House Office
Bldg.
Washington, DC 20515-0537
*Representative from California,
Democrat
Thirty-seventh District*

Tupou, King Taufa'ahau IV
The Palace
P.O. Box 6
Nuku'alofa, Tonga
Sovereign of Tonga

Turner, Janine
9830 Wilshire Blvd.
Beverly Hills, CA 90212
Actress

**Turner, Tina
(Anna Mae Bullock)**
c/o Roger Davis Mgmt.
3575 Cahuenga Blvd., W.
Los Angeles, CA 90068
Singer
birthdate 11/26/39

Tutti Frutti
Jimmijack Publishing Co.
807 Vivian Ct.
Baldwin, NY 11510
Teen fan magazine

Tutu, Bishop Desmond
Box 31190
Johannesburg, South Africa
Human rights activist

TV Picture Life
c/o Sanford Schwarz
355 Lexington Ave.
New York, NY 10017
Fan magazine

TV Radio Mirror
Macfadden Holdings
233 Park Ave. S.
New York, NY 10003
Fan magazine

Twentieth Century Fox
10201 W. Pico Blvd.
Beverly Hills, CA 90213
Film production company

**Twinless Twins Support
   Group**
11220 St. Joe Rd.
Ft. Wayne, IN 46835
Dr. Raymond W. Brandt,
   Director

Tyco Toys, Inc.
6000 Midlantic Dr.
Mt. Laurel, NJ 08054
Richard E. Grey, CEO
Game manufacturer

Tyson, Mike
#922335, Regional Diagnostic
   Center
Plainfield, IN 46168
Incarcerated boxer

It gives me the greatest pleasure to realize I have one more invisible friend at the other end of the post office. Nearly every week a new one turns up, and I feel like I am having a party, and the postman is a sort of Santa Claus every day, with letters from my new friends.

—VACHEL LINDSAY TO ALICE HENDERSON, 1913

U.S. Association for Blind Athletes
33 N. Institute St.
Colorado Springs, CO 80903
Dr. Roger E. Neppl, Executive Director

U.S. Bobsled and Skeleton Federation
Box 828
Lake Placid, NY 12946
Ray Pratt, Executive Director

U.S. Boomerang Association
P.O. Box 182
Delaware, OH 43015
Chet Snouffer, Director

U.S. Disc Sports Association
180 Norman Rd.
Rochester, NY 14623
Jim Palmieri, Director
Frisbee, etc.

U.S. Express
Scholastic Inc.
730 Broadway
New York, NY 10003
Magazine for English-as-a-second-language students

U.S. Hang Gliding Association
559 E. Pikes Peak, #101
P.O. Box 8300
Colorado Springs, CO 80933

U.S. Paddle Tennis Association
189 Seeley St.
Brooklyn, NY 11218
Greg Lawrence, President

U.S. Powerlifting Federation
P.O. Box 389
Roy, UT 84067
Jan Shendiow, Acting President

U.S. Sailing
P.O. Box 209
Newport, RI 02840
John B. Bonds, Executive Director

U.S. Sports Acrobatic Federation
c/o Dr. Jed Friend
3595 E. Fountain, #J1
Colorado Springs, CO 80910

U.S. Swimming Inc.
1750 E. Boulder St.
Colorado Springs, CO 80909
Ray B. Essick, Executive Director

U.S. Taekwondo Union
1750 E. Boulder St., #405
Colorado Springs, CO 80909
Robert K. Fujimara, Executive
Director

U.S. Team Handball
Federation
1750 E. Boulder St.
Colorado Springs, CO 80909
Michael D. Cavanaugh,
Executive Director

U.S.A. Field Hockey
Association
1750 E. Boulder St.
Colorado Springs, CO 80909
Carolyn L. Moody, Executive
Director

U.S.A. Hockey
4965 N. 30th St.
Colorado Springs, CO 80919
Baaron B. Pittienger,
Executive Director
Amateur hockey

U.S.A. Karate Federation
1300 Kenmore Blvd.
Akron, OH 44314
George E. Anderson, President

U.S.A. Toy Library Association
2530 Crawford Ave., #111
Evanston, IL 60201
Judith Q. Jacuzzi, Executive
Director
*Studies the roles of toys in child
development*

U.S.A. Wrestling
225 S. Academy Blvd.
Colorado Springs, CO 80910
Jim Sherr, Executive Director

U2
4 Windmill Lane
Dublin 4, Ireland
Rock group

Ueberroth, Peter
P.O. Box 2649
Los Angeles, CA 90053
Entrepreneur

Ugly Joe Kid
825 Eighth Ave.
New York, NY 10019
Rock group

Ullman, Tracy
9830 Wilshire Blvd.
Beverly Hills, CA 90212
Actress, comedienne
birthdate 12/30/59

Uncle Remus Museum
P.O. Box 3184
Eatonton, GA 31024
Madeleine Gooch, Secretary
Joel Chandler Harris Society

Uncle Scrooge
Walt Disney Publications
500 S. Buena Vista
Burbank, CA 91521
Comic

Underwater Society of
America
(Scuba)
P.O. Box 628
Daly City, CA 94017
George Rose, President

Underwood, Blair
5200 Lankershim Blvd., #260
N. Hollywood, CA 91601
Actor
birthdate 8/25

Underwriters Laboratories
333 Pfingsten Rd.
Northbrook, IL 60062
Tom Castino, President
Those UL guys on the labels

United Drag Racers
Association
7601 Hamilton Ave.
Burr Ridge, IL 60521
Jack C. Thomas, President

United Federation of Dull
Clubs
10920 N. Ambassador
Kansas City, MO 64153
Rita Johnston, President

United Nations Children's
Fund
3 United Nations Plaza
New York, NY 10017
James P. Grant, Executive
Director

United Press International
1400 Eye St. NW
Washington, DC 20005
Steve Germann, CEO

United States Aikido
Federation
98 State St.
Northampton, MA 01060
Susan Wolk, Secretary
Treasurer

United States Amateur Boxing
1750 E. Boulder St.
Colorado Springs, CO 80909
James J. Fox, Executive
Director

United States Amateur
Confederation of Roller
Skating
P.O. Box 6579
Lincoln, NE 68506
George Pickard, Executive
Director

United States Amateur Jai Alai
Players Association
c/o Howard Kalik
1935 NE 150th St.
N. Miami, FL 33181

United States Amateur Tug of
War Association
P.O. Box 9626
Madison, WI 53715
Robert Pulfer, Executive
Officer

United States Athletes
Association
3735 Lakeland Ave., N., #230
Minneapolis, MN 55422
Carl Eller, Executive Director
*Athletes for academic achievement
and drug-free sports*

United States Badminton
Association
1750 E. Boulder St., Bldg. 10,
Rm. 127
Colorado Springs, CO 80909
Mark Hodges, Executive
Director

United States Cerebral Palsy
Athletic Association
34518 Warren Rd., #264
Westland, MI 48185
Michael P. Mushett, Executive
Director

United States Committee for
the United Nations
Environment Program
2013 Q St. NW
Washington, DC 20009
Richard A. Hellman, President

United States Croquet
Association
500 Ave. of the Champions
Palm Beach Gardens, FL
33418
Rudulph E. Carter, President

United States Curling
Association
c/o David Garber
1100 Center Point Dr.
Box 866
Stevens Point, WI 54481

United States Cycling
  Federation
c/o USOC
1750 E. Boulder St.
Colorado Springs, CO 80909
Jerry E. Lace, Executive
  Director

United States Diving Inc.
Pan American Plaza
201 S. Capitol Ave., #430
Indianapolis, IN 46225
Todd B. Smith, Executive
  Director

United States Equestrian
  Team
Gladstone, NJ 07934
Robert J. Standish, Executive
  Director

United States Fencing
  Association
1750 E. Boulder St.
Colorado Springs, CO 80909
Carla-Mae Richards, Executive
  Director

United States Figure Skating
  Association
20 1st St.
Colorado Springs, CO 80906
Jan Anderson, Executive
  Director

United States Flag Football
  League
c/o John D. Carrigan
5834 Pine Tree Dr.
Sanibel, FL 33957

United States Gymnastics
  Federation
201 S. Capitol, #300
Indianapolis, IN 46225
Mike Jacki, Executive Director

United States Handball
  Association
930 N. Benton Ave.
Tucson, AZ 85711
Vern Roberts, Executive
  Director

United States International
  Speed Skating Association
P.O. Box 16157
Rocky River, OH 44116
Katie Marquard, Executive
  Director

United States Judo Association
19 N. Union Blvd.
Colorado Springs, CO 80909
Larry Lee, Executive Director

United States Lifesaving
  Association
P.O. Box 366
Huntington Beach, CA 92648
Joseph Pecoraro, President
Lifeguards

United States Luge Association
P.O. Box 651
35 Church St.
Lake Placid, NY 12946
Ronald Rossi, Executive
  Director

United States Naturalized
  Citizen Association
P.O. Box 19822
Alexandria, VA 22320
Rev. Dr. Peter P. S. Ching,
  President

United States of America
  Rugby Football
3595 E. Fountain Blvd.
Colorado Springs, CO 80910
Karen Kast, Director of
  Administration

United States Olympic Committee
1750 E. Boulder St.
Colorado Springs, CO 80909
William J. Hybl, President

United States Organization for Disabled Athletes
c/o John Hurley
143 California Ave.
Uniondale, NY 11553

United States Orienteering Federation
P.O. Box 1444
Forest Park, GA 30051
Robin Shannonhouse,
Executive Director
Compass sports

United States Parachute Association
1440 Duke St.
Alexandria, VA 22314
William H. Ottley, Executive Director

United States Polo Association
Kentucky Horse Park
4059 Iron Works Pike
Lexington, KY 40511
Allan D. Scherer, Executive Director

United States Professional Tennis Association
One USPTA Centre
3535 Briarpark Dr.
Houston, TX 77042
Tim Heckler, CEO

United States Rowing Association
201 S. Capitol Ave., #400
Indianapolis, IN 46225
Sandra Hughes, Executive Director

United States Skiing
P.O. Box 100
Park City, UT 84060
Howard Peterson, Contact

United States Snowshoe Association
c/o Candice Bowen Bosworth
R.D.#1, Box 170
Corinth, NY 12822

United States Soccer Federation
1801-1811 S. Prairie Ave.
Chicago, IL 60616
Hank Steinbrecher, Secretary General

United States Squash Racquets Association
P.O. Box 1216
23 Cynwyd Rd.
Bala Cynwyd, PA 19004
Craig W. Brand, Executive Director

United States Stickball League
P.O. Box 363
East Rockaway, NY 11518
Ronald B. Babineau, President

United States Surfing Federation
7104 Island Village Dr.
Long Beach, CA 90803
Bob Pace, President

United States Synchronized Swimming
Pan American Plaza
201 S. Capitol, #510
Indianapolis, IN 46225
Betty Watanabe, Executive Director

United States Table Tennis Association
1750 E. Boulder St.
Colorado Springs, CO 80909
Kae Rader, Executive Director

United States Tennis Association
1212 Ave. of the Americas
New York, NY 10036
M. Marshall Happer III, Executive Director

United States Twirling Association
P.O. Box 24488
Seattle, WA 98124
Kathy Forsythe, Executive Director
Baton twirlers

United States Volleyball Association
3595 E. Fountain Blvd.
Colorado Springs, CO 80910
Jerry Sherman, President

United States Water Polo
201 S. Capitol, #520
Indianapolis, IN 46225
Rich Foster, President

United States Weightlifting Federation
1750 E. Boulder St.
Colorado Springs, CO 80909
George Greenway, Executive Director

United States Youth Soccer Association
2050 N. Plano Rd., #100
Richardson, TX 75082
Robert Contigulia, Chairman
Youth division of U.S. Soccer Federation

United Way of America
701 N. Fairfax St.
Alexandria, VA 22314
Elaine Chao, President

Universal Autograph Collectors Club
P.O. Box 6181
Washington, DC 20044
Robert A. Erickson, Contact

Universal Pictures
100 Universal City Plaza
Universal City, CA 91608
Film production company

Unsoeld, Jolene
1527 Longworth House Office Bldg.
Washington, DC 20515-4703
Representative from Washington, Democrat
Third District

Untouchables, The
Paramount
5555 Melrose Ave.
Los Angeles, CA 90038
TV series

Upton, Fred
2439 Rayburn House Office Bldg.
Washington, DC 20515-2206
Representative from Michigan, Republican
Sixth District

Urich, Robert
8942 Wilshire Blvd.
Beverly Hills, CA 90211
Actor
birthdate 12/19/46

USA Basketball
1750 E. Boulder St.
Colorado Springs, CO 80909
William L. Wall, Executive Director
In charge of U.S. amateurs playing overseas (Olympics, etc.)

USA Network
2049 Century Park East, #2550
Los Angeles, CA 90067

Usagi Yojimbo
Fantagraphics Books Inc.
7563 Lake City Way N.E.
Seattle, WA 98115
Comic

USTA National Junior Tennis League
70 W. Red Oak Lane
White Plains, NY 10604
Henry Talbert, Contact

Utah Jazz
5 Triad Center
Salt Lake City, UT 84180
Professional basketball team

V

La Letter, l'épitre, qui n'est pas un genre mais tous les genres, la littérature même.

The letter, the epistle, which is not a genre but all the genres, literature itself.

—JACQUES DERRIDA, *"La Carte Postale"*

Valentine, Tim
2229 Rayburn House Office
  Bldg.
Washington, DC 20515-3302
*Representative from North
  Carolina, Democrat
Second District*

Valor
DC Comics, Inc.
1325 Ave. of the Americas
New York, NY 10019
Comic

Van Dyke, Dick
151 El Camino
Beverly Hills, CA 90212
Actor, comedian
birthdate 12/13/25

Van Dyke, Jerry
9300 Wilshire Blvd., #410
Beverly Hills, CA 90212
Actor
birthdate 7/27/31

Van Halen, Eddie
Premier Talent Agency
3 E. 54th St.
New York, NY 10022
Guitarist
birthdate 1/26/57

Van Peebles, Mario
8942 Wilshire Blvd.
Beverly Hills, CA 90211
Actor, director
birthdate 1/15/57

Van Shelton, Ricky
P.O. Box 121754
Nashville, TN 37212
Singer, songwriter

Vancouver Canucks
100 North Renfew St.
Vancouver, B.C. V5K 3N7
  Canada
Professional hockey team

Vandross, Luther
c/o Epic Records
51 W. 52nd St.
New York, NY 10019
Singer

Vanilla Ice
8730 Sunset Blvd., 5th Fl. W
Los Angeles, CA 90069
Rapper

Vanished Children's Alliance
1407 Parkmoor Ave., #200
San Jose, CA 95126
Georgia K. Hilgeman,
  Executive Director

Vanity
151 El Camino
Beverly Hills, CA 90212
Singer

Variety Clubs International
1560 Broadway, #1209
New York, NY 10036
Maria Boyder, Executive
Director
*Financially supports various
children's causes*

Vassilou, Dr. George
Presidential Palace
Nicosia, Cyprus
President of Cyprus

Velazquez, Nydia M.
132 Cannon House Office
Bldg.
Washington, DC 20515-3212
*Representative from New York,
Democrat
Twelfth District*

Vento, Bruce F.
2304 Rayburn House Office
Bldg.
Washington, DC 20515-2304
*Representative from Minnesota,
Democrat
Fourth District*

Veterans Bedside Network
250 W. 54th St., 9th Fl.
New York, NY 10019
Douglas Lutz, Administrator
*Radio and TV workers
volunteering in Veteran's
Administration Hospitals*

VH-1
Video Hits 1
1515 Broadway
New York, NY 10036

Viacom Inc.
1515 Broadway
New York, NY 10036
Sumner M. Redstone,
Chairman
MTV and VH-1 parent company

Vibe
Time/Warner Inc.
1271 Ave. of the Americas
Rockefeller Center
New York, NY 10020
Jonathan Van Meter, Editor
Hip hop magazine

Viera, Joao Bernardo
Conselho de Estado
Bissau, Guinea-Bissau
President of the Council of State

Viewers for Quality Television
c/o Dorothy Swanson
P.O. Box 195
Fairfax Station, VA 22039

Village of Childhelp
P.O. Box 247
14700 Manzanita Park Rd.
Beaumont, CA 92223
Robert Lippert, Administrator
*Residential program for abused
children and their families*

Viner, Michael
Dove Video
301 N. Canon Dr.
Beverly Hills, CA 90210
Audio book company

Virgin Records
338 N. Foothill Rd.
Beverly Hills, CA 90210
Jordan Harris, Co-Managing
Director
*Record label, also Charisma, Point
Blank*

(New York Office)
1790 Broadway, 20th Fl.
New York, NY 10019

Visclosky, Peter J.
2464 Rayburn House Office
  Bldg.
Washington, DC 20515-1401
Representative from Indiana,
  Democrat
First District

Voinovich, George
State House
Columbus, OH 43215
Governor of Ohio

Volkmer, Harold L.
2409 Rayburn House Office
  Bldg.
Washington, DC 20515-2509
Representative from Missouri,
  Democrat
Ninth District

Volunteer Lawyers for the Arts
1 E. 53rd St., 6th Fl.
New York, NY 10022
Daniel Y. Mayer, Esq.,
  Executive Director

Voodoo Child
Box 374
Des Plaines, IL 60016
Jimi Hendrix magazine

Vucanovich, Barbara F.
2202 Rayburn House Office
  Bldg.
Washington, DC 20515-2802
Representative from Nevada,
  Republican
Second District

Dear Pamela, the value of a letter can't be measured quantitatively. If you haven't time to write what you call a "real" letter, then write a few lines. I don't expect anyone to compose longwinded epistles, as I sometimes do. I write letters because I enjoy doing it. It doesn't matter too much whether the recipient takes pleasure in reading what I write; I've had my pleasure.

—"In Absentia"

Waddaulah, H.M. Sultan Sir Mud Hassanal Bolkia Mu'isuddin
Istana Darul Hana
Brunei
Ruler of Brunei

Waihee, John D.
State Capitol
Honolulu, HI 96813
Governor of Hawaii

**Waits, Tom
(Thomas Alan)**
c/o E. Smith
11 Eucalyptus Lane
San Rafael, CA 94901
Singer, composer

Walesa, Lech
Kancelaria Presydenta RP
Ul Wiejska 4/8
00-902 Warsaw, Poland
President of Poland

Walker, Robert S.
2369 Rayburn House Office
Bldg.
Washington, DC 20515-3816
*Representative from Pennsylvania,
Republican
Sixteenth District*

Wallop, Malcolm
237 Senate Russell Office
Bldg.
Washington, DC 20510-5001
*Senator from Wyoming,
Republican*

Walsh, James T.
1330 Longworth House Office
Bldg.
Washington, DC 20515-3225
*Representative from New York,
Republican
Twenty-fifth District*

Walt Disney Pictures
500 S. Buena Vista
Burbank, CA 91521
Film production company

**Walt Disney's Comics &
Stories**
Walt Disney Publications
500 S. Buena Vista
Burbank, CA 91521
Comic

Walters, David
State Capitol, Room 212
Oklahoma City, OK 73105
Governor of Oklahoma

Wangchuk, King Jigme Singye
Royal Palace
Thimphu, Bhutan
Ruler of Bhutan

Ward, Sela
8942 Wilshire Blvd.
Beverly Hills, CA 90211
Actress

Warheads
Marvel Entertainment Group
387 Park Ave., S.
New York, NY 10016
Comic

**Warlock and the Infinity
   Watch**
Marvel Entertainment Group
387 Park Ave. S.
New York, NY 10016
Comic

Warner Bros.
4000 Warner Blvd.
Burbank, CA 91522
Film production company

Warner Bros. Collections
Dept. TS
P.O. Box 60049
Tampa, FL 33660
*Mail order for Warner Bros.
   Looney Tunes shirts, jackets,
   etc.*

Warner Bros. Records
3300 Warner Blvd.
Burbank, CA 91510
Mo Ostin, Chairman
*Record label, also Reprise, Sire,
   Cold Chillin', Paisley
   Park, Quest, Slash*

(New York Office)
75 Rockefeller Plaza
New York, NY 10019

Warner, John W.
225 Senate Russell Office
   Bldg.
Washington, DC 20510-4601
Senator from Virginia, Republican

Warner, Malcolm-Jamal
151 El Camino
Beverly Hills, CA 90212
Actor
birthdate 8/18/70

Warner/Alliance Records
24 Music Square E.
Nashville, TN 37203
Neil Joseph, Vice-President,
   General Manager
Record label

Warner/Reprise Records
1815 Division St.
Nashville, TN 37203
Jim Ed Norman, President
Record label

Warwick, Dionne
December Twelve
144 S. Beverly Dr., #503
Beverly Hills, CA 90212
Singer
birthdate 12/12/41

Washington Bullets
1 Harry S. Truman Dr.
Landover, MD 20785
Professional basketball team

Washington Capitals
Capital Centre
Landover, MD 20785
Professional hockey team

Washington Redskins
P.O. Box 17247
Dulles International Airport
Washington, DC 20041
Professional football team

Washington, Craig
1711 Longworth House Office
Bldg.
Washington, DC 20515-4318
Representative from Texas,
Democrat
Eighteenth District

Washington, Denzel
9830 Wilshire Blvd.
Beverly Hills, CA 90212
Actor
birthdate 12/28/54

Wass, Ted
232 N. Canon Dr.
Beverly Hills, CA 90210
Actor

Waters, Maxine
1207 Longworth House Office
Bldg.
Washington, DC 20515-0535
Representative from California,
Democrat
Thirty-fifth District

Watley, Jody
8439 Sunset Blvd., #103
Los Angeles, CA 90069
Singer

Watt, Melvin L.
1232 Longworth House Office
Bldg.
Washington, DC 20515-3312
Representative from North
Carolina, Democrat
Twelfth District

Watts, Andre
IMG
22 E. 71st St.
New York, NY 10021
Concert pianist
birthdate 6/20/46

Waxman, Henry A.
2408 Rayburn House Office
Bldg.
Washington, DC 20515-0529
Representative from California,
Democrat
Twenty-ninth District

Wayans, Keenen Ivory
P.O. Box 900
Beverly Hills, CA 90213
Executive producer and star of
In Living Color

Web of the Spider-Man
Marvel Entertainment Group
387 Park Ave. S.
New York, NY 10016
Comic

Weekly Variety
475 Park Ave. S.
New York, NY 10016
Peter Bart, Editor
Weekly trade paper

Weicker, Lowell P., Jr.
State Capitol
Hartford, CT 06106
Governor of Connecticut

Weight Watchers International
500 N. Broadway
Jericho, NY 11753-2196
Lelio Parducci, Executive
Officer

Weld, William F.
State House
Boston, MA 02133
Governor of Massachusetts

Weldon, Curt
2452 Rayburn House Office
Bldg.
Washington, DC 20515-3807
Representative from Pennsylvania,
Republican
Seventh District

Wellstone, Paul D.
717 Senate Hart Office Bldg.
Washington, DC 20510-2303
Senator from Minnesota, Democrat

Wendy
Harvey Comics Entertainment
Inc.
100 Wilshire Blvd., #500
Santa Monica, CA 90401
Comic

Wendy's
4288 W. Dublin Granville Rd.
Dublin, OH 43017
R. David Thomas, Founder
Fast-food chain

Wenner, Jann Simon
Straight Arrow Publications,
Inc.
1290 Ave. of the Americas
New York, NY 10104
*Editor, publisher, Executive Vice-
President Rock & Roll Hall of
Fame*

Westminister Kennel Club
230 Park Ave., #644
New York, NY 10169
Ronald H. Menaker, Show
Chairman
Dog show group

Whalley-Kilmer, Joanne
9830 Wilshire Blvd.
Beverly Hills, CA 90212
Actress

Wheat, Alan
2334 Rayburn House Office
Bldg.
Washington, DC 20515-2505
*Representative from Missouri,
Democrat
Fifth District*

Wheel of Fortune
Merv Griffin Enterprises
9860 Wilshire Blvd.
Beverly Hills, CA 90210
Game show

Whitaker, Forest
8942 Wilshire Blvd.
Beverly Hills, CA 90211
Actor

**White House News
Photographers Association**
7119 Ben Franklin Station
Washington, DC 20044-7119
Michael Geissinger, President

White, Jaleel
1450 Belfast Drive
Los Angeles, CA 90069
Actor

White, Vanna
345 N. Maple Dr., #185
Beverly Hills, CA 90210
Letter turner
birthdate 2/18/57

Whitman, Christine Todd
State House, Office of the
Governor, CN-001
Trenton, NJ 08625
Governor of New Jersey

Whitney, Jane
Telepictures Productions
3300 Riverside Dr., #405
Burbank, CA 91522
Talk show host

Whitten, Jamie L.
2314 Rayburn House Office
Bldg.
Washington, DC 20515-2401
*Representative from Mississippi,
Democrat
First District*

Who, The
48 Harley House
Marylebone Rd.
London, NW1 England
Rock group

**Wild West C.O.W.—Boys of
  Moo Mesa**
King World Prods. Inc.
1700 Broadway, 35th Fl.
New York, NY 10019
Animated series

Wilder, L. Douglas
State Capitol
Richmond, VA 23219
Governor of Virginia

Wilderness Society, The
900 17th St. NW
Washington, DC 20006
George T. Frampton, Jr.,
  President

Will, George
1208 30th St. NW
Washington, DC 20007

William Shatner's Tekworld
Marvel Entertainment Group
387 Park Ave. S.
New York, NY 10016
Comic

Williams, Billy Dee
15301 Ventura Blvd., #345
Sherman Oaks, CA 91403
Actor
birthdate 4/6/37

Williams, John
151 El Camino
Beverly Hills, CA 90212
Conductor, composer

Williams, Montel
151 El Camino
Beverly Hills, CA 90212
Talk show host

Williams, Pat
2457 Rayburn House Office
  Bldg.
Washington, DC 20515-2601
*Representative from Montana,
  Democrat At Large*

Williams, Robin
10201 W. Pico Blvd., Bldg. #58
Los Angeles, CA 90035
Actor, comedian
birthdate 7/21/52

Williams, Vanessa
Rt. #100
Millwood, NY 10546
Singer

Williamson, Mykelti
9200 Sunset Blvd., #625
Los Angeles, CA 90069
Actor

Willis, Bruce
151 El Camino
Beverly Hills, CA 90212
Actor
birthdate 3/19/55

**Wilson
(Carnie Wilson, Wendy
  Wilson)**
1290 Ave. of the Americas
New York, NY 10104
Pop duo

Wilson, Brian
151 El Camino
Beverly Hills, CA 90212
Composer, singer, record producer

Wilson, Charles
2256 Rayburn House Office
  Bldg.
Washington, DC 20515-4302
*Representative from Texas,
  Democrat
Second District*

Wilson, Hugh
151 El Camino
Beverly Hills, CA 90211
Writer, producer

Wilson, Pete
State Capitol
Sacramento, CA 95814
Governor of California

Wilson, Sheree J.
9300 Wilshire Blvd., #400
Beverly Hills, CA 90212
Actress

Winfrey, Oprah
Harpo Productions
110 N. Carpenter St.
Chicago, IL 60607
Talk show host
birthdate 1/29/54

Wings
Paramount
5555 Melrose Ave.
Los Angeles, CA 90038
TV series

Winnipeg Jets
15-1430 Maroons Rd.
Winnipeg, Manitoba R3G OL5
  Canada
Professional hockey team

Winwood, Steve
151 El Camino
Beverly Hills, CA 90212
Musician, composer
birthdate 5/12/48

Wise, Bob
2434 Rayburn House Office
  Bldg.
Washington, DC 20515-4802
*Representative from West Virginia,
  Democrat
Second District*

Wish With Wings, A
P.O. Box 3457
Arlington, TX 76010
Pat Skaggs, Executive Director
Wish fulfillment for dying kids

WittyWorld
Box 1458
North Wales, PA 19454
John A. Lent, Editor
Cartoon magazine

Wm. Wrigley Jr. Co.
410 N. Michigan Ave.
Chicago, IL 60611
William Wrigley, CEO
Chewing gum manufacturer

Wofford, Harris
521 Senate Dirksen Office
  Bldg.
Washington, DC 20510-3803
*Senator from Pennsylvania,
  Democrat*

**Wolf Trap Foundation for the
  Performing Arts**
1624 Trap Rd.
Vienna, VA 22182
Shelton G. Stamfill, President

Wolf, Frank R.
104 Cannon House Office
  Bldg.
Washington, DC, 20515-4610
*Representative from Virginia,
  Republican
Tenth District*

Wolfman Jack
Rt. 1, Box 56
Belvidere, NC 27919
Perennial DJ

Wolverine
Marvel Entertainment Group
387 Park Ave. S.
New York, NY 10016
Comic

Woman of Mystery
WOM'N
Box 1616 Canal St. Station
New York, NY 10013
Agatha Christie magazine

WAR
(Women Against Rape)
Box 02084
Columbus, OH 43201

Women Associated With
Crossdressers
Communication Network
Box 17
Bulverde, TX 78163-0017
C. Philips, Contact

Women in Film
6464 Sunset Blvd., #530
Hollywood, CA 90028
Billie Beasley-Jenkins, Contact

Wonder Man
Marvel Entertainment Group
387 Park Ave. S.
New York, NY 10016
Comic

Wonder Woman
DC Comics
1325 Ave. of the Americas
New York, NY 10019
Comic

Wonder, Stevie
(Steveland Morris)
4616 W. Magnolia Blvd.
Burbank, CA 91505
Singer, musician, composer
birthdate 5/13/50

Woo, Roh Tae
Chong Wa Dae
1 Sejongno, Chougnogu
Seoul 110-050,
Republic of Korea
President of the Republic of Korea

Wood, Elijah
151 El Camino
Beverly Hills, CA 90212
Actor

Woodard, Alfre
8942 Wilshire Blvd.
Beverly Hills, CA 90211
Actor
birthdate 11/2/53

Woodward, Joanne
1120 5th Ave, #1C
New York, NY 10128-0144
Actress
birthdate 2/27/30

Woody Woodpecker
Harvey Comics Entertainment,
  Inc.
100 Wilshire Blvd., #500
Santa Monica, CA 90401
Comic

Woolsey, Lynn
439 Cannon House Office
  Bldg.
Washington, DC 20515-0506
Representative from California,
  Democrat
Sixth District

World Bicycle Polo Federation
P.O. Box 1039
Bailey, CO 80421
Lou Gonzalez, Co-Chair

World Championship
  Wrestling
Marvel Entertainment Group
387 Park Ave. S.
New York, NY 10016
Comic

World Footbag Association
1317 Washington Ave., #7
Golden, CO 80401
Bruce Guettich, Director

World Masters Cross-Country Ski Association
c/o Dick Hunt
Box 5
Bend, OR 97709

World of Archie
Archie Comic Publications, Inc.
325 Fayette Ave.
Mamaroneck, NY 10543
Comic

World Organization for Human Potential
8801 Stenton Ave.
Philadelphia, PA 19118
Neil Harvey, Ph.D., President
Specializes in the treatment of brain-injured children

World Pen Pals
1694 Como Ave.
St. Paul, MN 55108
Christina Burkhouse, Coordinator

World Robotic Boxing Association
183 N. Main St.
Cumberland, IA 50843
Keith Namanny, Executive Officer

World Waterpark Association
P.O. Box 14826
Lenexa, KS 66285
Al Turner, Executive Director

World Wildlife Fund
1250 24th St. NW
Washington, DC 20037
Kathryn Fuller, President

World's Wristwrestling Championship
423 E. Washington St.
Petaluma, CA 94952
Bill Soberanes, Executive Director

Worldwide Friendship International
3749 Brice Run Rd., #A
Randallstown, MD 21133
Elton Smith, President

Wow!
Pilot Communications
25 W. 39th St.
New York, NY 10018
Steve Korte, Editor
Entertainment magazine

Wrangler
P.O. Box 21488
Greensboro, NC 27420
Mackey McDonald, President
Jeans/clothing manufacturer

Writers Guild of America, West
8955 Beverly Blvd.
West Hollywood, CA 90048-2456
Del Reisman, President

Wyden, Ron
1111 Longworth House Office Bldg.
Washington, DC 20515-3703
Representative from Oregon, Democrat
Third District

Wyeth, Andrew
c/o General Delivery
Chadds Ford, PA 19317
Artist

Wylie, Adam
14724 Ventura Blvd., #401
Sherman Oaks, CA 91403
Actor

Wynn, Albert R.
423 Cannon House Office
  Bldg.
Washington, DC 20515-2004
Representative from Maryland,
  Democrat Fourth District

Wynnona
3907 Alameda Ave., 2nd Fl.
Burbank, CA 91505
Singer

I see you understand the pleasure that can be got from writing letters. In other centuries this was taken for granted. Not any longer. Only a few people carry on true correspondences. No time, the rest will tell you. Quicker to telephone. Like saying a photograph is more satisfying than a painting. There wasn't all that much time for writing letters in the past, either, but time was found, as it generally can be for whatever gives pleasure.

X-Factor
Marvel Entertainment Group
387 Park Ave. S.
New York, NY 10016
Comic

XYY
Standard X Press
82 Kimball Ave.
Yonkers, NY 10704
Comic

Xenozoic Tales
Kitchen Sink Press
2 Swamp Rd.
Princeton, WI 54968
Comic

But I want music and intellectual companionships and affection. Well, perhaps I'll get all that one day. And in the meantime there are little things to look forward to, letters and the unexpected.

Yahoo
Fantagraphics Books, Inc.
7563 Lake City Way N.E.
Seattle, WA 98115
Comic

Yankovic, "Weird" Al
8383 Wilshire Blvd., #954
Beverly Hills, CA 90211
Performer

Yanni
6714 Villa Madera Dr. SW
Tacoma, WA 98499
Singer

Yates, Sidney R.
2109 Rayburn House Office
   Bldg.
Washington, DC 20515-1309
Representative from Illinois,
   Democrat
Ninth District

Yeltsin, Boris
The Kremlin
Moscow, Russia
President of Russia

YM
(Young and Modern)
Gruner & Jahr
685 Third Ave., 30th Fl.
New York, NY 10017
Bonnie Hurowitz, Editor
Teen fashion and beauty
   magazine

Yoakum, Dwight
c/o Reprise
3300 Warner Blvd.
Burbank, CA 91510
Singer

Yogi Bear
Harvey Comics Entertainment,
   Inc.
100 Wilshire Blvd., #500
Santa Monica, CA 90401
Comic

Young Actors Guild
c/o Aaron White
120 S. 3rd St.
Connellsville, PA 15425
Works to protect child performers

Young American Bowling Alliance
5301 S. 76th St.
Greendale, WI 53129
Joseph Wilson, Executive Director

Young Concert Artists
250 W. 57th St., #921
New York, NY 10019
Susan Wadsworth, Director

Young Entrepreneurs Organization
1010 N. Glebe Rd., #600
Arlington, VA 22201
Mohamed Fathelbab, Executive Officer
Under-40 millionaires

Young Indiana Jones Chronicles
Dark Horse Comics, Inc.
10956 SE Main St.
Milwaukie, OR 97222
Comic

Young Life
720 W. Monumental
P.O. Box 520
Colorado Springs, CO 80904
Douglas Burleigh, President
Christian adolescents

YWCA
Young Women's Christian Association of the United States of America
726 Broadway
New York, NY 10003
Gwendolyn Calvert Baker, Executive Director

Young, C. W. Bill
2407 Rayburn House Office Bldg.
Washington, DC 20515-0910
Representative from Florida, Republican
Tenth District

Young, Don
2331 Rayburn House Office Bldg.
Washington, DC 20515-0201
Representative from Alaska, Republican At Large

Young, Neil
c/o Geffen Records
9126 Sunset Blvd.
W. Hollywood, CA 90069
Songwriter, musician
birthdate 11/12/45

Youth For Christ (USA)
P.O. Box 22822
Denver, CO 80222
Roger Cross, President

Youth Policy
Youth Policy Institute
1221 Massachusetts Ave. N.W. #B
Washington, DC 20005
Information and analysis on federal youth programs

I have now attained the true art of letter writing, which, we are always told, is to express on paper exactly what one would say to the same person by word of mouth; I have been talking to you almost as fast as I could the whole of this letter.

—JANE AUSTEN

Zamor, Jaime Paz
Palacio de Gobierno
Plaza Murillo
La Paz, Bolivia
President of Bolivia

Zappas
(Moon Unit, Dweezil)
P.O. Box 5265
N. Hollywood, CA 91616
Musicians

Zeliff, Bill
224 Cannon House Office
  Bldg.
Washington, DC 20515-2901
*Representative from New
  Hampshire, Republican
First District*

Zemeckis, Robert
9830 Wilshire Blvd.
Beverly Hills, CA 90212
Writer, director

Zenawi, Meles
c/o Ethiopian People's
  Revolutionary Democratic
  Front
Addis Ababa, Ethiopia
President of Ethiopia

Zero Patrol
Continuity Publishing, Inc.
62 W. 45th St.
New York, NY 10036
Comic

Zero Population Growth
1400 16th St. NW, #320
Washington, DC 20036
Susan Weber, Executive
  Director

Zia, Begum Khaleda
Office of the Prime Minister
Dhaka, Bangladesh
Prime Minister of Bangladesh

Zillions
Consumers Union of U.S. Inc.
101 Truman Avenue
Yonkers, NY 10703
Kids' consumer magazine

Zimmer, Dick
228 Cannon House Office
  Bldg.
Washington, DC 20515-3012
*Representative from New Jersey,
  Republican
Twelfth District*

Zindel, Paul
151 El Camino
Beverly Hills, CA 90211
Playwright, screenwriter

Zippy Quarterly
Fantagraphics Books, Inc.
7563 Lake City Way N.E.
Seattle, WA 98115
Comic

Zoobooks
Wildlife Education Inc.
3590 Kettner Blvd.
San Diego, CA 92101
Ken Kitson, Publisher
Animal magazine

Zuniga, Daphne
c/o Murphy
2401 Main St.
Santa Monica, CA 90405
Actor

ZZ Top
P.O. Box 19744
Houston, TX 77024
Pop group

ZZ Top International Fan Club
P.O. Box 19744
Houston, TX 77224

Write to Me

The Address Book is updated every two years, and you can play an active role in this procedure. If you are notable in any field, or know someone who is, send the name, mailing address, and some documentation of the notability (newspaper clippings are effective) for possible inclusion in our next edition.

Also, we are very interested in learning of any success stories resulting from *The Address Book*.

During the last few years, I have received tens of thousands of letters, ranging from loving to vituperative, from owners of *The Address Book*. Despite the overwhelming task of answering this mail, I really enjoy the letters.

But, please, remember a couple of rules if you write:

- Remember to include a *self-addressed stamped envelope*. For reasons of both time and expense, this is the only way I can respond to mail; so, unfortunately, I've had to draw the line—no S.A.S.E., no reply.
- I need your comments. While I confess I'm partial to success stories, comments from purchasers of the book have helped me a great deal for future editions; so fire away.
- Many people have written to request addresses of people not listed in the book. As much as I would like to, I simply can't open up this can of worms. Requests for additional addresses are carefully noted and considered for future editions.

Receiving a photo from someone who writes adds an entirely new dimension to the letter, so feel free. That's right, enclose a photo of yourself. After all, from the photo on the back cover, you know what I look like, and I'm rather eager to see you.

Keep those cards and letters coming.

Michael Levine
8730 Sunset Blvd., 6th Floor
Los Angeles, CA 90069